Microsoft Inforr Protection Administrator SC-400 Certification Guide

Advance your Microsoft Security & Compliance services knowledge and pass the SC-400 exam with confidence

Shabaz Darr

Viktor Hedberg

BIRMINGHAM—MUMBAI

Microsoft Information Protection Administrator SC-400 Certification Guide

Group Product Manager: Wilson D'souza

Publishing Product Manager: Meeta Rajani

Senior Editor: Shazeen Iqbal

Content Development Editor: Rafiaa Khan

Technical Editor: Arjun Varma

Copy Editor: Safis Editing

Project Coordinator: Shagun Saini

Proofreader: Safis Editing

Indexer: Manju Arasan

Production Designer: Nilesh Mohite

First published: February 2022
Production reference: 2060722

Published by Packt Publishing Ltd.
Livery Place
35 Livery Street
Birmingham
B3 2PB, UK.

ISBN 978-1-80181-149-1

www.packt.com

To my wife, Reema, you are my rock. To my children, Zoya and Mikaeel, for being my motivation and inspiration. To my mother, Sajida Darr, and to the memory of my late father, Mohammed Arshad Darr, for their sacrifices and love.

– Shabaz Darr

To my wife, Matilda, you are my everything. To my children, Jack and Theo, for helping me with motivation and giving me the time to finish the project. To my mother, Anna, and my father, Stefan, for everything during my upbringing, making me the person that I am today.

– Viktor Hedberg

Foreword

The Information Protection Administrator plans and implements controls that meet organizational compliance needs. This person is responsible for translating requirements and compliance controls into technical implementation. They assist organizational control owners to become and stay compliant.

That is how the description for the SC-400 exam starts. To me, and, hopefully, to you who read this book, this is the core of information protection.

One of the greatest assets an organization has today is its data. You can only understand whether data is valuable or not if you understand the business goals and requirements of the organization itself. Once you have done that, this book will give you the crucial knowledge needed to protect the valuable data, thereby also making it more accessible.

Information protection and information security can sometimes be seen as cumbersome, complex, and difficult. I am convinced that proper continuous and value-driven work around information protection will only unlock new potential, new opportunities, and an increased ability to collaborate inside and between organizations.

Use this book to pass your SC-400 exam, use these learnings to bring value and compliance to your organization, and use information protection to help your organization to reach its goals.

– Simon Binder

Contributors

About the authors

Shabaz Darr is a senior infrastructure specialist for Netcompany, based in the United Kingdom. He is a Microsoft MVP in Enterprise Mobility, specializing in Microsoft cloud technologies including Endpoint Manager, Security & Compliance, and Azure Virtual Desktop. He has over 15 years' experience in the IT industry, with 7 of those spent working with Microsoft cloud technologies. During this period, he has assisted several global organizations with designing and implementing information protection strategies.

Viktor Hedberg is a cybersecurity consultant/security advisor for Truesec, based in Sweden. He is a Microsoft MVP in the Cloud and Datacenter Management category, specializing in Microsoft technologies, whether on-premises or in the cloud, Viktor strives to secure all workloads, while also taking part in incident response to help organizations respond, recover, and rebuild from an attack. He has 10 years of experience in the IT industry, and during this time, he has worked for a number of government entities and as a consultant, helping several global organizations with designing and implementing various Microsoft workloads, including information protection.

About the reviewer

Richard Hagerwald is a certified Microsoft Enterprise Administrator Expert with a heavy focus on security technologies. He has a career in IT spanning 20 years, covering the full range of service deliveries, from end user support to his current role as an Enterprise Solutions Architect. In his current position, he is guiding private and public customers to a safer overall IT environment using mainly Microsoft technologies with a primary focus on Microsoft 365. Richard has a passion for continuous improvements in all things IT-related and has a genuine passion for technology that also influences his free time, with a home that is highly automated.

I'd like to thank my wife and daughter for having provided me with the time and opportunity to review this fantastic book from Packt Publishing. Furthermore, I wish to thank Packt Publishing for allowing me to review this extraordinary book, and I would like to thank the authors for taking me on their journey.

Table of Contents

Preface

Section 1: Exam Overview and Introduction to Information Protection

1

Preparing for Your Microsoft Exam and SC-400 Exam Objectives

2

Introduction to Information Protection

Section 2: Implementing Information Protection

3

Creating and Managing Sensitive Information Types

4

Creating and Managing Trainable Classifiers

5

Implementing and Managing Sensitivity Labels

6

Planning and Implementing Encryption for Email Messages

Section 3: Implementing Data Loss Prevention

7

Creating and Configuring Data Loss Prevention Policies

8

Implementing and Monitoring Microsoft Endpoint Data Loss Prevention

9

Managing and Monitoring Data Loss Prevention Policies and Activities

Section 4: Implementing Information Governance

10

Configuring Retention Policies and Labels

11

Managing Data Retention in Microsoft 365

12
Implementing Microsoft Purview Records Management

Practice Exam

Other Books You May Enjoy

Index

Preface

Microsoft Purview Information Protection in Microsoft 365 is the solution tasked with discovering, classifying, and protecting sensitive information wherever it may reside or travel. This book will act as an in-depth, walk-through guide, taking you through the features available and how to implement them in order to protect data successfully. The book is written to cover each topic present in the SC-400 exam "Information Protection Administrator Associate," and, after completing the book, you should possess sufficient skills to achieve a pass grade on examination day.

Who this book is for

This book is intended for compliance administrators, Microsoft 365 administrators, and information protection administrators. You should have a basic understanding of the fundamental services within Microsoft 365 and Compliance & Security.

What this book covers

Chapter 1, Preparing for Your Microsoft Exam, provides guidance on getting prepared for a Microsoft exam, along with the resources that can assist in your learning plans.

Chapter 2, Introduction to Information Protection, provides an introduction to information protection, including what it is and why it is so important. This chapter will also discuss the benefits of implementing information protection in your organization.

Chapter 3, Creating and Managing Sensitive Information Types, focuses on creating sensitive information types of data and how to manage these in an organization.

Chapter 4, Creating and Managing Trainable Classifiers, introduces trainable classifiers, and how to identify, create, and manage them. We will also look at how to verify that they are performing correctly and how to retrain a classifier.

Chapter 5, Implementing and Managing Sensitivity Labels, examines the roles and permissions required to administer sensitivity labels as well as create and manage policies and how to apply them to Microsoft 365 SaaS applications. We will also look at the integration of classification with on-premises data and the application of protections and restrictions to files.

Chapter 6, Planning and Implementing Encryption for Email Messages, provides an overview of what encryption in Microsoft 365 looks like and then focuses on email encryption specifically. We will look at defining requirements and then implementing Office 365 Message Encryption.

Chapter 7, Creating and Configuring Data Loss Prevention Policies, covers how to create data loss prevention policies in Microsoft 365 in order to discover, classify, and protect sensitive and business-critical content throughout its life cycle across your organization.

Chapter 8, Implementing and Monitoring Microsoft Endpoint Data Loss Prevention, examines the planning and implementation of Microsoft Endpoint data loss prevention, which extends the activity monitoring and protection capabilities of data loss prevention to sensitive items that are on Windows 10 devices.

Chapter 9, Managing and Monitoring Data Loss Prevention Policies and Activities, discusses how to respond to and mitigate data loss policy violations using the Microsoft Purview Compliance Portal and **Microsoft Defender for Cloud Apps**.

Chapter 10, Configuring Retention Policies and Labels, examines the planning and implementation of retention labels and policies. This will include deploying, managing, and configuring retention labels and policies for your Microsoft 365 tenant.

Chapter 11, Managing Data Retention in Microsoft 365, discusses how to manage retention for Microsoft 365, and how retention solutions are implemented in the individual Microsoft 365 services.

Chapter 12, Implementing Microsoft Purview Records Management, covers how to use intelligent classification to automate and simplify the retention schedule for regulatory and business-critical records in your organization.

To get the most out of this book

You will need a Microsoft 365 tenant with either a Microsoft 365 E5 subscription or an add-on subscription to Azure AD P2 or an Enterprise Mobility & Security E5 subscription.

Software/hardware covered in the book	OS requirements
Microsoft 365 tenant	Windows
Relevant Microsoft 365 subscription	N/A

Download the color images

We also provide a PDF file that has color images of the screenshots/diagrams used in this book. You can download it here: https://static.packt-cdn.com/downloads/9781801811491_ColorImages.pdf.

Conventions used

There are a number of text conventions used throughout this book.

Code in text: Indicates code words in text, database table names, folder names, filenames, file extensions, pathnames, dummy URLs, user input, and Twitter handles. Here is an example: "To configure the host site of the network, you need the tunctl command from the **User Mode Linux** (**UML**) project."

A block of code is set as follows:

```
#include <stdio.h>
#include <stdlib.h>
int main (int argc, char *argv[])
{
    printf ("Hello, world!\n");
    return 0;
}
```

Any command-line input or output is written as follows:

```
$ sudo tunctl -u $(whoami) -t tap0
```

Bold: Indicates a new term, an important word, or words that you see on screen. For example, words in menus or dialog boxes appear in the text like this. Here is an example: "Click **Flash** from Etcher to write the image."

> **Tips or important notes**
> Appear like this.

Get in touch

Feedback from our readers is always welcome.

General feedback: If you have questions about any aspect of this book, mention the book title in the subject of your message and email us at customercare@packtpub.com.

Errata: Although we have taken every care to ensure the accuracy of our content, mistakes do happen. If you have found a mistake in this book, we would be grateful if you would report this to us. Please visit www.packtpub.com/support/errata, selecting your book, clicking on the Errata Submission Form link, and entering the details.

Piracy: If you come across any illegal copies of our works in any form on the internet, we would be grateful if you would provide us with the location address or website name. Please contact us at copyright@packt.com with a link to the material.

If you are interested in becoming an author: If there is a topic that you have expertise in and you are interested in either writing or contributing to a book, please visit authors.packtpub.com.

Reviews

Please leave a review. Once you have read and used this book, why not leave a review on the site that you purchased it from? Potential readers can then see and use your unbiased opinion to make purchase decisions, we at Packt can understand what you think about our products, and our authors can see your feedback on their book. Thank you!

For more information about Packt, please visit packt.com.

Share Your Thoughts

Once you've read *Microsoft Information Protection Administrator SC-400 Certification Guide*, we'd love to hear your thoughts! Scan the QR code below to go straight to the Amazon review page for this book and share your feedback.

https://packt.link/r/1801811490

Your review is important to us and the tech community and will help us make sure we're delivering excellent quality content.

Section 1: Exam Overview and Introduction to Information Protection

This part of the book will focus on the objectives and an overview of what to expect in the exam, along with an introduction to information protection.

This section comprises the following chapters:

- *Chapter 1, Preparing for Your Microsoft Exam and SC-400 Exam Objectives*
- *Chapter 2, Introduction to Information Protection*

1
Preparing for Your Microsoft Exam and SC-400 Exam Objectives

You are starting your journey with **Microsoft role-based** certifications. The **SC-400** exam is based on **Information protection administration**. Within this chapter, we will provide direction on getting equipped for the Microsoft exam, as well as outlining resources that can aid you in your learning strategy. We will provide useful links and explain how you can obtain access to *Microsoft 365 subscriptions* on a trial basis, which will allow you to gain hands-on experience. This chapter will give you the understanding and knowledge you need to prepare for the exam and become an information protection administrator.

In this chapter, we're going to cover the following main topics:

- Preparing for a Microsoft exam
- Accessing resources and Microsoft Learn
- Creating a Microsoft 365 trial account
- Introducing the SC-400 exam objectives
- Why should I take this exam?

Technical requirements

To allow you to follow and complete the exercises within the book, you will need to have access to a **Microsoft 365 tenant**. This can be attained by signing up for a trial subscription. Additionally, Microsoft Purview Information Protection services will require one of the following licenses:

- Enterprise Mobility + Security E5/A5
- Microsoft 365 E5/A5

Preparing for a Microsoft exam

There are several parts of the process to prepare for a Microsoft exam, including the resources you use to prepare for the exam, being able to access a subscription for hands-on labs, and the method by which you are going to physically take the exam. Understanding the format of Microsoft exams is vitally important, especially if this is your first exam.

Accessing resources to prepare for the exam

You can find multiple resources to help you prepare for Microsoft exams. These include online video content from learning companies, live tutorials from **Microsoft Learning Partners**, content from members of the wider community, and Microsoft blog articles. All the resources mentioned are helpful. However, the video content from learning companies and live courses are not free and this may not be within your learning budget. Microsoft blog articles and community-based content can provide you with a route you can follow for each topic, but do not go into enough detail to fully cover the scope of the certification.

Microsoft provides one of the best resources that are available. You can find documentation on all services within Microsoft Docs, which will enable you to search for and find the information you need to help you better prepare. The information is all public and free, with Microsoft Docs being very closely knit to the Microsoft Learn content.

You can access and search Microsoft Docs by going to the following link in an internet browser: `https://docs.microsoft.com`.

How to access a Microsoft 365 subscription

Having hands-on experience with the services within the objectives as part of your preparation for a Microsoft certification is highly recommended. Microsoft courses have GitHub repositories for labs that are publicly available and free.

Guides for the labs can be found at the following link: `https://www.microsoft.com/learning`.

You can take advantage of Microsoft trial subscriptions for both Azure and Microsoft 365. We will provide further information on setting up a trial subscription later in this chapter.

Exam locations

One of the key elements of the exam preparation process is physically going to take your exam. Traditionally, there has only ever been the option to take the exams at a *proctored exam site*, which some people may still prefer as it is a controlled environment. Ensuring you understand the setup of the location where you are taking the exam can be helpful, minimizing the level of stress and allowing you to focus on the actual exam.

In more recent times, roughly when role-based exams were made available, Microsoft provided the option of taking *online proctored* exams. These allow the individual to take the exam from home or a work office location, rather than going to an already authorized exam site. Some people may prefer this option as it allows you to utilize your own equipment and environment. Please note that the online-proctored option is not available in all regions; however, if it is available in your region, you will see something similar to the following:

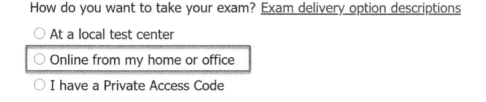

Figure 1.1 – Location selection when scheduling an exam

Preparing for the online-proctored exam is very different from preparing for a local test center exam. In relation to physical equipment, you must have a device with speakers, a microphone, and a webcam. You are only permitted to use a single monitor, so be sure to have a high resolution to avoid any issues with visibility in the exam. Testing the equipment in advance of taking the exam is highly recommended as this will allow you to avoid any delays on exam day. You must ensure the environment in which you are taking the exam is clear of any papers, books, pens, and pencils. It must also be an area that is quiet and isolated so no one can enter while you are taking the exam. Before starting the exam, you will be asked to provide photos of the surrounding area to both the left and right side, as well as the front and back of where you are sat. Valid photo identification (such as a passport or driving license) is required as well. You must remain within the view of the camera for the duration of the exam.

Microsoft exam format

All Microsoft exams are usually made up of four to six question types. There are multiple-choice questions, drag and drop, true/false, dropdowns, best answer scenarios, and case studies. The following is additional detail on question types:

1. **Multiple-Choice** questions are simple. A question may have more than one answer. The exam questions are transparent about how many correct answers you need to choose for each question, and you will be alerted if you choose the incorrect number of choices.

2. **Drag-and-Drop** questions are typically based on actions of a process to test your understanding of the order of operations to configure a service. There are more potential answers given than you need, and you are required to move the steps that are appropriate to the question over to the right-hand side in the correct sequence.

3. **True/False** questions are slightly different than traditional questions. You are usually provided with some screenshots are an exhibit from within the relevant Microsoft portals that show you what has been configured. You will then find three to four statements based on whether the statements are correct based on the information provided.

4. **Drop-down** questions are typically the ones with PowerShell or Azure CLI code in them. You are asked to achieve certain steps within a string of code where the blank sections provide the drop-down selections to choose from.

5. **Best-answer scenario** questions are used to test for a genuine understanding of a subject area. You will receive a warning when you get to this section that you will be unable to navigate back on these questions. The question will provide a specific scenario that needs to be solved, along with a potential solution. You will be required to establish whether the solution is the best one to solve the scenario. You can select yes or no, after which you will get the same scenario but with a different possible solution, to which you must again select yes or no.

6. **Case study** questions give a pretend company setting with an existing environment, future environment, and business and technical requirements. You will then be asked multiple (five to seven) questions that cover multiple objective areas of the exam you are sitting. You will find one to three of the case study questions on the associate level exam.

The various question types test your level of understanding in different ways, and all go into the weighted exam goals that will be discussed later in this chapter.

So far, we have covered the exam question types as well as the different locations where you can sit the exam. In the following sections, we will cover the various resources that will aid you in the process of learning the exam topics covered within the SC-400 exam and how you can gain access to the solutions, which will enable you to follow along with the exercises in this specific guide.

Accessing resources and Microsoft Learn

We referred to some of the resources available to you when preparing for the exam earlier in this chapter. Microsoft Learn was one of those, along with **Microsoft Docs**, but due to the amount of information, we have dedicated a whole section to this due to the amount of free content that it provides to aid you in preparing for the exam.

Accessing Microsoft Learn

Microsoft Learn is a good resource to get your learning path started. One of the major benefits of this content is the fact that it is free. When you create a Microsoft account, you are able to track your progress and you can acquire badges along your journey. Microsoft also creates learning challenges intermittently, with prizes such as free exam vouchers. You can create a free account by selecting the button at the top right of the page and then selecting **Sign in**, as shown in the following screenshot:

Figure 1.2 – Microsoft Learn Sign in

You have the option of signing in with an existing Microsoft account or creating one to get access to the content, as shown here:

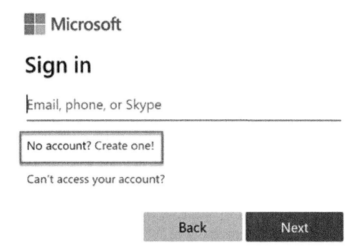

Figure 1.3 – Sign in or create a new Microsoft account

To access Microsoft Learn content, you can use the following link: `https://www.microsoft.com/learn`.

Relevant content can be found on Microsoft Learn in many ways. You can search for specific roles, products, or certification codes. You can find these options on the selection ribbon at the top of the **Learn** page as shown in *Figure 1.4*. You can also find several recommendations to start your learning on the same page:

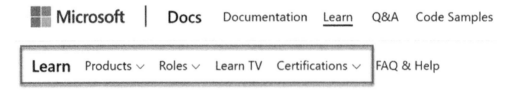

Figure 1.4 – Microsoft Learn navigation

You can select the drop-down arrows from the **Learn** site navigation tabs to filter for content in the specific **Roles**, **Products**, or **Certifications**, as shown in the following screenshot:

Figure 1.5 – Category filter drop-down arrow

After you have chosen the subject that you want to learn about, you can then search a specific topic of that subject and filter even further on particular topics or individual courses, and even learning paths, as shown in the following screenshot:

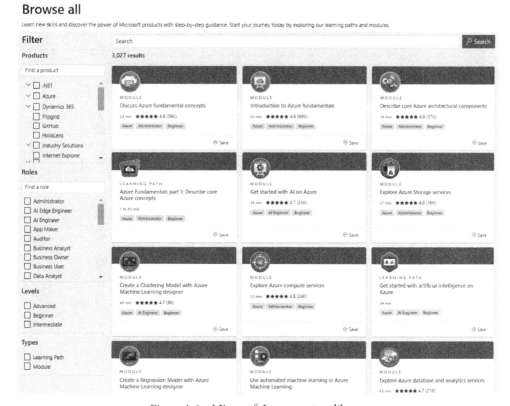

Figure 1.6 – Microsoft Learn content library

In this section, we took a look at the information needed to access the Microsoft Learn content library and how to browse for learning modules and learning paths. In the next section, we will guide you through finding content that is particular to the **SC-400 exam**.

Microsoft exam information pages

An additional common area within the Microsoft Learn site is the *exam pages*. There is an exam page for every Microsoft exam and a certification page. These pages deliver an overview of the exam certification, the objectives of the exam, the roles of individuals that may be interested in the exam, scheduling the exam, and the learning path to prepare for the exam. These pages are very helpful when you are planning for a specific exam, rather than just gaining general tech knowledge. The following screenshot shows an SC-400 exam search:

Figure 1.7 – Browsing for the SC-400 exam

The following screenshot shows the SC-400 exam page:

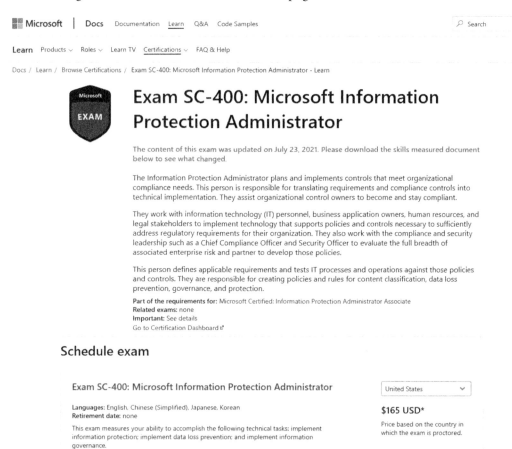

Figure 1.8 – SC-400 exam page

It is recommended that you use this exam page for reference when preparing for the SC-400 certification. At this stage of the chapter, you should have access to Microsoft Learn to log in and browse for content. In the following section, we will provide advice on creating a trial subscription to **Microsoft 365** services.

Creating a Microsoft 365 trial account

For those people who are new to Microsoft cloud services such as Azure and Microsoft 365, it is important to get hands-on experience, not only for the exam you are taking but also for professional development. You must understand the admin portals and how they work if you are looking to get certified. In this book, we will provide exercises that will get you familiar with how to work within the Microsoft 365 and Azure portals and how to navigate when in them. In order to follow along with the steps, we recommend you get a subscription to both Microsoft 365 and **Azure Active Directory Premium P2**. We will detail the steps required to obtain a 30-day trial in the next section.

Microsoft 365 or Office 365 trial subscription

The features and abilities discussed within the SC-400 exam objectives need a Microsoft 365 enterprise-level license, which *E3* and *E5* licenses are classed as. Microsoft offers a 30-day trial license for both. Therefore, as you prepare for the exam, you can create these subscriptions and follow the exercises.

You can navigate to the following link to get started, and select **Try for free**, as shown in *Figure 1.9* under the **Office 365 E5** plan: `https://www.microsoft.com/en-us/microsoft-365/enterprise/compare-office-365-plans`:

Office 365 E5

All the features of Office 365 E3 plus advanced security, analytics, and voice capabilities[1].

£30.80 user/month
(annual subscription–auto renews)
Price does not include VAT.

Buy now
Try for free >
Contact sales >
Learn more >

Figure 1.9 – Office 365 E5 trial subscription

To create an account, follow the process as shown in *Figure 1.10*. If you have created an account before, you will need to use a different email address to obtain a free trial again:

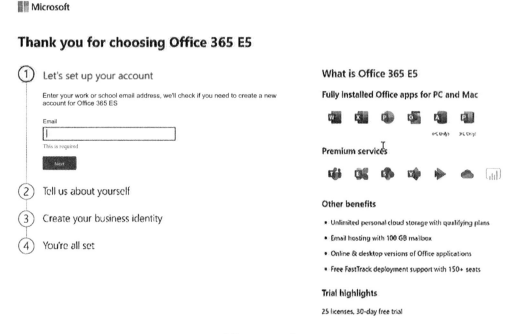

Figure 1.10 – Office 365 trial sign-up process

Once you have completed the process and created the Microsoft 365 tenant, you will have access to the full Microsoft 365 suite of services as well as all the different admin panels. In the next section, we will walk you through the process of setting up an additional service that will be required to follow along with the exercises within this book and complete the hands-on labs to prepare you for the exam.

Obtaining the relevant license

You will need an **Azure Information Protection (AIP)** Premium P2 license for the advanced information protection features that are discussed within the SC-400 exam objectives. The best way to get these features is by obtaining an **Enterprise Mobility + Security E5** license. As with most Microsoft 365 licenses, you can also get a 30-day trial of this. Let's perform the following steps:

1. Navigate to the following link: `https://www.microsoft.com/en-us/microsoft-365/enterprise-mobility-security/compare-plans-and-pricing`.

2. Once you have navigated to this web page, select **Try now** under the **Enterprise Mobility + Security E5 plan**, as shown in the following screenshot:

£11.20
user/month
(annual commitment)

Price does not include VAT.

Enterprise Mobility + Security E5

Try now >

Buy E5

Figure 1.11 – EMS E5 trial subscription

Please note that this is an add-on license to Microsoft 365, so you should enter the details of your email address that you used to sign up for the Office 365 subscription earlier in this chapter, as shown in the following screenshot:

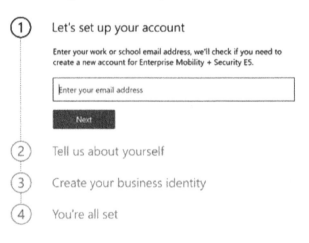

Figure 1.12 – EMS E5 sign-up form

The topics you have learned about so far in this chapter have enabled you to understand the different types of questions you can expect in all Microsoft's role-based certification exams, where you can find free study resources, and finally, how to obtain a free trial of the relevant Microsoft subscription and add-on license to allow you to follow the hands-on lab assignments within this book.

Introducing the SC-400 exam objectives

In this book, we will cover the exam objectives for the **SC-400 Information Protection Administration** exam. The objectives of the exam are closely followed within the structure of this book. Each exam objective is weighted differently. The weight of the objective is used as a compass for understanding the knowledge required for that section as well as a guide to understanding the potential number of questions you can expect in the exam for the specific topic. The following table shows the objectives covered within the SC-400 exam:

Objective	Weight
Implement Information Protection	35-40%
Implement Data Loss Prevention	30-35%
Implement Information Governance	25-30%

Table 1.1 – Objectives of the SC-400 exam

You can find further details on the topics that are covered in the SC-400 exam objectives at the following link: `https://query.prod.cms.rt.microsoft.com/cms/api/am/binary/RE4Mr80`.

The weight percentage does not mean that if an objective is at 10%, then you will only get 6 questions out of 60 on this area. Microsoft exams use a scoring scale of 1000 based on the type of question and the objectives covered in that question. The weights of the objectives will aid you in understanding the standing that is placed on the specific objective.

The next section will provide information on, and insight into, the types of roles that this exam highlights and how the SC-400 exam can assist you in your professional development.

Why should I take this exam?

The SC-400 exam is the Microsoft Purview Information Protection *associate level* exam, so the focus is on the areas of protecting information stored in the cloud, protecting data from being lost, and record management to ensure information governance is protected. You should take this exam if you have goals and aspirations to work with *Microsoft Cloud* technologies, and the exam should prepare you for the role of security administrator, specifically, protecting information in the Microsoft cloud.

Summary

Within this chapter, we covered all the areas that will help prepare you for the Information Protection Administration exam, which included how to prepare for your exam, accessing resources and Microsoft Learn, creating a Microsoft 365 trial account, introducing exam objectives, and a quick overview of why you should take this exam.

These key topics have given you the understanding and knowledge you need to use Microsoft's free learning resources and create a trial subscription, which will allow you to complete the hands-on labs throughout this book. Additionally, you have learned about the types of exam questions you will find within all of Microsoft's role-based certifications.

The next chapter will introduce the information protection topic and how it has progressed.

2
Introduction to Information Protection

This chapter will introduce **Information Protection**, what it is, and why it is so important to your organization. This is an introductory chapter, as we are going to cover all the features of Information Protection to give you a toolbox to tackle the rest of the book in an orderly fashion.

First, we will give you an overview of the features available in Information Protection and how the different components interact. Next, we'll provide some examples of where we could use Information Protection to safeguard our data. This is followed by some examples of what features are supposed to work on your on-premises data center or your cloud environment. We'll also have a discussion on the importance of protecting data and how Information Protection can assist us. You will also get insight into some examples of how you can benefit from an implementation of the features both in regard to data security and raising information security awareness within the organization. We are going to cover the following main topics:

- What is Information Protection?
- Information Protection use cases

- Understanding the scope of Information Protection
- Why is Information Protection important?
- What are the benefits of implementing Information Protection in your organization?

Technical requirements

To follow the chapter, you will need to have a **Microsoft 365 tenant** as described in the previous chapter. The tenant and your computer(s) need to at least meet the following requirements:

1. An **Azure Information Protection** plan for classification, labeling, and protecting information.

2. **Azure Active Directory**, to use *user accounts* synchronized from your on-premises Active Directory Domain Services. You also need to configure *directory integration* using **Azure Active Directory Connect**.

3. To use the **Azure Information Protection** client for Windows, the following operating systems are supported:

- Windows 10 (x86, x64)
- Windows 8.1 (x86, x64)
- Windows 8 (x86, x64)
- Windows Server 2019
- Windows Server 2016
- Windows Server 2012 and Windows Server 2012 R2

4. Applications supported for labeling and protection using the Azure Information Protection client are as follows:

- Microsoft 365 Apps for enterprise
- Office Professional Plus 2019
- Office Professional Plus 2016
- Office Professional Plus 2013 with Service Pack 1
- Office Professional Plus 2010 with Service Pack 2

5. The requirements for using the Azure Information Protection clients are listed at the following link: `https://docs.microsoft.com/en-us/azure/information-protection/rms-client/clientv2-admin-guide-install`.

Now let's dive into our first topic and explore what Information Protection is.

What is Information Protection?

Microsoft Purview Information Protection brings together the features of Azure Information Protection with the *Information Governance* features of Microsoft 365. Microsoft Purview Information Protection helps your organization to do the following:

- Identify your data.

- Provide protection for your data.

- Govern your data.

We will explore each of these in the following sections.

Identify your data

To understand the data landscape in your organization across a hybrid or cloud environment, Microsoft Purview Information Protection offers the following capabilities:

- **Sensitive information types**: These help you identify sensitive data in your organization by using a function, the provided regular expressions in the portal, or by creating your own custom regular expressions.

- **Trainable classifiers**: These help you identify sensitive data by using examples you provide rather than RegEx-based pattern matches.

- **Data classification**: This is a dashboard from where you can follow the amount of data using a specific retention label, sensitivity label, or classification. This dashboard will allow you to gain several insights as to what actions your users are taking on the listed items.

Now that we have covered how to identify our data, let's take a look at what capabilities Information Protection gives us to protect it.

Provide protection for your data

In order to provide protection for your data, applying encryption, access restrictions, and visual markings, Microsoft Purview Information Protection offers the following capabilities:

- **Sensitivity labels**: This is a solution that helps you to label and protect your data regardless of which device it is stored on, which application or service it is stored in, and whether it travels inside or outside your organization.

- **Azure Information Protection unified labeling client**: An extra set of features and functionality is added to the Windows client for sensitivity labels. Labeling and protecting all files from File Explorer and Powershell are included.

- **Double Key Encryption**: This is a feature that guarantees that under any circumstances, only your organization can ever decrypt content using Double Key Encryption or for regulatory requirements, you must keep encryption keys within a geographical boundary.

- **Office 365 Message Encryption (OME)**: By encrypting email messages and attachments sent to any user on any device, this ensures that only authorized recipients can access the information contained therein.

- **Service encryption with Customer Key**: This helps you protect data against viewing by unauthorized systems or personnel and complements BitLocker disk encryption in Microsoft data centers.

- **SharePoint Information Rights Management (IRM)**: This helps you protect SharePoint lists and libraries so that when a document gets checked out, the file is protected in order for only people with the correct authorization to be able to read and edit the file according to policies specified by you or your company.

- **Rights Management connector**: For servers existing in on-premises deployments that use *Exchange* or *SharePoint* or run *Windows Server* and *File Classification Infrastructure* (*FCI*), the Rights Management connector offers protection using encryption from Microsoft Purview Information Protection.

- **Azure Information Protection unified labeling scanner**: This is a feature that helps you to discover, label, and protect sensitive data stored in your on-premises environment.

- **Microsoft Defender for Cloud Apps**: With this feature, you can discover, label, and protect sensitive data stored in your cloud environment regardless of the cloud provider.

- **Microsoft Information Protection (SDK)**: This extends the usage of sensitivity labels to third-party applications and services.

That is all the protection capabilities of the Information Protection suite. Let's delve into what it has to offer when it comes to information governance and protection from either non-malicious or malicious sharing of data.

Govern your data

The following capabilities help you to prevent accidental oversharing of sensitive information:

- **Data loss prevention**: This is a feature intended to help prevent the unintentional sharing of sensitive information.
- **Endpoint data loss prevention**: This extends the data loss prevention capabilities to items used and shared on Windows 10 computers.
- **The protection of sensitive information** in Microsoft Teams chat and channel messages. This extends some data loss prevention capabilities to Teams chat and channel messages.

This features list does indeed help you to safeguard any information, regardless of its storage location, from unauthorized access and accidental or malicious sharing, and strengthens your compliance status with regulatory requirements.

These features are listed on the following website:

```
https://docs.microsoft.com/en-us/microsoft-365/compliance/
information-protection?view=o365-worldwide
```

We have covered the fundamentals regarding the capabilities of Information Protection, what features are available, and how they could help us safeguard our data throughout its life cycle. It is required of you as an Information Protection Administrator to have knowledge of these capabilities in order to understand where to use which feature and explain why it should be implemented.

Information protection use cases

Microsoft Purview Information Protection is commonly used to identify your data, supply protection for your data, and govern your data to minimize the risk of data leakage or oversharing. The features listed in the previous section provide you and your organization with the tools to achieve all of this.

The following diagram depicts the features of Information Protection that can be applied to sensitive data, and how they interact with each other:

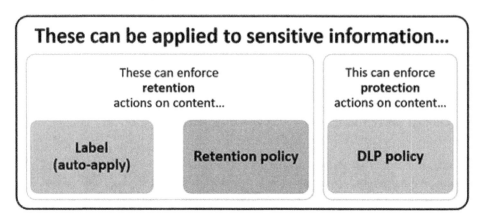

Figure 2.1 – Safeguarding mechanisms that can be applied to protect sensitive information

We will present **Example A**. Let's say that we have produced a document containing sensitive information regarding one of the employees in your organization. It could range from HR-related information to specific information that could cause harm to the individual if said information wound up in the wrong person's mailbox.

This is a perfect example of where Information Protection would swoop in with both *labeling* and *encryption* to make sure of the following:

1. The document containing the sensitive information is labeled automatically by leveraging sensitive information types.

2. The information in the document cannot be read by anyone not in possession of the correct access to it.

3. The document is labeled in such a way that, visually, it is easy to identify that it contains sensitive information.

Keeping example A in mind, the information is of such a nature that it must not leave the organization under any circumstances.

This calls for **data loss prevention (DLP), Example B**. With DLP, we could apply policies stating that information labeled with a certain label must not be shared outside the organization using email, SharePoint, OneDrive, or Teams chat and channel messages. Here, a DLP policy would interact with the end user stating that the item they are about to share or are trying to share externally is labeled such that external sharing is forbidden.

The following diagram is a brief overview of what a DLP policy consists of. The rules are paired to their own conditions and actions:

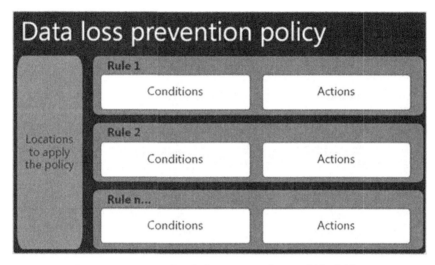

Figure 2.2 – Example of what a DLP policy could look like

In Example A, we are using sensitive information types, sensitivity labels, and encryption to safeguard the information on a document level.

As specified in *Figure 2.1*, the capabilities to label and/or retain information can work with a data loss prevention policy to further govern access to your data and make sure that no oversharing of sensitive information occurs. The following diagram shows what a data loss prevention policy consists of:

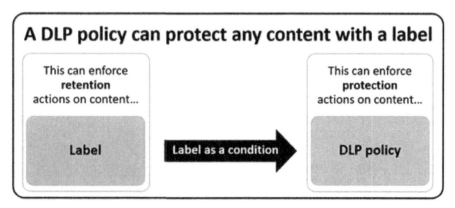

Figure 2.3 – How sensitivity labels and DLP policies interact with each other to apply protection

In Example B, we are leveraging the capabilities of DLP accompanied by our sensitivity labels to make sure that no accidental sharing of this information occurs.

The examples use a few features of Microsoft Purview Information Protection that can help you and your organization safeguard your information in a cost-effective and user-friendly manner.

Other use cases for Microsoft Purview Information Protection could have an even broader sense than one document.

Say that your organization needs insight into whether you are staying compliant with the **General Data Protection Regulation (GDPR)**. This is a situation where Microsoft Purview Information Protection could come into play as well. Leveraging the capabilities of sensitive information types, sensitivity labels, trainable classifiers, Azure Information Protection unified labeling scanners, **Microsoft Defender for Cloud Apps**, and the data classification dashboard, you would gain a lot of insight into which types of information are being stored where, such as whether it is **on-premises** or in a **cloud instance**.

The following diagram shows a brief overview of how **Microsoft Defender for Cloud Apps** operates in your cloud and on-premises environment. We will discuss the feature Microsoft Defender for Cloud Apps in more depth later in the book:

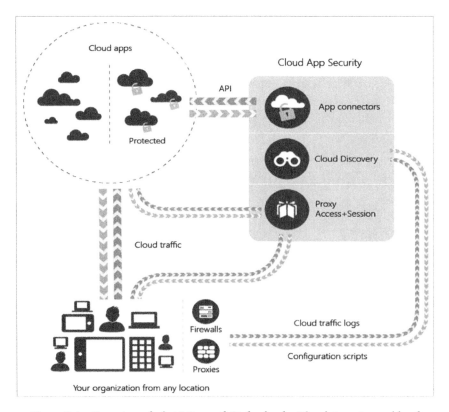

Figure 2.4 – Overview of what Microsoft Defender for Cloud Apps is capable of

In summary, for you to gain knowledge and insight into what information is being processed in your on-premises or cloud environment, you need to search for it, label it, and protect it to stay compliant with regulatory standards and make sure that the intellectual property of your organization stays inside the organization.

Microsoft Purview Information Protection helps with all of this, and when you have completed this book and the certification exam it is intended to help you prepare for, you will also have the toolset to implement these features in your organization.

We have covered some Information Protection use cases and will proceed with our next topic, which discusses the scope of Information Protection.

Understanding the scope of Information Protection

For information stored on-premises, we rely on the features designed to help us govern access and protect information stored there, such as the following:

- Sensitive information types
- Trainable classifiers
- Sensitivity labels
- The Azure Information Protection unified labeling client
- Double Key Encryption
- The Rights Management connector
- The Azure Information Protection unified labeling scanner
- Data loss prevention
- Endpoint data loss prevention

The same goes for the cloud environment, where we rely on the features in the cloud to help us achieve the same result, such as the following:

- Sensitive information types
- Trainable classifiers
- The data classification dashboard
- Sensitivity labels
- The Azure Information Protection unified labeling client

- Double Key Encryption

- **Office 365 Message Encryption** (OME)

- Service encryption with Customer Key

- **SharePoint Information Rights Management** (IRM)

- **Microsoft Defender for Cloud Apps**

- Microsoft Information Protection SDK

- Data loss prevention

- Endpoint data loss prevention

- Protect sensitive information in Microsoft Teams chat and channel messages

As you can see, the capabilities are largely intended to be used both in your own on-premises environment and in the cloud. Microsoft Purview Information Protection is intended to help you safeguard your information regardless of where the information is stored, processed, or travels to. All of these features will be covered in the coming chapters of the book, providing you with the theoretical and practical skillset to understand, explain, and implement these features in your organization.

To summarize, the scope of Information Protection is basically everywhere you are storing data.

The following diagram shows us the capabilities of Information Protection and how they all work together in order to keep our data as safe as possible:

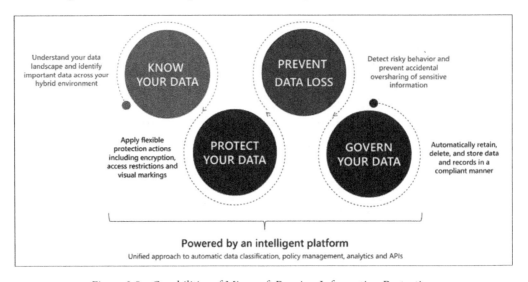

Figure 2.5 – Capabilities of Microsoft Purview Information Protection

As we have just covered, the scope of Information Protection is not limited to a specific workload in cloud apps, on-premises data centers, or information stored on an employee's computer. It is all three. To fully cover every inch of intellectual property with labels, protection via encryption, and prevention against data leaks is the main goal of implementing Information Protection capabilities. Next, we will talk more about the regulatory requirements Information Protection can help us stay compliant with.

Why is Information Protection important?

Information Protection is an important feature to help you stay compliant with regulatory requirements such as the following:

- GDPR
- LGPD
- HIPAA-HITECH

Information Protection helps you with insights and technical enforcement to stay compliant with all three mentioned previously.

Regulatory requirements are of course a big part of why Information Protection is important, but the intellectual property of your organization could be a big part of this as well, making sure that sensitive information about your organization or your business does not fall into the wrong hands.

Bear in mind that the implementation of Information Protection does not automatically protect you from any harm on its own. The implementation must be accompanied by policies with regard to information and sharing it internally, as well as the will of your employees to understand why it is important to label information, protect it, and minimize the risks of accidental or malicious sharing.

Information Protection is important to stay compliant with regulatory requirements, and as we have talked about in the previous sections, to keep your data safe and accessible by intended users only.

Next, we will cover the topic of the benefits of implementing Information Protection in your organization.

What are the benefits of implementing Information Protection in your organization?

Some *benefits* have been covered previously when it comes to regulatory compliance and protection from insider risk. But something we have not talked about yet is the importance of raising **security awareness** inside your organization.

Here, an implementation of Information Protection would help your users to understand which types of information are subject to protection using encryption or information barriers.

Information Protection not only safeguards any information protected by it, but it also will help with making your users aware of how to interact with information within your organization in a safe manner, due to visual markings on labeled information, notifications from data loss prevention policies, and the requirement to set permissions on data labeled as classified.

Summary

This chapter has been about providing an introduction to Information Protection, what capabilities it has, and how it could help your organization to safeguard data and protect it from accidental or malicious sharing of information.

In order to implement and administer Information Protection, you will need to have knowledge about all of the capabilities presented. Perhaps not in depth, as there are quite a few features available, but knowing about them will make the implementation and administration of the platform easier.

In the next chapter, we will cover the subject of how to create and manage sensitive information types, which is the first step of implementing Information Protection.

Section 2: Implementing Information Protection

This part of the book will focus on implementing information protection within a Microsoft 365 tenant. This will include custom sensitive information types, document fingerprinting, and keyword dictionaries.

This section comprises the following chapters:

- *Chapter 3, Creating and Managing Sensitive Information Types*
- *Chapter 4, Creating and Managing Trainable Classifiers*
- *Chapter 5, Implementing and Managing Sensitivity Labels*
- *Chapter 6, Planning and Implementing Encryption for Email Messages*

3
Creating and Managing Sensitive Information Types

In the previous chapter, we introduced Microsoft Purview Information Protection, by looking at some use cases, understanding the scope of Information Protection, and seeing why it is such an important security service for Microsoft 365. In this chapter, we will go into further detail about how specific aspects of the service are *configured* and *implemented*.

In this chapter, we're going to cover the following main topics:

- Selecting a sensitive information type based on an organization's requirements
- Creating and managing custom sensitive information types
- Creating custom sensitive information types with an exact data match
- Implementing document fingerprinting
- Creating a keyword dictionary

Technical requirements

In this chapter, we will start to explore configuring Information Protection and its use within Microsoft 365. There will be exercises that will require access to the **Microsoft Purview Compliance Portal** with *Global Administration* rights. If you have not created the trial licenses for Microsoft 365, please follow the instructions in *Chapter 1, Preparing for Your Microsoft Exam and SC-400 Exam Objectives.*

Accessing the Microsoft Purview Compliance Portal

The various information protection policies and configurations are managed via the Microsoft Purview Compliance Portal. The following steps will show you how to navigate the Microsoft 365 admin center to gain access to the relevant compliance center:

1. Open a web browser and navigate to `https://login.microsoftonline.com/`.

2. Log into the Microsoft 365 portal using the Global Admin account in your tenant where you have enabled the Microsoft 365 trial license.

3. Once you are logged in, navigate to the **Microsoft 365 admin center** icon on the left-hand side of the screen and click it:

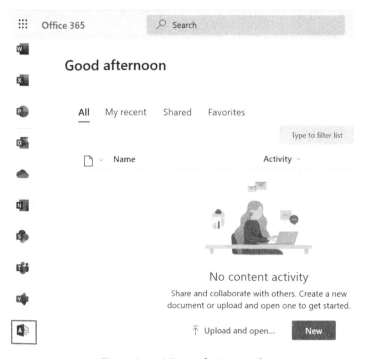

Figure 3.1 – Microsoft 365 portal

4. This will open an additional tab on your explorer window for the Microsoft 365 admin center. Navigate to the left-hand side of the window, where you will see **… Show all**. Click on this to view the entire menu.

5. Navigate to the **Compliance** option and click it. An additional tab will open on your browser. Now, you will be able to start configuring the different information protection settings:

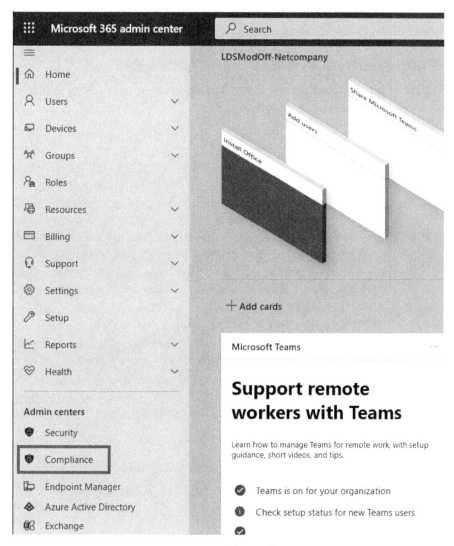

Figure 3.2 – Microsoft 365 admin center

You should now know how to access the Microsoft Purview Compliance Portal so that you can take part in the exercises in this and future chapters of this book.

Selecting a sensitive information type based on an organization's requirements

Before you can select **sensitive information types**, it is important to understand what they are used for and the fundamental components that make up a sensitive information type. They are used to identify sensitive items within pieces of information, such as credit card numbers. Sensitive information types look for patterns and validate information by looking at the relevant keywords, the format of the data, and its checksum.

Sensitive information type components

The following table describes the fundamental components of sensitive information types for both *custom* and *built-in* information types:

Component	Information Contained
Primary pattern	Typically identified by a regular expression but can be keywords, such as project numbers and employee ID numbers.
Character proximity	You are more likely to find the detected content you are looking for if the primary pattern and supporting evidence of the data are close to each other. To increase the accuracy of finding actual sensitive data and reducing the number of false positives, you can specify the distance between the primary pattern and the supporting evidence, which is called the proximity window.
Confidence level	By assigning higher levels of confidence, you will increase the likelihood of false positives being detected. Having higher amounts of supporting evidence will increase the likelihood that a match contains the sensitive information you are looking for.
Additional evidence	Also known as supporting or corroborative evidence, this increases the likelihood that, for example, a nine-digit number found in the data is an employee ID number. This lowers the chance of false positives.

Table 3.1 – Sensitive information type components

The next part of this chapter will focus on the key features of the custom sensitive information type.

Custom sensitive information type features

The **custom sensitive information type**'s special features and their use cases are detailed as follows:

- **Document fingerprinting**: This converts a standard form into a sensitive information type. You can use this on a government form, an employee information form, or a patent template. In an ideal world, businesses will already have an established practice of using specific forms to send and receive sensitive information, though it is recommended that after uploading an empty form, it should be converted into a document fingerprint. Then, you should set up a corresponding policy so that any documents being shared that match that fingerprint are detected.

- **Keyword dictionaries**: This is a solution for managing reused keyword lists when matching large amounts of businesses' information/data. It supports up to 1 MB of keywords in any language. When looking to identify inappropriate or explicit language, keyword dictionaries can be used to detect specific words and take the required actions on them, such as enforcing organization guidelines.

- **Exact Data Match (EDM)-based classification**: This enables you to generate databases with custom sensitive information types that refer to specific data. There are daily refreshes that can contain up to 100 million rows of information. These are best for businesses that are required to store large amounts of personal data, including hospitals. They can benefit from EDM-based classification to ensure no personal information is being shared.

You should now understand how to access the Microsoft Purview Compliance Portal, the components that are part of a sensitive information type and the information they store, as well as the key features of custom sensitive information. Because you have this knowledge, you are ready to create a custom sensitive information type, which we are going to cover in the next part of this chapter.

Creating and managing custom sensitive information types

Protecting stored employee IDs, cost center numbers, and other **human resources (HR)** and finance-specific data are all common usage scenarios for custom sensitive information types. The recommended way to make a new custom sensitive information type is to look for a built-in sensitive information type and modify the rules. Once you have fully completed your customization, you can upload it with a new name.

We will now go through the steps required to create a new sensitive information type that is completely defined:

1. From the **compliance center**, navigate to **Data classification** and then **Sensitive info types**. At this point, select **Create sensitive info type**, as shown here:

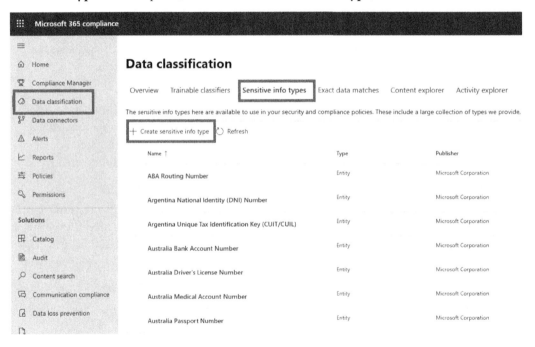

Figure 3.3 – Create info types

2. Fill in the values for **Name** and **Description** and click **Next**:

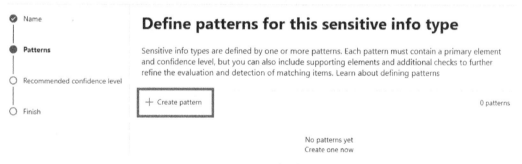

Sensitive info types > Create sensitive info type

Name your sensitive info type

This name and description will appear in compliance policies that support sensitive info types, so be sure to enter text that helps admins easily understand what info will be detected.

Name *

Enter a friendly name

Description *

Enter a friendly description

Figure 3.4 – Name and Description

3. On the next screen, you will need to click on **Create pattern**, as shown in the following screenshot. You have the option of creating many patterns, and in every case, different elements and confidence levels, which will enable you to build the new sensitive information type:

Name

Patterns

Recommended confidence level

Finish

Define patterns for this sensitive info type

Sensitive info types are defined by one or more patterns. Each pattern must contain a primary element and confidence level, but you can also include supporting elements and additional checks to further refine the evaluation and detection of matching items. Learn about defining patterns

+ Create pattern

0 patterns

No patterns yet
Create one now

Figure 3.5 – Creating a pattern for the sensitive info type

4. The next option will be to select the default **Confidence level** setting, as shown in the following screenshot. The available options are *low*, *medium*, and *high*:

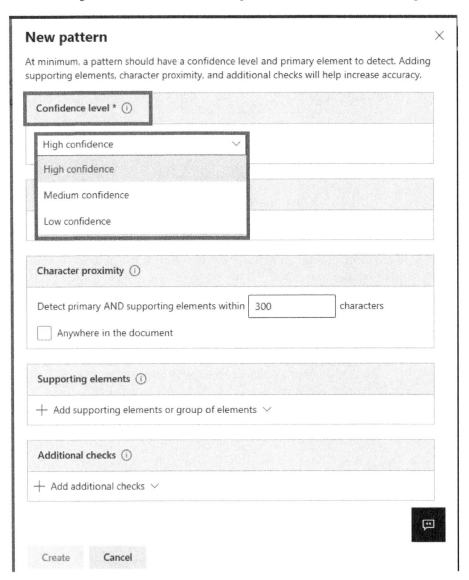

Figure 3.6 – Choosing a confidence level

5. Next, you must define **the primary element**. The available settings are that you can set it to a regular expression with an optional validator, **Keyword list**, **Keyword dictionary**, or a pre-constructed function, as follows:

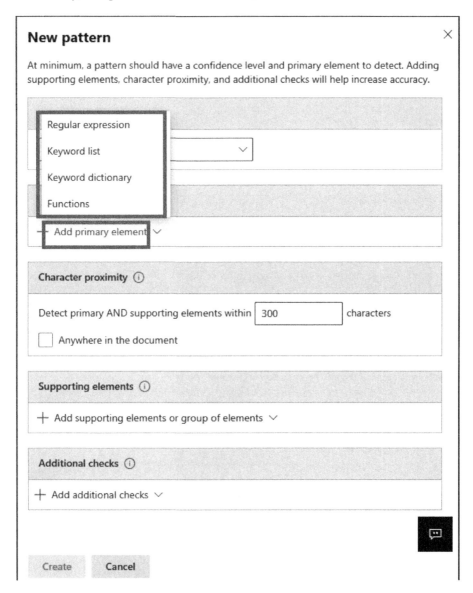

Figure 3.7 – Primary element

6.   Enter a value for **Character proximity**, as shown here:

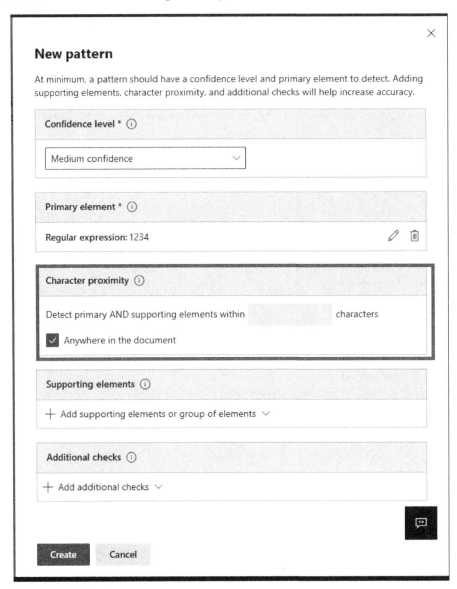

Figure 3.8 – Character proximity

7.   As you can see, you have the option of adding supporting elements if you have any.

8. In the final box at the bottom, add any additional checks you want to include from the available options, including **Exclude specific matches**, **Start** or **Doesn't start with characters**, or **Exclude duplicate characters**, as well as options that you will find in the list:

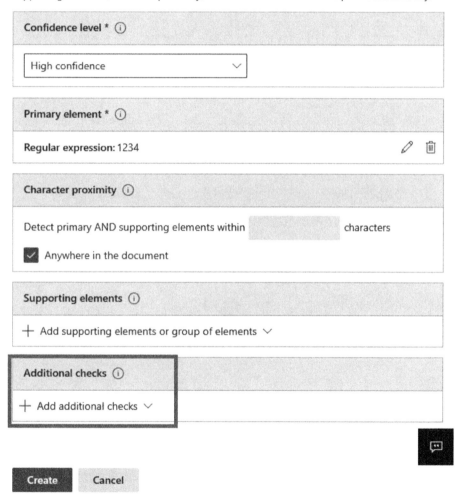

Figure 3.9 – Additional checks

9. Click on **Create**:

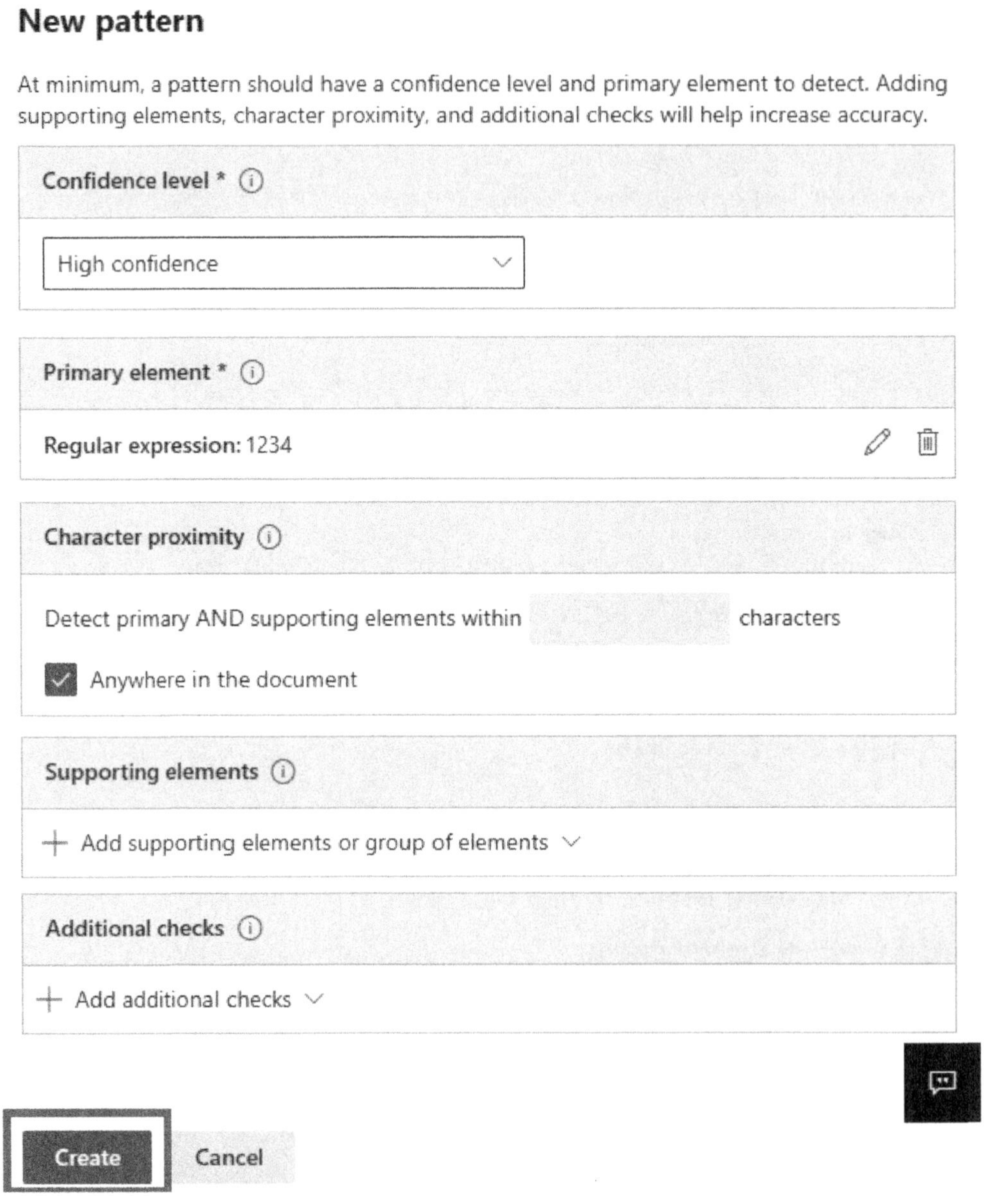

New pattern

At minimum, a pattern should have a confidence level and primary element to detect. Adding supporting elements, character proximity, and additional checks will help increase accuracy.

Confidence level * ⓘ

High confidence ⌄

Primary element * ⓘ

Regular expression: 1234   ✏ 🗑

Character proximity ⓘ

Detect primary AND supporting elements within [   ] characters

☑ Anywhere in the document

Supporting elements ⓘ

\+ Add supporting elements or group of elements ⌄

Additional checks ⓘ

\+ Add additional checks ⌄

💬

Create	Cancel

Figure 3.10 – Create button

10. Click on **Next**:

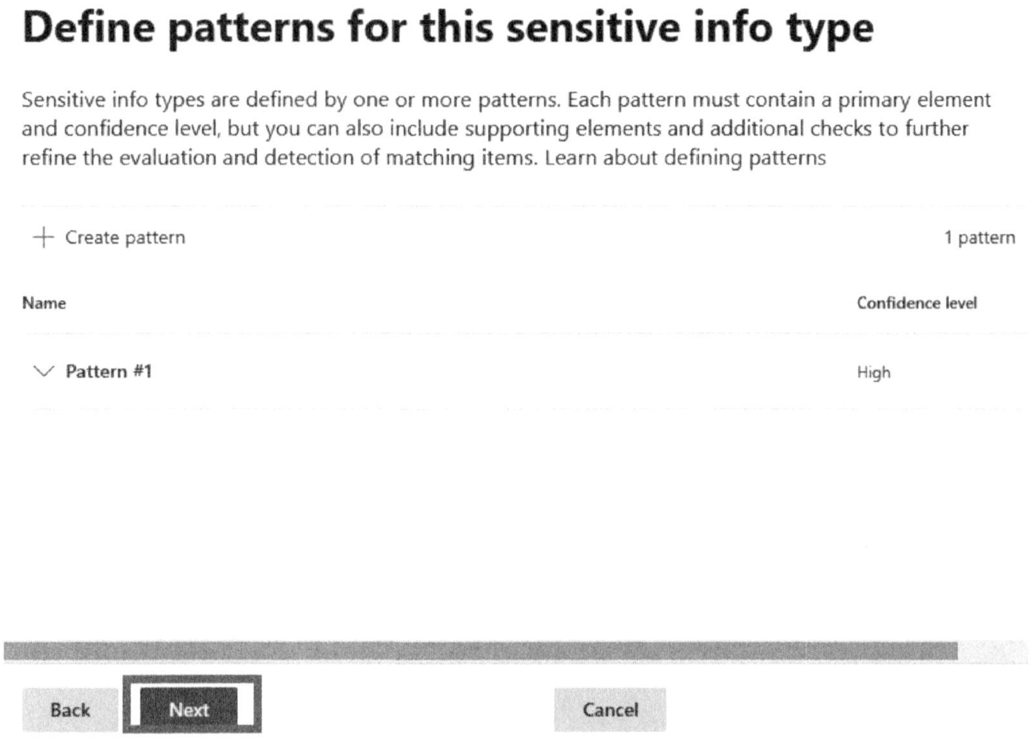

Define patterns for this sensitive info type

Sensitive info types are defined by one or more patterns. Each pattern must contain a primary element and confidence level, but you can also include supporting elements and additional checks to further refine the evaluation and detection of matching items. Learn about defining patterns

Name	Confidence level
⌄ Pattern #1	High

+ Create pattern   1 pattern

Back   Next   Cancel

Figure 3.11 – Next button

11. You will now need to set **Choose the recommended confidence level** to show in compliance properties, as shown in the following screenshot. Here, you have the following choices:

- **High confidence level**: Matched items will contain the fewest false positives but the most false negatives.

- **Medium confidence level**: Matched items will contain an average amount of false positives and false negatives.

- **Low confidence level**: Matched items will contain the fewest negatives but the most false positives:

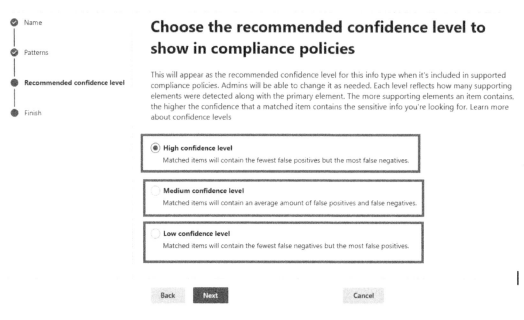

Figure 3.12 – Confidence level

12. Check that all the settings are correct and choose **Submit**.

13. You may need to click **Refresh** on the **Data Classification** page, which will cause the custom sensitive information type you have just created to appear.

Once you have created the sensitive information type, you can test, modify, and remove it later if you so wish. The following steps will explain how to test a sensitive information type and how to modify a custom sensitive information type in the compliance center.

Testing a sensitive information type

Microsoft's best practice recommendation is that once you have created a sensitive information type, it should be tested to ensure it is working as expected. You can then deploy this to the wider organization. Let's explore this by performing the following steps:

1. Create two files; for example, two Microsoft Word documents. Add data that matches the components you configured in your sensitive information type to one of the documents, and then add content that does not match the other.

2. From the Microsoft compliance center, navigate to **Data Classification | Sensitive info types** and select the sensitive information type. This will open a pane containing the specific configuration. Now, select **Test**.

3. Upload the files, then select **Test**.

4. Review the findings on the **Matches results** page and click on **Finish**.

Although the sensitive information type is available to the entire tenant, once you have created and tested the custom sensitive information type, you can assign this to groups and users. However, you may need to edit this in the future, which will be covered in the next part of this chapter.

Modifying custom sensitive information types in the compliance center

In this next section, we will go through the steps you need to follow to modify an already existing custom sensitive information type from the Microsoft Purview Compliance Portal. Let's get started:

1. From within the compliance center, navigate to **Data Classification | Sensitive info types**, select the sensitive information type you want to amend, and choose **Edit**.

2. From within this menu, you can add other patterns with supporting elements, character proximity, confidence levels, and additional checks. You can also modify or delete the existing ones if you so wish.

Once you have modified the custom sensitive information type, you will find yourself back on the sensitive information type pane, where we will now look at how to delete an existing sensitive information type.

Removing custom sensitive information types in the compliance center

It is important to note that at this stage, you can't remove *built-in* sensitive information types. You are only able to remove any custom sensitive information types that are created by you or another administrator. Let's take a look at how to do this:

1. From within the compliance center, navigate to **Data Classification | Sensitive info types** and select the sensitive information type that needs to be removed.

2. Select **Delete** in the pop-up window that opens.

You should now be able to create, test, modify, and delete a custom sensitive information type from the Microsoft Purview Compliance Portal. Next, we are going to cover the same tasks, but this time with custom sensitive information types with exact data matches.

Creating custom sensitive information types with exact data matches

Custom sensitive information types match several business needs for a lot of organizations. However, there is also a use case where you may want a custom **sensitive information type** that uses exact data values, rather than the sensitive information types that have matched based on common patterns.

EDM-based classifications will enable you to build a custom sensitive information type that is design to be more scalable and secure, as well as having integration with the Microsoft 365 and Azure ecosystem.

EDM-based classification will allow an admin to build custom sensitive information types that apply to *particular values* in a database. This database of sensitive information can be rejuvenated daily and may contain up to 100 million rows of information. You can also utilize EDM-based classifications with multiple different policies, including **data loss prevention (DLP)** policies.

Please note that EDM-based classification is available as part of the following subscriptions:

*   Office 365 E5

*   Microsoft 365 E5

*   Microsoft 365 E5 Compliance

*   Microsoft 365 E5/A5 Information Protection and Governance

There are three parts to creating and implementing an EDM-based classification, as follows:

1. Saving sensitive data in a `.csv` or `.tsv` file structure
2. Defining your sensitive information in your database schema
3. Building a ruler package

We'll look at these closely in the next few sections.

Saving sensitive data in .csv or .tsv file format

The following steps will explain how you can save sensitive data in `.csv` or `.tsv`, which are the two supported file formats:

1. First, you will need to identify the sensitive information that you wish to utilize and transfer that data to an app, such as *Microsoft Excel*. The file then needs to be kept in either **comma-separated values** (`.csv`), **tab-separated values** (`.tsv`), or **pip-separated** (`|`) format. Microsoft's best practice recommendation is to save the file in `.tsv` format in case the information values include commas. The file can include the following:

    *   Up to 32 columns per data source
    *   Up to 100 million rows of sensitive data
    *   Up to 5 columns marked as searchable

2. You must configure the sensitive data in your file so that the first row contains the names of the field that will be used for EDM-based classification; for example, `firstname` and `lastname`. Ensure that the column header names do not consist of spaces or underscores.
3. Fields that might contain commas will be parsed as two individual fields; for example, `London, UK` for a street address. You can use a `.tsv` file to avoid this or utilize double quotes around the comma values. If, for example, the value with the comma also has a space in it, you will be required to build a custom sensitive information type that meets the resultant format.

Now that we understand how to save data and sensitive information in the supported file formats, this will enable us to define the schema for the database, which we will cover in the next section.

Defining the schema for your database of sensitive information

You can build a **schema** and EDM-sensitive information type pattern with both PowerShell and the **Exact Data Match Schema and Sensitive Information Type** wizard. Note that the wizard is only available for the *Worldwide* and *GCC clouds*. You can find additional information on the wizard at the following *Microsoft Docs* link: `https://docs.microsoft.com/en-us/microsoft-365/compliance/sit-edm-wizard?view=o365-worldwide`. Let's look at the following steps:

1. First, you need to utilize an XML format file to identify the schema for the database of sensitive information. Name the file `edmtest.xml` and ensure it has been configured so that for each column, there is a line that uses the following composition:

    `\<field name="" searchable=""/\>`

    Field name values should be used for column names.

    If you would like the fields to be searchable, use `searchable="true"`. Please note that at least one field must be searchable.

2. For a full example of an EDM XML file that you can use for your lab, please refer to the following *Microsoft Docs* link: `https://docs.microsoft.com/en-us/microsoft-365/compliance/create-custom-sensitive-information-types-with-exact-data-match-based-classification?view=o365-worldwide&viewFallbackFrom=o365-worldwide%3Fazure-portal%3Dtrue`.

3. You will need to connect to the **Security & Compliance Center** using PowerShell. Follow the steps at the following *Microsoft Docs* link to complete these tasks: `https://docs.microsoft.com/en-us/powershell/exchange/connect-to-scc-powershell?view=exchange-ps`.

4. To upload the database schema, you will be required to complete two **cmdlets** in the following order:

    ```
    $edmSchemaXml=Get-Content .\\edm.xml -Encoding Byte
    -ReadCount 0
    New-DlpEdmSchema -FileData $edmSchemaXml -Confirm:$true
    ```

Once these cmdlets have been entered, you will be requested to confirm you want to proceed.

Setting up a rule package

We will now explain the steps you need to follow when setting up a rule package:

1. First, you will need to create a rule package in XML format. When creating the rule package, ensure you reference the `.csv` or `.tsv` file, as well as the `edm.xml` file. In this example, the resulting fields will need to be adapted to create the EDM sensitive type, as follows:

    *   **Datastore**: This field is specific to the EDM lookup datastore. You must provide the data source name of the configured EDM schema.

    *   **idMatch**: This field points to the primary element for EDM:

        RulePack id and **ExactMatch id**: Use the `New-GUID` command to generate a **GUID**. You can find more information on how to do this at the following *Microsoft Docs* link: `https://docs.microsoft.com/en-us/powershell/module/microsoft.powershell.utility/new-guid?view=powershell-7.1&viewFallbackFrom=powershell-6`.

    *   **Match**: In this field, you will point to additional proof that can be found in the proximity of `idMatch`.

    *   **Resource**: This segment identifies the name and description of a sensitive type in multiple locales.

    > Tip
    > You can find some example. `xml` code at the following *Microsoft Docs* site that will help you with this exercise: `https://docs.microsoft.com/en-us/microsoft-365/compliance/create-custom-sensitive-information-types-with-exact-data-match-based-classification?view=o365-worldwide#save-sensitive-data-in-csv-or-tsv-format`.

2. Once the rule package has been created, you will need to use PowerShell to upload it. Use the following cmdlets to do so:

    ```
    $rulepack=Get-Content .\\rulepack.xml -Encoding Byte
    -ReadCount 0

    New-DlpSensitiveInformationTypeRulePackage -FileData
    $rulepack
    ```

Once the rule package has been imported with the EDM sensitive info type and the sensitive data table, you will be able to test this by utilizing the **Test** task in the EDM wizard from within the compliance center.

Once you have created the EDM sensitive information type, you can modify and remove the schema later if you so wish.

Modifying the schema for EDM-based classification

The following steps explain how to test a sensitive information type and how to modify a custom sensitive information type in the compliance center:

1. Edit the `edm.xml` file (this is the file we discussed in the *Defining the schema for your database of sensitive information* section of this chapter).

2. Next, you will need to connect to the **Security & Compliance Centre** by utilizing PowerShell. You can find instructions for this by going to the link that was shared in the *Defining the schema for your database of sensitive information* section, earlier in this chapter.

3. You can update the database schema by running the following cmdlets, one at a time:

```
$edmSchemaXml=Get-Content .\\edm.xml -Encoding Byte
-ReadCount 0
```
```
Set-DlpEdmSchema -FileData $edmSchemaXml -Confirm:$true
```

You will be asked to confirm your action within the PowerShell window, where you can hit the *Enter* key to accept the changes.

Removing the schema for EDM-based classification

If you must remove the schema you are using for the EDM-based classification, you do the following:

1. First, you will need to connect to the **Security & Compliance Center** by utilizing PowerShell. You can find instructions on how to do this in the *Defining the schema for your database of sensitive information* section, earlier in this chapter.

2. Now, run the following cmdlet, where you can replace the datastore's name (`patientrecords`) with the name of whatever it is you want to remove:

```
Remove-DlpEdmSchema -Identity patientrecords
```

As with the previous examples in PowerShell, you will be prompted to confirm your action from within this window.

You should now have the required knowledge and understanding of what a custom sensitive information type is due to **EDM**, the three parts that define it, as well as how to create, modify, and delete it from the Microsoft Purview Compliance Portal and PowerShell. This completes the sensitive information type section of the chapter. Next, we will take a deeper dive into *document fingerprinting*.

Implementing document fingerprinting

Employees in an organization that have the responsibility of dealing with information manage many kinds of sensitive information when completing their regular daily tasks. **Document fingerprinting** within the Microsoft 365 ecosystem makes it simpler for you, as the admin, to protect that information by identifying standard forms that are used by all users within the business.

To prevent unintentionally sharing information that's been created from official company templates, you can configure and implement document fingerprinting as a *custom sensitive information type*. A good example of this is documents managed by HR workers that can potentially contain personal information, which can be identified by document fingerprinting. This is regardless of whether the information from within the document does not meet other sensitive information type conditions.

Although documents do not have actual fingerprints, much like a person's fingerprint, documents have unique identifiers and word patterns. When a file is uploaded, **DLP** detects that unique pattern in the document, creates a fingerprint built on that pattern, and utilizes the document fingerprint to detect outbound documents that may encompass the same pattern.

The following diagram and flow demonstrate how the basic functionality of document fingerprinting works:

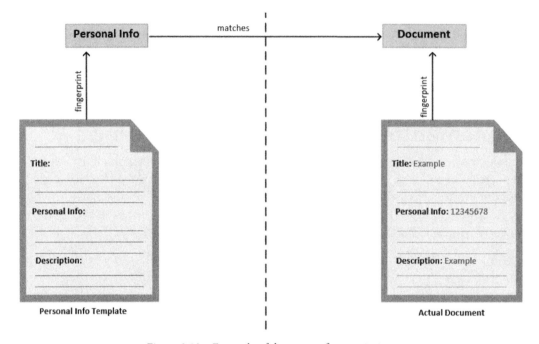

Figure 3.13 – Example of document fingerprinting

Here, the **Personal Info Template** document contains blank fields under **Title**, **Personal Info**, and **Description**, as well as descriptions for each of those fields, which is the *word pattern*.

The word pattern is then converted into a document fingerprint and a small *Unicode XML* file with a unique hash value is created. This represents the original text. Active Directory also stores the fingerprint as a security measure because the original document is not stored on the service.

The personal information fingerprint will become a sensitive information type that can be associated with a policy, or even any outbound email, that contains the document that was created from the same template.

There are some cases, however, where document fingerprinting cannot be detected in sensitive information, as follows:

- A password-protected file
- A document that only contains images

- A document that does not contain all the text that was in the original template that was used to create the document fingerprint

In this section, we learned about the theory behind document fingerprinting and how this relates to sensitive information types. You should now understand how the functionality works and the uses cases where it is not detected. In the final section of this chapter, we will discuss keyword dictionaries and how to implement them from the Microsoft Purview Compliance Portal and PowerShell.

Creating a keyword dictionary

A **keyword dictionary** is an effective method of managing a big list of words that regularly change. You can create keyword lists in a sensitive information type; however, lists have size limitations, and you will be required to edit an XML file to make any changes to them.

You can configure keyword dictionaries from the *Microsoft Purview Compliance Portal* or via the *Security & Compliance* PowerShell module. There are some Microsoft best practice recommendations you should be aware of when implementing keyword dictionaries:

- Create an employee audit and create the list from the outcome.

- Collect typical words from some departments using **Microsoft Forms**.

- Collaborate with some employees, such as those from HR or legal, to create a list of typical words.

- Remember that you can edit the list, so you can improve your results by revising them regularly.

We will now go through the actions you need to complete to build a keyword dictionary from both the Microsoft 365 *Security & Compliance Center* and a file using PowerShell.

Building a keyword dictionary using the Security & Compliance Center

You need to perform the following steps:

1. Ensure you are logged into the Microsoft 365 Security & Compliance Centre with an account with **Global Admin** privileges (`https://protection.office.com/`).

2. Next, go to **Classification | Sensitive info types**, as shown in the following screenshot:

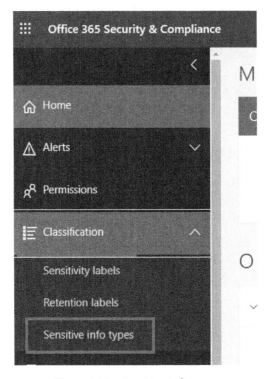

Figure 3.14 – Sensitive info types

3. Click on **Create sensitive info type** and then enter a name and a description for the sensitive info type you want, as shown in the following screenshot. Then, click **Next**:

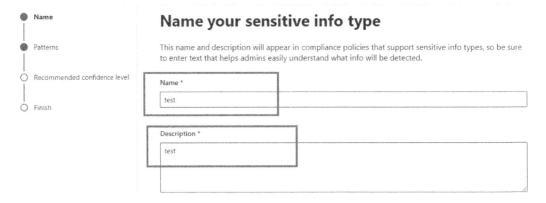

Figure 3.15 – Name and Description

4. Select **Create pattern | Add primary element** and choose **Keyword dictionary**:

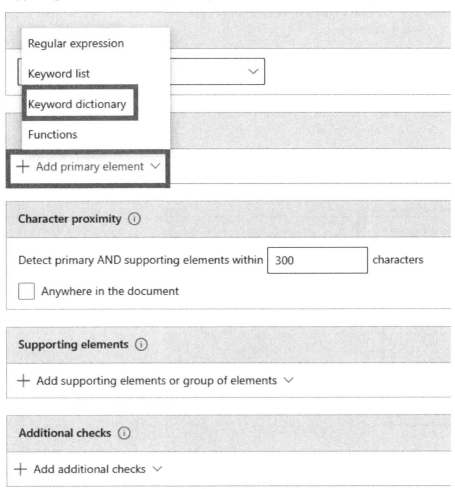

Figure 3.16 – Add primary element

5.   You now have a few different options, as follows:

- You can enter a name and a list of keywords in the policy.

- Click on **Choose from existing dictionaries** to select a built-in list of predefined words.

- Click on **Upload a dictionary** to upload either a `.csv` or `.txt` file that has been created in advance:

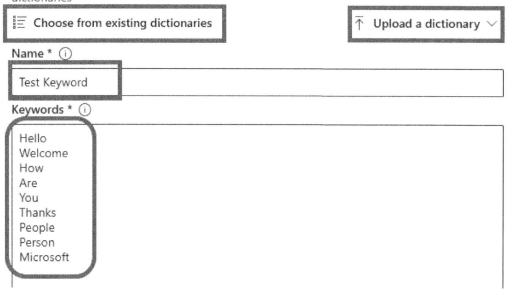

Figure 3.17 – Add keyword dictionary

6.   Now, click on **Done** and then **Create**. Review your configuration and click on **Next** and then **Create** to complete the configuration.

Next, we will learn about creating a keyword dictionary from a file using PowerShell.

Creating a keyword dictionary from a file using PowerShell

A lot of the time, you will use keywords from a file or a list that have been exported from some other source when creating a large dictionary. To complete this exercise, you will need to link up to the *Security & Compliance Center* in PowerShell, as shown in the *Defining the schema for your database of sensitive information* section, earlier in this chapter:

1. Place the keywords into a text file and ensure that each one is on a separate line.

2. Save the file with *Unicode* encoding.

3. Run the following cmdlet in PowerShell to read the file into a variable. Replace `<filename>` with the full URL of where you saved the keywords file:

```
$fileData = Get-Content <filename> -Encoding Byte
-ReadCount 0
```

4. Run the following cmdlet to create the dictionary:

```
New-DlpKeywordDictionary -Name <name> -Description
<description> -FileData $fileData
```

Replace `<name>` and `<description>` with whatever name and description you wish to give the keyword dictionary. You can use keyword dictionaries in custom sensitive information types and DLP policies. For further information on this, you can refer to the following Microsoft Docs link: `https://docs.microsoft.com/en-us/microsoft-365/compliance/create-a-keyword-dictionary?view=o365-worldwide`.

Summary

In this chapter, we have covered a lot of different topics, including selecting a sensitive information type based on your organization's requirements, how to create and manage a custom sensitive information type via the Microsoft Purview Compliance Portal and PowerShell, how to create custom sensitive information types with an exact data match, what document fingerprinting is and why you should implement it, and how to create a keyword dictionary via the Microsoft Security & Compliance Center and PowerShell.

We have run through multiple exercises and if you have not followed these as of yet, I strongly recommend that you do them before moving on to the next chapter.

The next chapter will cover creating and managing trainable classifiers.

4
Creating and Managing Trainable Classifiers

In this chapter, we will introduce trainable classifiers, including how to identify, create, and manage them. We will also look at how to verify that they are performing correctly and how to retrain a classifier. Classifying and labeling content in bulk is a challenge for many organizations, which is where trainable classifiers come to play.

In this chapter, we are going to cover the following main topics:

- What are trainable classifiers?
- Identifying when to use trainable classifiers
- Creating a trainable classifier
- Verifying a trainable classifier is performing properly
- Retraining a classifier

Technical requirements

The technical requirements for using trainable classifiers are any one of these licenses:

- Microsoft 365 E5 license
- Microsoft 365 E5 Compliance license

More information about the licensing requirements for using trainable classifiers can be found at the following link:

```
https://docs.microsoft.com/en-us/microsoft-365/compliance/
classifier-get-started-with?view=o365-worldwide#licensing-
requirements
```

When it comes to administrative privileges required to create and manage classifiers, you will need the following.

To access classifiers in the user interface, the global admin will need to perform an opt-in for the tenant in order to create custom classifiers.

Compliance administrator privileges are required to perform the training of a classifier.

You will need these permissions to use classifiers in the following scenarios:

- Retention label scenario:

    a. Record management role

    b. Retention management role

- Sensitivity label scenario:

    a. Compliance data administrator

    b. Compliance administrator

    c. Security administrator

- Communication compliance scenario:

    a. Insider risk management admin

    b. Supervisory review administrator

These privilege requirements are listed at the following site:

```
https://docs.microsoft.com/en-us/microsoft-365/compliance/
classifier-get-started-with?view=o365-worldwide#permissions
```

Now that we have covered the requirements part, let's dive into our first topic and start exploring what trainable classifiers are.

What are trainable classifiers?

There are three ways to classify content in your **Microsoft 365 tenant**:

- **Manually**: The responsibility of classifying the data falls on the end user or the administrator, using the sensitivity labels created in the previous chapter.

- **Automated pattern matching**: Automated pattern matching includes finding content by using the following:

    a. Metadata values or keywords

    b. Sensitive information types to identify data

    c. Document fingerprinting to recognize data

    d. Exact data match by finding the presence of exact strings

- **Trainable classifiers**: The classification method of *trainable classifiers* is very well suited for content that is not easily identified by automated pattern matching or the manual approach.

Trainable classifiers are fed examples of data you want to train the classifier to identify, meaning that the classifier looks at data you provide in order to train its identification algorithm.

There are two separate types of classifiers available in **Microsoft 365**, the pretrained classifiers created by Microsoft, which you can start using directly without the need to train them, and the custom classifiers, which you create on your own if there are classification needs within your organization where the pretrained classifiers are insufficient.

We will explore each of these classifiers in the following sections.

Pretrained classifiers

There are five pretrained classifiers in Microsoft 365 and, as was mentioned earlier, they are created and maintained by Microsoft Corporation. These are the following:

- **Source code**: Detects items that are written in any of the top 25 computer programming languages on GitHub:

    - **ActionScript**

    - **C**

    - **C#**

    - **C++**

    - **Clojure**

    - **CoffeeScript**

    - **Go**

    - **Haskell**

    - **Java**

    - **JavaScript**

    - **Lua**

    - **MATLAB**

    - **Objective-C**

    - **Perl**

    - **PHP**

    - **Python**

    - **R**

    - **Ruby**

    - **Scala**

    - **Shell**

    - **Swift**

    - **Tex**

    - **Vimscript**

- **Threat**: Detects offensive language with threats of committing acts of violence, physical harm, or damage to property or a person.

- **Harassment**: Detects offensive language directed at one or several individuals based on traits such as ethnicity, national origin, gender, religion, age, sexual orientation, or disability.

- **Profanity**: Detects offensive language that contains expressions listed as profane, with the purpose of embarrassing users.

- **Resumes**: Detects information related to resumes present in Microsoft 365, such as an applicant, personal or professional qualifications, work experience, or other **personally identifiable information (PII)** related to resumes.

These classifiers can be found in the **Microsoft Purview Compliance Portal**, https://compliance.microsoft.com, under **Data classification | Trainable classifiers**, as illustrated in the following screenshot:

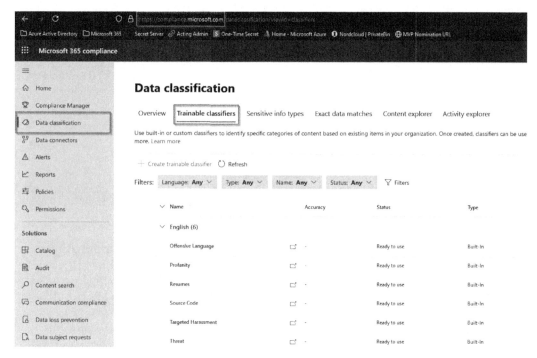

Figure 4.1 – Screenshot showing the location of Trainable classifiers in the Microsoft Purview Compliance Portal

As you can see in the preceding screenshot, a sixth classifier appears called **Offensive Language**. This classifier is deprecated by Microsoft as it is prone to generate many false positives, which is why we're not going to cover it to any extent and will rather focus on the ones listed earlier as they cover the areas of offensive language as well.

Custom classifiers

Custom classifiers are not present in the Microsoft Purview Compliance Portal by default; as stated earlier, a global administrator will need to consent to the usage of classifiers before being able to create any customized ones. The consent popup looks as in the screenshot shown next:

Figure 4.2 – The opt-in popup visualized in the Microsoft Purview Compliance Portal

To create your own custom classifiers, you need to click on the **Start scanning process** button highlighted in *Figure 4.2*. This will initiate a scan of your data in your Microsoft 365 tenant to better understand what data lives therein. The scan will take 7 to 14 days to complete, and you will have to complete it before creating your custom classifier.

The custom classifier differentiates itself from the pretrained classifier in the previous section in that they are untrained and you need to feed them with data in order to train them. The process flow of creating a custom classifier looks as in the following diagram:

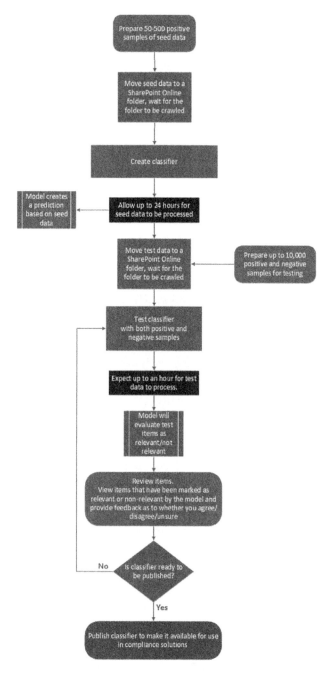

Figure 4.3 – The process flow of creating a custom classifier with each step described

This concludes this section of the chapter. Up next, we will delve deeper into the topic of trainable classifiers and try to distinguish when they are a good choice for classifying data.

Identifying when to use trainable classifiers

When do you use trainable classifiers? Well, to answer that, we will need to revisit the different options we have at our disposal to classify data in our environment:

- **Manually**: The responsibility of classifying the data falls on the end user or the administrator, using the sensitivity labels created in the previous chapter, *Chapter 3, Creating and Managing Sensitive Information Types*.

- **Automated pattern matching**: Automated pattern matching includes finding content by using the following:

  a. Metadata values or keywords

  b. Sensitive information types to identify data

  c. Document fingerprinting to recognize data

  d. Exact data match by finding the presence of exact strings

- **Trainable classifiers**: The classification method of *trainable classifiers* is very well suited for content that is not easily identified by automated pattern matching or the manual approach.

As the list makes it known, when we have data that is not easily detected by our unified labeling client for automatic labeling or when the manual approach cannot quite get us all the way there, the trainable classifiers make their entrance known.

A classifier learns how data is constructed by looking at hundreds and thousands of examples of the content of interest.

The following table visualizes when there is a need for using trainable classifiers:

Information type	Manually	Automatic	Classifier
Business data containing sensitive information about a project	✔	✔	✘
GDPR-related information in a large volume, such as social security numbers, credit card numbers, and so on	✘	✔	✘
Harassment: data that consists of a number of comments with offensive language targeting ethnicity, religion, or national origin	✘	✘	✔

Figure 4.4 – This table shows us the use cases for trainable classifiers rather than manual or automatic (pattern match) classification

So, identifying when to use trainable classifiers really boils down to the description of the classifiers themselves, namely, *trainable classifiers are very well suited for content that is not easily identified by automated pattern matching or the manual approach.*

If the data is hard to identify as sensitive, profane, harassment, or threats, there is no other option but to use trainable classifiers to gain knowledge of such content and label it accordingly.

Now that we have covered the introduction to trainable classifiers and when to use them, it is time to start trying this out ourselves and create some classifiers in our tenant.

Creating a trainable classifier

First things first, in order to create our custom trainable classifiers, we need to opt in to this feature in the Microsoft Purview Compliance Portal, as shown in the following screenshot:

Figure 4.5 – Opting in to trainable classifiers in the Microsoft Purview Compliance Portal

Bear in mind that this initial scan of data in your tenant might take as long as 14 days to complete. Prior to the completion of this, we will not be able to create any new classifiers in our environment.

Before we start creating our first custom classifier, it is important to note that there is a timeline to adhere to since the training takes some time for the classifier to get right, as described in the screenshot here:

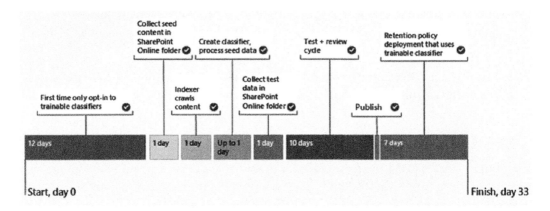

Figure 4.6 – A timeline of deployment for a classifier

Figure 4.6 is perhaps not accurate for each classifier created, but as you can see, we do have at least 26 days before we can publish a classifier to our environment. The initial step in the timeline will, of course, not be there for the next classifier we create as it is a one-and-done thing to opt-in.

So, let's start with creating a trainable classifier. There is a requirement here that the seed content (used for training our classifier) is stored in SharePoint Online. You can train your classifier using several different file types. The standard Office files, Word (.docx), Excel (.xlsx), PowerPoint (.pptx), Visio (.vsdx), and Text (.txt) files, are fully supported and most commonly used. The full list of supported file extensions can be found at the following link: https://docs.microsoft.com/en-us/sharepoint/technical-reference/default-crawled-file-name-extensions-and-parsed-file-types.

There need to be at least 50 files present in the SharePoint storage space, and the latest 500 files are the ones that will be scanned. The content must not be encrypted, and the language must be English.

In my example, I have uploaded some **Right Management Services (RMS)** logs to SharePoint Online to a `.txt` file, to be able to crawl them:

1. Sign in to the Microsoft Purview Compliance Portal.

2. Click on **Create trainable classifier**.

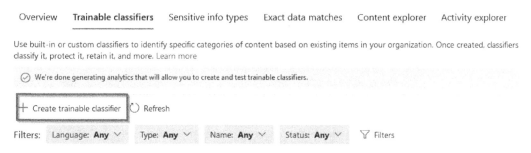

Figure 4.7 – Create trainable classifier

3. Specify a name for the classifier and add a description to help you identify what it is used for.

Figure 4.8 – Adding a name and description for the classifier

4. Specify the SharePoint site where you have added the seed content and the folder the content resides in.

Figure 4.9 – Specifying the SharePoint site and folder where the seed content is located

5. Now we have created our first classifier, but as shown in the following screenshot, it can take up to 24 hours to analyze the content you have provided, so patience is a virtue:

Trainable classifier > **New trainable classifier**

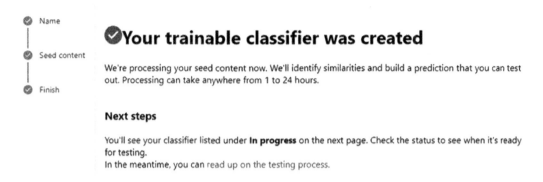

○ Name

○ Seed content

○ Finish

✅Your trainable classifier was created

We're processing your seed content now. We'll identify similarities and build a prediction that you can test out. Processing can take anywhere from 1 to 24 hours.

Next steps

You'll see your classifier listed under **In progress** on the next page. Check the status to see when it's ready for testing.
In the meantime, you can read up on the testing process.

Figure 4.10 – The processing of data can range from 1 to 24 hours to complete

6. You can follow the status of your classifier in the **Trainable classifiers** section of the Microsoft Purview Compliance Portal.

Data classification (preview)

Overview   **Trainable classifiers**   Sensitive info types   Content explorer   Activity explorer

Use built-in or custom classifiers to identify specific types of info and items in your organization. Once created, classifiers can be compliance solutions to detect related content and classify it, protect it, retain it, and more. Learn more

⊘ We're done generating analytics that will allow you to create and test trainable classifiers.

+ Create trainable classifier   ↻ Refresh

⌄ Name	Accuracy	Status	Created by	Last modified
⌄ **In progress (1)**				
○ RMS Logs ⌕ ·		Need test items		

Figure 4.11 – Showing the location of the newly created classifier

7.   Once the classifier is presented under **In progress**, we can start testing it. In the following example, I used two Word documents. One document contained RMS log data, while the other one contained log data from another source and thus should not be identified by the classifier:

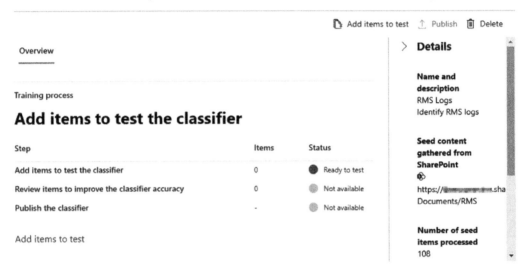

Figure 4.12 – Add items to test the classifier

8. Here, we will have to give our take on what the classifier has identified. Does it behave as we configured it to?

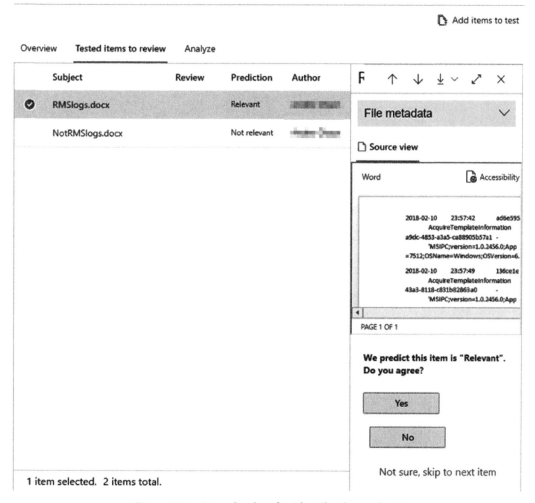

Figure 4.13 – Does the classifier identify relevant data?

9. Since it is relevant, we will click on the **Yes** button to let the classifier know that it has found relevant data.

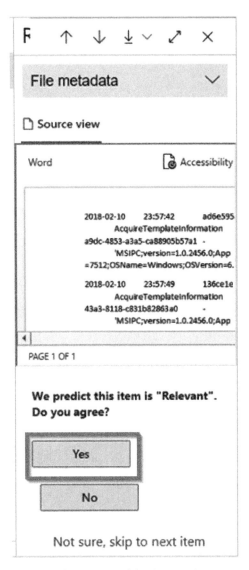

Figure 4.14 – Clicking on Yes if the data is relevant, No if not

10. This brings us to the following screen, stating **Auto-retrain performed**. This means that we have successfully told the classifier it identified relevant data and it will hone its performance further:

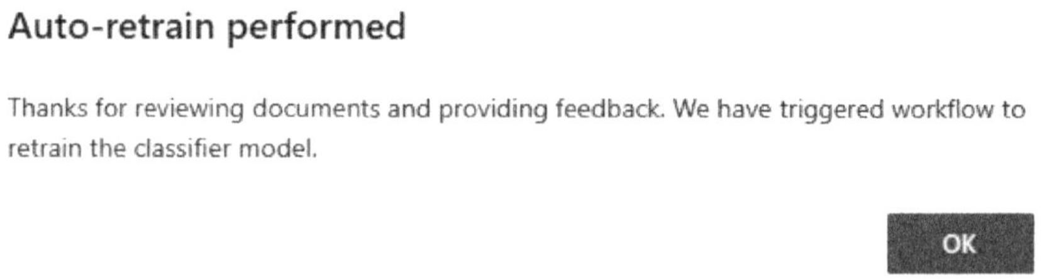

Auto-retrain performed

Thanks for reviewing documents and providing feedback. We have triggered workflow to retrain the classifier model.

Figure 4.15 – Auto-retrain performed

11. We then see the following screen before us, stating what we have just performed and what the recommended steps are moving forward. The portal states **Classifier accuracy is not available yet** since we have only tested this classifier on two data points; the recommended number of items to train your classifier on is at least 200. We can also see that the portal does not recommend this classifier to be published:

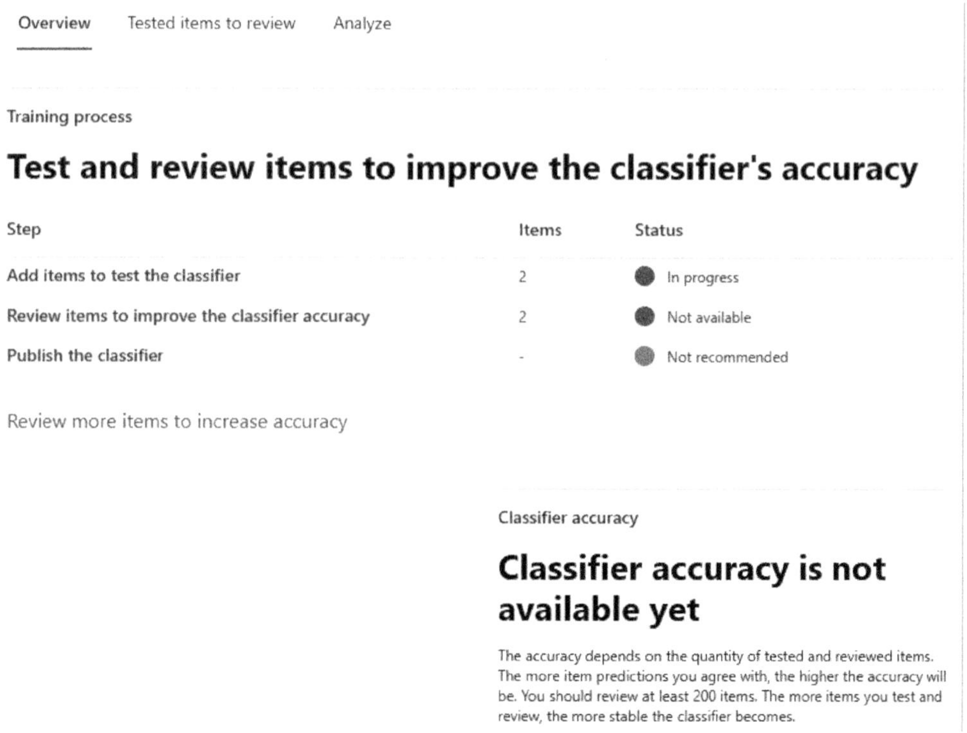

Overview   Tested items to review   Analyze

Training process

Test and review items to improve the classifier's accuracy

Step	Items	Status
Add items to test the classifier	2	● In progress
Review items to improve the classifier accuracy	2	● Not available
Publish the classifier	-	● Not recommended

Review more items to increase accuracy

Classifier accuracy

Classifier accuracy is not available yet

The accuracy depends on the quantity of tested and reviewed items. The more item predictions you agree with, the higher the accuracy will be. You should review at least 200 items. The more items you test and review, the more stable the classifier becomes.

Figure 4.16 – Information about your classifier after performing the first test

12. Now we need to upload even more data to test the classifier on. In my example, continuing with logs, I uploaded more than 200 files with a mix of RMS logs and from other sources. I performed *steps 8-11* once again to see whether my classifier is good enough to publish in my Microsoft 365 tenant.

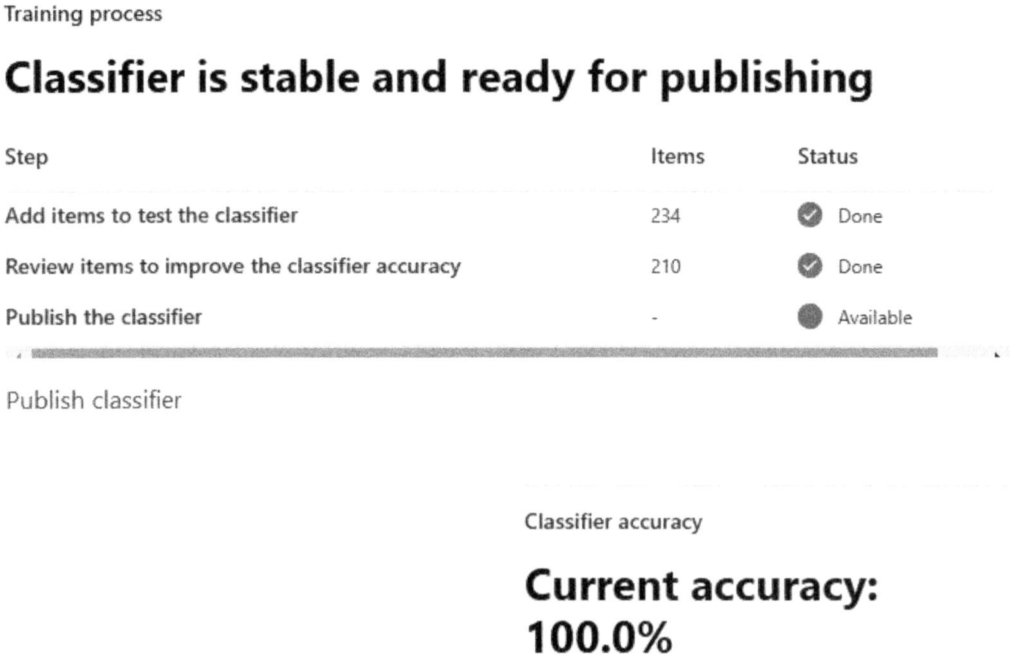

Training process

Classifier is stable and ready for publishing

Step	Items	Status
Add items to test the classifier	234	✅ Done
Review items to improve the classifier accuracy	210	✅ Done
Publish the classifier	-	◉ Available

Publish classifier

Classifier accuracy

Current accuracy: 100.0%

Figure 4.17 – Information about the classifier after retraining it with over 200 items

13. We can now, finally, publish our classifier.

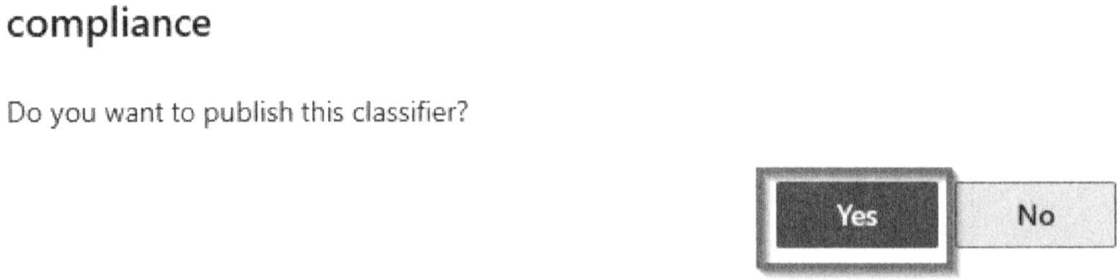

compliance

Do you want to publish this classifier?

Figure 4.18 – Click Yes to publish the classifier

14. And we are done with our first classifier, well done!

| Overview | Trainable classifiers | Sensitive info types | Content explorer | Activity explorer |

Use built-in or custom classifiers to identify specific types of info and items in your organization. Once created, classifiers can b in several compliance solutions to detect related content and classify it, protect it, retain it, and more. Learn more

⊘ We're done generating analytics that will allow you to create and test trainable classifiers.

+ Create trainable classifier   ↻ Refresh

∨ Name	Accuracy	Status	Created by	Last modified
∨ **Ready to use (7)**				
RMS Logs ⌕ 100 %		Ready to use		03/02/2020

Figure 4.19 – The published classifier in the Microsoft Purview Compliance Portal

In this section, we have covered the topic of how to create a custom classifier in Microsoft 365, touching on some of the remaining topics. Up next, we will look at how we can make sure that a trainable classifier is performing properly.

Verifying that a trainable classifier is performing properly

Verification of a classifier is important to make sure that data does not get classified in an incorrect manner. To make sure that your classifier is doing what it is supposed to, follow the steps outlined here.

To verify our trainable classifier, we could go back to the list in the previous section and look at *steps 8-12*. Here, we will have to give our take on what the classifier has identified. Does it behave as we configured it to?

1. Go to your classifier and test it on new content.

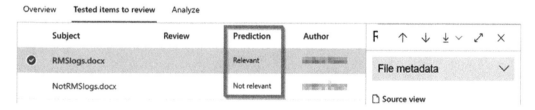

| Overview | Tested items to review | Analyze |

	Subject	Review	Prediction	Author	F ↑ ↓ ↧∨ ↗ ✕
⊘	RMSlogs.docx		Relevant		**File metadata** ∨
	NotRMSlogs.docx		Not relevant		
					⎙ Source view

Figure 4.20 – Does the classifier identify relevant data?

2. Make sure to add your input for whether the data is relevant.

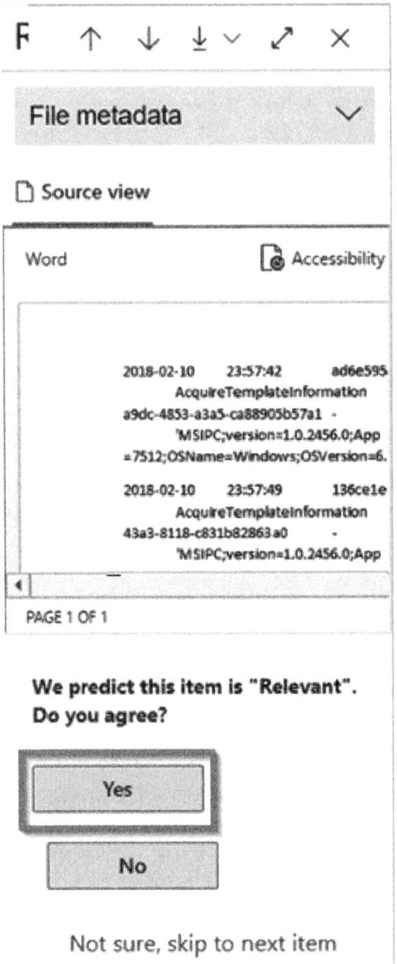

Figure 4.21 – Click on Yes if the data is relevant, No if not

3. Simply put, we let our classifier scour through even more data and make our decisions based on the assumptions from the classifier. If there are errors or data gets classified in an insufficient manner, we need to look deeper into how the classifier operates and how it identifies data.

We need to remember that the classifier will always look at the seed content from which it was trained. If data gets classified the wrong way, we might need to retrain our classifier using new seed content, which we will cover in the next topic.

Retraining a classifier

Say that a classifier is behaving wrongly or we need to use it to classify other data than the original purpose. The following figure shows the process involved with retraining a classifier:

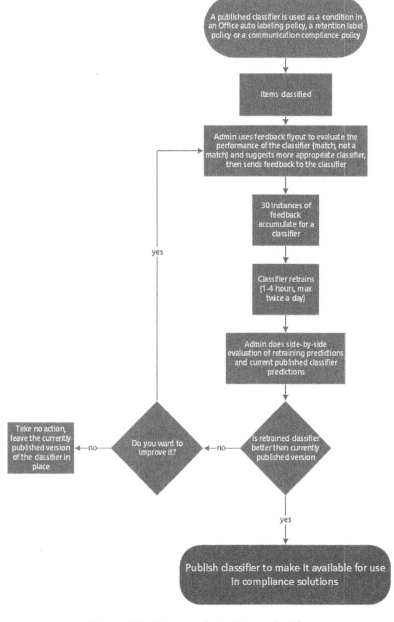

Figure 4.22 – Process of retraining a classifier

This calls for retraining and the steps involved are listed as follows:

1. To start the retraining process, let's head over to the content explorer in the Microsoft Purview Compliance Portal to start retraining our classifier. You'll find the **Content explorer** tab under **Data classification**:

Figure 4.23 – Screenshot showing the location of Content explorer in the compliance center

2. Here, we will go to **Filter on labels | Info types or categories**, expand **Trainable Classifiers**, and select the classifier we wish to retrain.

3. Choose an item the classifier has processed and select **Provide feedback**.

4. In the **Detailed feedback** pane, we can provide feedback on whether or not data is true positives (**Match**) or false positives (**Not a Match**).

5. Once we have provided our feedback to the classifier, it will automatically start retraining. The timeline here is 1-4 hours, and any classifier can be retrained a maximum of 2 times per day.

When retraining finishes, we get an overview of the classifier looking like this:

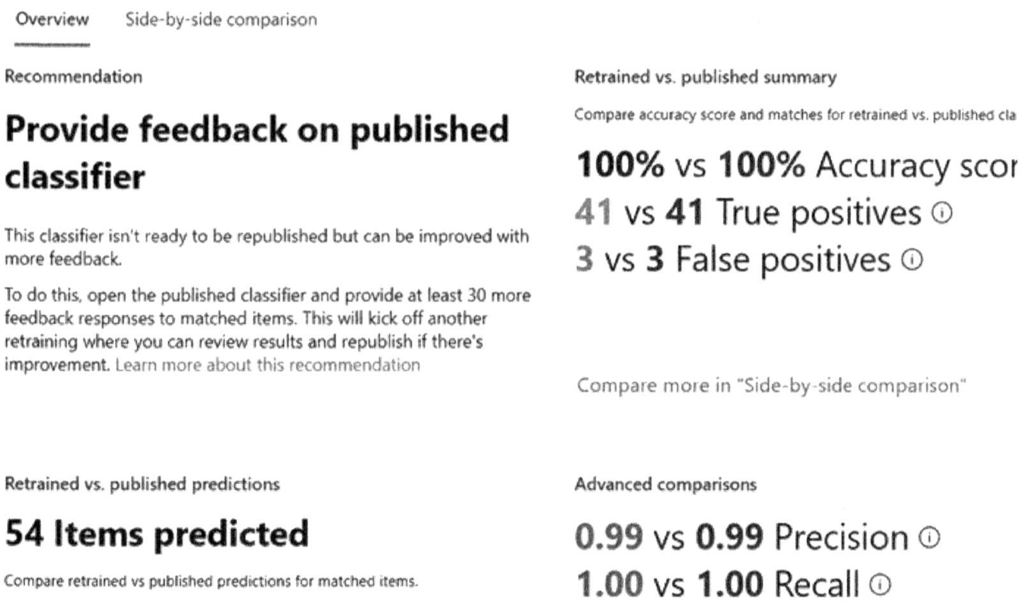

Overview   Side-by-side comparison

Recommendation

Provide feedback on published classifier

This classifier isn't ready to be republished but can be improved with more feedback.

To do this, open the published classifier and provide at least 30 more feedback responses to matched items. This will kick off another retraining where you can review results and republish if there's improvement. Learn more about this recommendation

Retrained vs. published summary

Compare accuracy score and matches for retrained vs. published cla

100% vs **100%** Accuracy scor

41 vs **41** True positives ⓘ

3 vs **3** False positives ⓘ

Compare more in "Side-by-side comparison"

Retrained vs. published predictions

54 Items predicted

Compare retrained vs published predictions for matched items.

Advanced comparisons

0.99 vs **0.99** Precision ⓘ

1.00 vs **1.00** Recall ⓘ

Figure 4.24 – Overview of our classifier after retraining

6. Here, we can choose to republish the classifier if the results are satisfactory, start the retraining process once more, or simply do nothing, in which case the classifier will be published as it was before starting the first retraining process.

In this section, we have covered how to retrain our classifier in order to make it even more sensitive to how we store data.

Summary

This chapter has been about trainable classifiers, and we have discussed what they are, how they can be used, how to create classifiers, and lastly, how to manage them to make sure they are working as intended.

In the next chapter, we will take a deep dive into how to create and manage sensitivity labels.

5
Implementing and Managing Sensitivity Labels

The previous chapter discussed the creation and management of sensitive information types, including selecting a sensitive information type based on an organization's requirements, creating, and managing custom sensitive information types, creating custom sensitive information types with exact data matches, implementing document fingerprinting, and creating a keyword dictionary.

In this chapter, we're going to cover the following main topics:

- Identifying roles and permissions for administering sensitivity labels
- Creating and managing sensitivity labels and applying sensitivity labels to Microsoft SaaS applications
- Configuring automatic labeling policies and monitoring label usage
- Applying bulk classification to on-premises data and managing protection settings
- Applying and managing protections and restrictions

Technical requirements

In this chapter, we continue to explore the configuration of information protection within Microsoft 365. There will be an exercise that will require access to the **Microsoft Purview Compliance Portal** with Global Administration rights. If you have followed the exercise from the previous chapters, you should by now have the relevant trial licenses; however, if you have not yet created this for Microsoft 365, please follow the instructions from *Chapter 1*, *Preparing for Your Microsoft Exam and SC-400 Exam Objectives*.

Identifying roles and permissions for administering sensitivity labels

It is important to give members of the IT administration team the relevant permissions to allow them to create and manage sensitivity labels within the Microsoft Purview Compliance Portal and, in some cases, from the older Security & Compliance Center.

All global admins can administer both the compliance center and the Security & Compliance Center by default. They can then assign the relevant permissions to the compliance officer or any other user without granting them access to the entire tenant. There are three roles to which you can add users that will grant them the relevant permissions to access both the Microsoft Purview Compliance Portal and the older Security & Compliance Center:

- Compliance Data Administrator role group
- Compliance Administrator role group
- Security Administrator role group

There is also an alternative option to using the standard roles, which is to create a new role group and add the **Organization Configuration** or the **Sensitive Label Administrator** roles to the new group. If you want to grant the new group read-only access, then you would need to use the **Sensitivity Label Reader** role.

In this section, we have explained the names of the different role groups you can assign to a user to grant them access to the compliance center. The following section of this chapter will describe the part played by **Role-Based Access Control** (**RBAC**).

Security & Compliance Center permissions

The RBAC model is utilized by the Security & Compliance Center, which is also used by Exchange Online. Therefore, if you are familiar with Exchange permissions, giving permissions in **the Security & Compliance Center** will be very familiar to you.

Please remember that role groups in **Exchange Online** and **the Security & Compliance Center** do not share permissions or membership. However, both do have an Organization Management role group. You can find a list of compliance center role groups by navigating to **Permissions & roles** > **Azure AD roles** from within the Microsoft Purview Compliance Portal, as shown in the following screenshot:

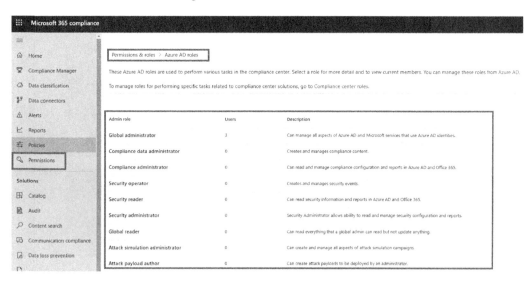

Figure 5.1 – Compliance center roles and permissions

Relationship between roles, members, and role groups

Three permission elements work together and form a relationship with regard to access rights:

- A **Role** gives permissions to perform specific set tasks. An example of this would be the "Case Management" role, which allows users to operate eDiscovery.

- A **Role Group** is a number of specific roles that enable users to do their jobs within the Security & Compliance Center.
- A **Member** is an individual user who can be added or assigned to the default role groups.

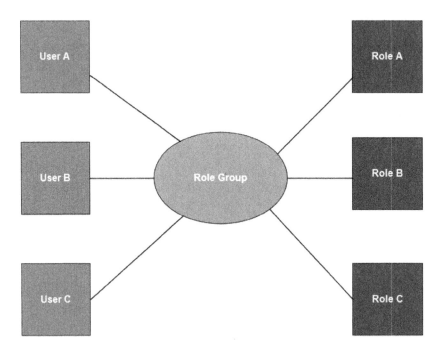

Figure 5.2 – Role, member, and role group relationship

Now that you understand the relationship between roles, members, and role groups, we will take a closer look at the specific role groups that are available within the Microsoft Security and Compliance Center and what features they give to members.

Role groups within the Security and Compliance Center

Controlling permissions within the Security and Compliance Center will only grant access to the features from this specific admin center. If you are required to assign permissions to other security and compliance features within other admin centers, you will need to access the relevant one to assign those permissions (for example, to assign the SharePoint Contributor role, you will need to access the SharePoint Admin Center).

You can find a full list of the default role groups that are accessible in the Security and Compliance Center, as well as the roles that are assigned to those groups by default at the following Microsoft docs link: `https://docs.microsoft.com/en-us/microsoft-365/security/office-365-security/permissions-in-the-security-and-compliance-center?view=o365-worldwide`.

As you can see, there are a lot of role groups available within the Microsoft 365 Security and Compliance Center. You will not need to know each one for the exam; however, it is important to understand the main differences between the Reviewer, Reader, Operator, and Administrator level groups. In the next section of this chapter, we will do a lab exercise in which you will add a user as a member of a role group within the Microsoft 365 Security and Compliance Center and by using PowerShell.

Providing users with access to the Security and Compliance Center

The following steps will guide you through how to give a user the relevant permissions to allow them access to the Security and Compliance Center. Here, users will then be able to configure and administer sensitivity labels. Before you start these steps, there is some information you need to be aware of:

- The account you are using for these steps needs to be a global admin or assigned to the **OrganizationManagement** role group within the Microsoft 365 Security and Compliance Center.

- Exchange Online and the Security & Compliance Center may have similar role group names, but they are not the same.

- Exchange Online and the Security and Compliance Center do not share Role Group membership.

The steps are as follows:

1. You cannot access the Security and Compliance Center when you are **Delegated Access Permission (DAP)** partners with **Administer On Behalf Of (AOBO)** permissions. Now that you understand these points, we will walk through how to assign users to different role groups. Navigate to the **Permissions** tab from within the **Security and Compliance Center** at https://protection.office.com:

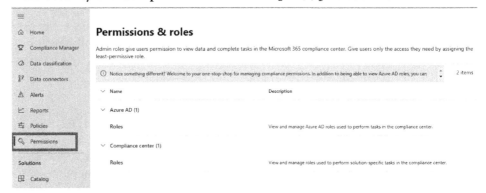

Figure 5.3 – Permissions tab within the Security and Compliance Center

2. Select the role group from the **Compliance center list** within the central pane, choose the group you want to edit, and then **Edit role group**:

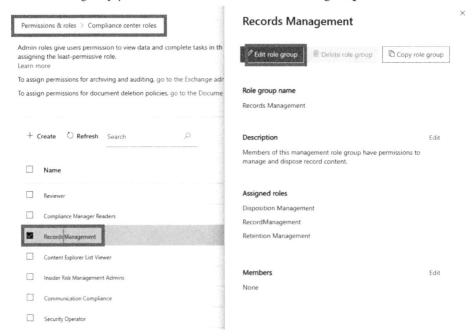

Figure 5.4 – Edit role group

3. Within the properties page, next to **Members**, click on **Edit**:

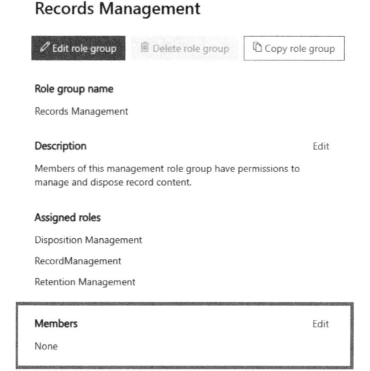

Figure 5.5 – Editing members of the role group

4. Click on **Choose members** and add the users you wish to be a member and then click **Done** followed by **Save**:

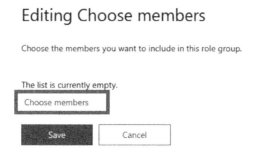

Figure 5.6 – Choosing members to add to the role group

The preceding screenshot shows how to select the option to choose members you wish to add to the role group. The following screenshot is what you will see once you have selected **Choose members**. As you can see, you have the option to click on **Add** and find the specific users you wish to assign to this specific role group:

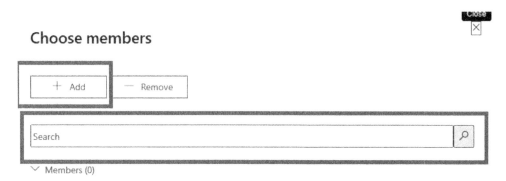

Figure 5.7 – Searching for and adding members

You should now understand how to assign users to different role groups from within the Microsoft Security and Compliance Center. In the following section, we will complete the same task, but we will do this from PowerShell rather than the Admin Center.

Utilizing the Security and Compliance Center PowerShell to grant another user permission to the Security and Compliance Center

We will not look at the steps you need to follow when utilizing PowerShell to grant a user permission to the Security and Compliance Center:

1. You will need to first connect to the **Security and Compliance Center PowerShell**. Follow the steps at this link to complete this task: https://docs.microsoft.com/en-us/powershell/exchange/connect-to-scc-powershell?view=exchange-ps.

2. Use the following command composition:

```
Add-RoleGroupMember -Identity <Insert RoleGroup> -Member
<Insert UserIdentity>
```

-Identity is the role group. -Member is the user, or **universal security group** (**USG**). You can only specify one member at a time.

The next example adds AllenB to the Organization Management role group:

```
Add-RoleGroupMember -Identity "Organization Management"
-Member AllenB
```

3. You can check whether the changes have worked by running the following cmdlet:

```
Get-RoleGroupMember -Identity "<InsertRoleGroupName>"
```

So far in this chapter, we have covered the relationship between roles, members, and role groups and you have then gone on to configure user permissions and role group assignments via the Admin Center and PowerShell. The next section of the chapter will focus on configuring the sensitivity labels and applying them to Microsoft 365 SaaS applications.

Creating and managing sensitivity labels and applying sensitivity labels to Microsoft SaaS applications

When sensitivity labels are configured in your tenant and your business has been utilizing them for some time, you should assess their usefulness and look at fine-tuning label policies. Utilizing label analytics will help identify which sensitivity labels trigger the false positives.

You can apply sensitivity labels to SharePoint sites and Microsoft 365 Groups. This allows the life cycle management of information within the various types of containers of Microsoft 365.

The following list shows containers where labels can be published:

- Microsoft 365 Groups
- Microsoft Teams
- SharePoint Sites

In the following section, you will apply labels to both SharePoint Online and Microsoft 365 Groups via the SharePoint Admin Center and the Microsoft Teams Admin Center.

Applying labels to SharePoint Online and Microsoft 365 Groups

In this section, we will look at how we can apply sensitivity labels at different locations through various applications. The following steps will explain how to apply labels via the SharePoint Admin Center and the Microsoft Teams Admin Center.

1. Go to the SharePoint Admin Center via the **Microsoft 365 Admin Center**, as shown in the following screenshot:

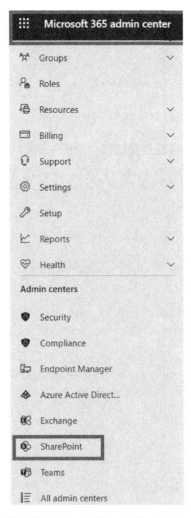

Figure 5.8 – Navigating to SharePoint Admin Center

2. Navigate to **Sites** > **Active sites**:

Figure 5.9 – Selecting active sites

3. Select the SharePoint site you want to apply a published sensitivity label to, go to the **Policies** tab, and then click on **Edit**, as shown in the following screenshot:

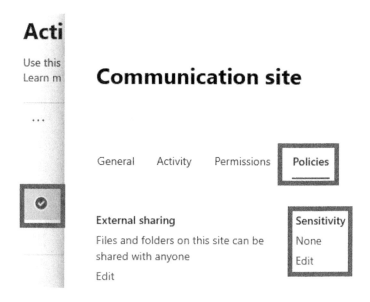

Figure 5.10 – Editing the sensitivity label on the SharePoint site

Microsoft Teams Admin Center

A Microsoft Teams Administrator can amend or chose a sensitivity label from within the admin center. Once you have selected a team and navigated to the settings, the label can be chosen or changed for the team:

1. Go to the Microsoft Teams Admin Center via the **Microsoft 365 admin center**, as shown in the following screenshot:

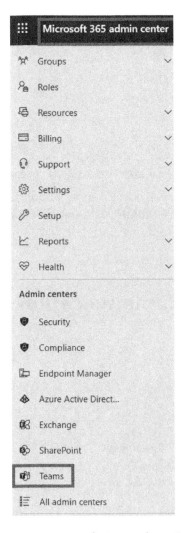

Figure 5.11 – Microsoft Teams Admin Center

2. From within the Microsoft Teams Admin Center, go to **Teams** > **Manage Teams**.

3. Choose the checkmark to the left of any current team that you wish to apply the published sensitivity label to.

4. Click on **Edit**, select **Sensitivity**, and then chose the label you want for the team.

You now know how to edit sensitivity labels from a SharePoint site and a Microsoft Teams channel. In the next section, we will look at creating controls for sensitivity labels.

Creating controls for sensitivity labels from within Microsoft Teams

When a sensitivity label is made with a group and site setting and the member has an Azure AD P1 license, it's possible to control the creation of Microsoft Teams with sensitivity labeling:

1. Navigate to the Microsoft Teams desktop application client.

2. Select **Join or create a team** from the bottom-left menu:

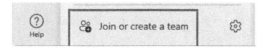

Figure 5.12 – Creating or joining a new Microsoft Teams chat

3. Chose **Create Team**.

4. You will now need to select a team template.

5. Choose a published sensitivity label.

6. Choose the **Privacy** option. Please note that these options are set within the sensitivity label.

7. Enter an appropriate team name and description.

8. As an option, you can choose team members who should have secure access to the team.

9. Click **Close**.

Setting the sensitivity label from the SharePoint site wizard (user)

You have the option of selecting a sensitivity label from within the default wizard when setting up a new SharePoint site. Please be aware that this is only available when the feature is active and enabled. You can choose the relevant label under the topic *Sensitivity*, as described in the following steps:

1. Navigate to the SharePoint Admin Center via the **Microsoft 365 admin center**:

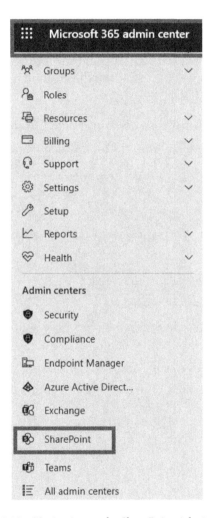

Figure 5.13 – Navigating to the SharePoint Admin Center

2. Go to **Sites** > **Active sites** and select **Create**.

3. Choose the applicable design and insert a relevant site name and group owner in the appropriate fields.

4. Choose the **Published sensitivity** label and then click on **Finish** to create the SharePoint site:

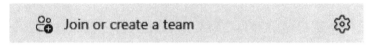

Figure 5.14 – Published sensitivity label

Employing a label for a pre-existing SharePoint site

You can apply or change a sensitivity label if a SharePoint site is already deployed. This option is shown under site information for site admins only. The following steps describe how you can achieve this:

1. Browse to your existing *SharePoint online site.*

2. Choose the **Setting** icon (*gear/cog icon*) in the top-right corner of the screen.

3. Browse to **Site Information**.

4. Select **Sensitivity label** and then click **Save**.

So far, in the *Creating and managing sensitivity labels and applying sensitivity labels to Microsoft SaaS applications* section of this chapter, we have discussed applying sensitivity labels to new teams, existing teams, new SharePoint sites, and existing SharePoint sites. To complete this section of the chapter, we will discuss how to apply and change a label to a Microsoft Teams team as a user with a life cycle.

Applying and changing a label to a Microsoft Teams team as a user with a life cycle

If you are a Microsoft Teams owner, you have permission to amend the label of a team to handle the life cycle:

1. From inside the Teams application, browse to **Teams**.

2. Select your team from within the list.

3. Click on [...] > **Edit team**.

4. Configure **Sensitivity label** and then click on **Done**.

At this stage of the chapter, you should understand how to identify roles, the different role groups available within the Security and Compliance Center, and how to apply security labels to Microsoft 365 SaaS applications. In the next section of the chapter, we will look at automatic labeling and monitoring label usage.

Configuring automatic labeling policies and monitoring label usage

You can automatically designate a sensitivity label to emails and files when they match the conditions you have stipulated. It is important to automatically apply sensitivity labels for the following reasons:

- There is no need to train users in terms of when to use each of the classifications.

- Users do not need to classify all content correctly.

- Users do not need to know about the policies you have set.

Automatic labeling cannot replace content that has been labeled manually; however, it can with lower-priority labels that have been created automatically. When it comes to automatic labeling, there are two methods you can use when applying sensitivity labels to data in Microsoft 365:

- **Client-side labeling when users edit a document or compose emails**: This automatic labeling method supports both recommending a label and automatically applying a label.

- With client-side labeling, the user decides to accept or reject the label, which helps ensure the right labeling of content. Auto-labeling is not supported on all client apps; it is supported by the Azure Information Protection unified labeling client, and some versions of Office. You can find a full list of supported Office apps at the following link: `https://docs.microsoft.com/en-us/microsoft-365/compliance/sensitivity-labels-office-apps?view=o365-worldwide#support-for-sensitivity-label-capabilities-in-apps`.

- **Service-side labeling when content is already saved or emailed**: This method is also referred to as *auto-labeling for data at rest and data in transit*. For Exchange, this does not include emails in the mailbox (at rest).

You do not need to be concerned with what apps and versions users have because this type of labeling is applied by services instead of applications. This means it is the best choice for labeling at scale throughout your business.

Creating an auto-labeling policy

The following are the steps to create an auto labeling policy:

1. From within the Microsoft Purview Compliance Portal, browse to **Solutions > Information protection**:

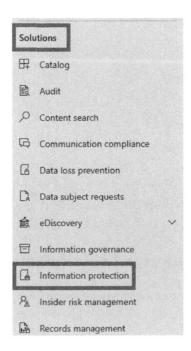

Figure 5.15 – Information protection menu

2. From within the **Information protection** menu, choose **Auto-labeling**:

Create auto-labeling policies to automatically apply sensitivity labels to email messages or OneDrive a contain sensitive info. To confirm that labels will be applied to the correct items, you'll first run policies can review items that will be labeled when the policy is activated. In addition to these policies, you can Office client apps by editing the "Auto-labeling" settings for a specific label. Learn more about auto-la

Figure 5.16 – Auto-labeling menu

3. Choose **+ Create auto-labeling policy**, which will open up the new policy wizard:

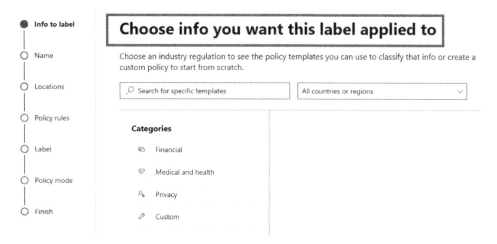

Figure 5.17 – New policy wizard

4. On the **Choose info you want this label applied to** screen, choose the relevant template from the available choices and then click **Next**:

Figure 5.18 – Template choices

5. From the **Name your auto-labeling policy** screen, you will be required to insert a relevant and unique name as well as an optional description, and then click **Next**:

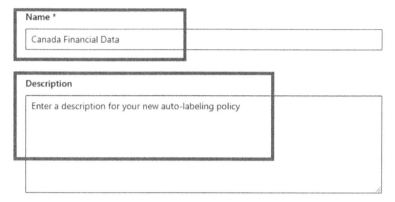

Name your auto-labeling policy

This policy will automatically apply a label to items that match rules and conditions you'll define.

Name *

Canada Financial Data

Description

Enter a description for your new auto-labeling policy

Figure 5.19 – Name and description

6. From the **Choose locations where you want to apply the label** screen, you will need to choose the locations for SharePoint sites, OneDrive, and Exchange, and then click **Next**:

Choose locations where you want to apply the label

Exchange will automatically apply the label to unlabeled emails, regardless of which device or platform is used to send and receive the email. OneDrive and SharePoint will automatically apply the label to unlabeled Office documents.

ⓘ **Tip** Edit the "Auto-labeling" settings for this label to ensure that that it's automatically applied to documents when they're saved and emails when they're sent.

Status	Location	Included	Excluded
⬤ Off	📧 Exchange		
⬤ Off	🔵 SharePoint sites		
⬤ Off	☁ OneDrive accounts		

Figure 5.20 – Label location

7. From the **Set up common or advanced rules** menu, you have two options:

-   **Common rules**: Keep this default setting to classify rules that identify content that will be labeled across the selected locations.

-   **Advanced rules**: Select this option if you are required to configure different rules per location:

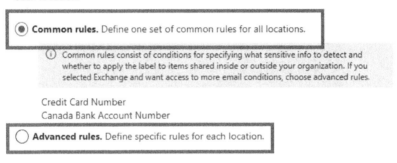

Figure 5.21 – Common or Advanced rules

8. In this next step, you have the option of configuring new rules by utilizing conditions and exceptions; however, this is dependent on the previous choices you have made.

Note

The sensitivity information types are the same as the ones you chose for auto-labeling for Office apps.

---

9. On the **Choose a label to auto-apply** screen, you will need to click on **+ Choose a label**, and then choose a label from the **Choose a sensitivity label** screen. Once completed, click **Next**:

Users will see this label applied to files that match the rules and conditions you chose. Where will this label appear?

Label to auto-apply

+ Choose a label

Figure 5.22 – Choose a label to auto-apply

10. On the **Decide if you want to test out the policy now or later** screen, you have two options:

-   **Run policy in simulation mode**: This is if you feel you are ready to test straight away. No content is amended in simulation mode.

-   **Leave policy turned off**: If you select this option, then the policy will remain inactive until you are ready to test in simulation mode.

11. On the **Summary** screen, you can review the entire label configuration before completing the steps.

In this section of the chapter, we have covered an overview of auto-labeling and then run through a lab exercise to configure auto-labeling. In the following section, we will discuss monitoring label usage and information protection in general.

Monitoring information protection

Within the Microsoft Purview Compliance Portal, you can utilize the **Data Classification** section, which provides intelligence about your business data after it has been classified. This will assist you in finding areas that are exposed and risks to inform policies that enable you to protect and govern your content:

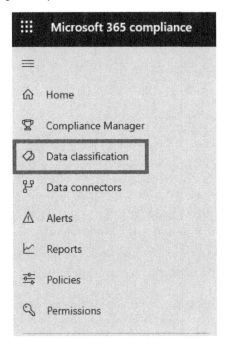

Figure 5.23 – Data classification

Not only does it help when developing an understanding of your data, but it also helps you to monitor the status of the classification on an ongoing basis. The following tabs from the **Overview** pane are the most relevant to information protection:

- **Top sensitive info types**
- **Top sensitivity labels applied to content**
- **Top retention labels applied to content**
- **Top activities detected**
- **Locations where sensitivity labels are applied:**

Figure 5.24 – Monitoring information protection

You should now understand where you can monitor and gather data about sensitivity labels that have been implemented in your tenant and which classifications are the most relevant ones. In the next section of the chapter, we will take a closer look at applying bulk classification to on-premises data and managing protection settings.

Applying bulk classification to on-premises data and managing protection settings

Having the ability to protect on-premises data and files with an information protection solution is crucial in a hybrid scenario and also when looking to migrate to cloud platforms.

Unified the labeling scanner

The unified labeling scanner allows you to label on-premises data. The following list is an example of situations when you may need to utilize the labeling scanner:

- Data privacy conditions from the data protection team, for example:

    A. Before uploading files into the cloud, they should be labeled.

    B. Sensitive data being handled in a special way.

    C. Specific requirements from legal and purchasing departments.

    D. Only storing data in a certain territory.

    E. Understanding your on-premises data by running a scan.

The previous list is just a few examples of when you would look at utilizing the unified labeling scanner.

Unified labeling best practice requirements

The unified labeling scanner scans and protects data within your on-premises infrastructure, including files shares, local SharePoint servers, and NAS storage devices.

The scanner utilizes sensitivity labels that are configured in the following Microsoft 365 labeling admin centers, including the following:

- Microsoft 365 Security Center
- Microsoft Purview Compliance Portal
- Microsoft 365 Security and Compliance Center

Before you can implement and install the unified labeling scanner, you need to meet the following requirements:

- Install SQL Server Database (SQL Express will suffice).
- Download the unified labeling client .exe file, including the scanner.
- Any of the following roles:

    A. Compliance Data Administrator

    B. Security Administrator

    C. Global Admin
- Azure AD token.
- Windows Server 2016 or 2019 with a user interface.
- A service account with the following requirements:

Requirement	Information
Log on locally as a user right assignment	This permission is needed to install and configure the scanner. Please note that it is not automatically set.
Log on as a service user right assignment	This permission right is automatically enabled to the account during installation.
Permissions to the data repositories	Read, write, and modify permissions on local files are required for canning them and then applying classification and protection.
Labels that re-protect or remove protection	Make the account an information protection super user for Azure so that it can always have access to the protected files.
Specific URL scanning	Site collector auditor rights are required to allow the scanning and discovery of sites and subsites under specific URLs.

Configuring on-premises labeling

The AIPService PowerShell module is utilized for the installation and configuration of the unified labeling scanner. This module is traditionally installed on a server that will act as the unified labeling scanner within the infrastructure. Please note that the PowerShell module is installed automatically during the AIPService installation.

Unified labeling scanner install

After ensuring that all the prerequisites have been met, it will be possible to install the unified labeling scanner by completing the following steps:

1. Log in to the Windows server that will be used as the on-premises scanning server.
2. Run the unified labeling client install on the server.
3. Once the install is complete, start PowerShell as an Administrator for elevated permissions.
4. Utilize the following cmdlet from the AIPService PowerShell module to install the AIP scanner:

```
Install-AIPScanner -SqlServerInstance <name> -Cluster
<cluster name>
```

5. You can check whether the installation has been successful by checking in the Services Administrative tool for the Azure Information Protection Scanner service and that it is configured to run by utilizing the scanner service account you made.

At this stage, the unified label should be installed on the server, and it should be connected to the SQL server. The following steps will explain how to connect the service to the Azure environment by utilizing an Azure AD token.

Obtaining an Azure AD token

You will be required to complete the following steps to acquire an Azure AD token for the unified scanner:

1. In the Azure portal, type `App Registrations` and select this service.
2. Click on **New Registration**.
3. Type in a relevant name.
4. Choose a **Supported account** type. You also have the option of leaving this as the default option.
5. Configure the redirect URL to `https://localhost`.
6. Click on **Register**.
7. Make a note of the **Application (client) ID** value, as we will need this in a later step.
8. Click on the **Certificates & Secrets** option.
9. Browse to **Client Secrets**, and then select **New client secret**.
10. Enter a description and select the expiration interval.
11. Make a copy of the new secret to a safe and secure location. Please note that this value is only displayed once so you need to ensure you make a copy and store it.
12. Click **Add**.
13. Browse to **API permissions**.
14. Click on **Add permission**.
15. Choose **Azure rights management services** > **application permissions**.
16. Expand **content permissions**.
17. Choose `Content.DelegateReader` and `Content.DelegatedWriter`.
18. Choose **Add permission**.
19. Choose **+ Add a permission** > **APIs my organization uses**.
20. Browse for **Microsoft Information Protection Sync Service**.

21. Click on **Microsoft Information Protection Sync Service** > **Application Permission**.

22. Choose **content permissions**.

23. Choose `UnifiedPolicy.Tenant.Read`.

24. Choose **Add permission**.

25. Choose **Grant admin consent**.

26. Browse to **Azure Active Directory**.

27. Copy the `Tenant ID` value to a notepad.

28. Start the PowerShell session by utilizing the `AzureInformationProtection` module. Use the following `cmdlet`:

```
Set-AIPAuthentication -AppId <ID of the registered app>
-AppSecret <client secret sting> -TenantId <your tenant
ID> -DelegatedUser <Azure AD account>
```

Once these steps have been followed and are complete, the scanner will have an Azure AD token and will be enrolled as an app in the Azure tenant. We will now take a look at monitoring label performance by utilizing label analytics.

Utilizing label analytics to monitor label performance

Having the functionality to label content within the Microsoft 365 tenant is a good option to allow control of access and sharing. As part of this functionality, having the ability to look at the analytics on performance is also very important.

Obtaining a report

The reporting system within the Security and Compliance Center includes the ability to report on sensitivity labels. For this specific element of reporting, we will focus our attention on the compliance center reports.

If you have an existing sensitivity label, you can access a report for this by performing the following steps:

1. Browse to the **Microsoft Purview Compliance Portal**, `https://compliance.microsoft.com`, and log in with an account that has the required permissions.

2. Browse to **Reports**:

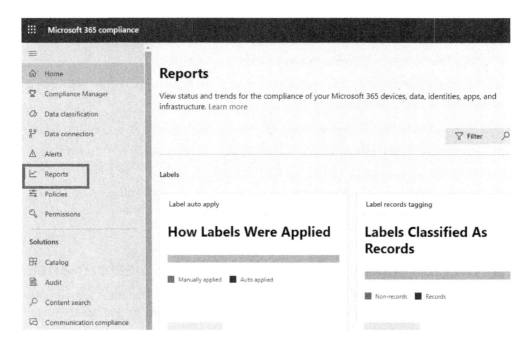

Figure 5.25 – Reports

3. From the **Sensitivity labels** section, click on **View details**.

Permissions and roles for label analytics

Like most analytical services within Microsoft 365 and Azure, you need a certain level of permission, or a specific role assigned to your user account, to be able to view and run reports. To enable a user to create a log analytics workspace as well as custom queries, you will need to assign them one of the following roles:

- Azure Information Protection administrator
- Security administrator
- Compliance administrator

- Compliance data administrator
- Global administrator

Once the workspace has been created you can assign a role to the user with limited access that will only allow them to view content and data that has been collected:

- Security reader
- Global reader

You will need to be wary of costs when it comes to storing all the analytics data. With the data being stored in Azure monitor and log analytics, it means there will be **Usage and estimated cost** features to aid you in estimating the amount of data you have stored, which will, in turn, enable you to estimate a cost.

Azure Sentinel integration

You can integrate Azure Sentinel with sensitivity label monitoring and analyzing. With this feature, log files are collected in an Azure Sentinel workspace to get an overview of the whole environment.

A lot of information has been covered so far in this chapter. The last section took a look at how you can monitor and manage your sensitivity labels within the Microsoft 365 and Azure tenant. In the final section of the chapter, we will look at applying protections and restrictions to data, specifically, emails and files.

Applying and managing protections and restrictions

Any user can apply a single label to each document and email. Email attachments added to messages do not inherit the label, apart from in the following scenario:

1. If a label that does not apply encryption is applied to the attachment, and the file attached to the email is an office document, then the file will inherit the email label's encryption settings.

   In all other cases, the following applies:

- The attachments will keep their original label if one has been applied.

2. If the email attached has existing encryption that has not been applied via a label, it will keep that encryption, but it will not be applied by any label.

3. If there are attachments within the email that do not have any labels applied, then they will stay that way.

Manual label application

It is possible to apply a sensitivity label in Outlook Desktop (for both Mac and Windows), a mobile Outlook app (iOS, Android), or in the web app manually.

Utilizing auto-apply to apply labels by default

You can utilize the auto-apply functionality to apply sensitivity labels by default. The following options are available when applying labels to a file and an email:

- New emails and documents can get the default label.

- Auto-apply via sensitive information types, including or not including a hint.

- Auto-apply via trainable classifiers.

Summary

Within this chapter, we have covered a lot of different topics, including identifying roles and permissions for administering sensitivity labels, creating and managing sensitivity labels and applying them to Microsoft SaaS applications, configuring automatic labeling policies and monitoring label usage, applying bulk classification to on-premises data and managing protection settings, and applying and managing protections and restrictions.

By the end of this chapter, you will have completed multiple lab exercises; however, if you have not followed any of these, I strongly recommend that you do before moving on to the next chapter.

The next chapter will cover planning and implementing encryption for email messages.

6
Planning and Implementing Encryption for Email Messages

Encryption is a highly sought-after feature when it comes to protecting your data from illegitimate access. In this chapter, we are going to cover the subject of encryption in **Microsoft 365** in general, as well as undertake a deep dive into defining the requirements for, and implementing, **Office 365 Advanced Message Encryption** in the following order:

- Introduction to encryption in Microsoft 365
- Defining requirements for implementing Office 365 Advanced Message Encryption
- Implementing **Office 365 Advanced Message Encryption**

Technical requirements

The requirements for utilizing Office 365 Advanced Message Encryption are roughly the same as for the other technical features listed both previously and that are forthcoming in this book. By way of a refresher, however, in order to implement Office 365 Advanced Message Encryption, you need one of the following subscriptions present in your Microsoft 365 tenant:

- **Microsoft 365 E5**

- **Office 365 E5**

- **Microsoft 365 E5 (Nonprofit Staff Pricing)**

- **Office 365 Enterprise E5 (Nonprofit Staff Pricing)**

- **Office 365 Education A5**

- **Microsoft 365 E5 Compliance add-on for Microsoft 365 E3**

- **Office 365 Advanced Compliance add-on for Microsoft 365 E3**

- **Microsoft 365 E5 Information Protection and Governance add-on for Microsoft 365 E3**

If you would like to delve deeper into the licensing requirements for Office 365 Advanced Message Encryption, you can refer to this link: `https://docs.microsoft.com/en-us/microsoft-365/compliance/ome-advanced-message-encryption?view=o365-worldwide`.

With the technical requirements all sorted out, let's now dive into our first topic, which will give us an introduction to encryption in Microsoft 365.

Introduction to encryption in Microsoft 365

Encryption is the common process of cryptographically encoding information in a way that only individuals or organizations with correct authorization are permitted to read it. The use of encryption greatly increases the resilience to the following threats:

- The theft of data.

- Failures in physical security.

- The interception of data while in transit.

- Within **Microsoft 365**, there are multiple layers of encryption working together to safeguard customer data both at rest and in transit.

Examples of **data-at-rest** include the following:

- Files uploaded to a SharePoint site
- Teams chat messages
- Files shared in Microsoft Teams meetings
- Attachments in email messages stored in a mailbox
- Files uploaded to OneDrive for Business

Examples of **data-in-transit** include the following:

- Conversations taking place in a Teams meeting
- Email messages in the process of being delivered
- Whenever a user's laptop or other device is communicating with Microsoft 365 services.

When it comes to encryption, this is a topic not taken lightly by Microsoft in their efforts to keep their customer's data as safe as possible. The data provided and uploaded by customers to **Microsoft 365** is encrypted at rest and in transit using **Federal Information Processing Standard** (**FIPS**) 140-2-compatible encryption algorithms and technologies, including:

- **Advanced Encryption Standard** (**AES**)
- **Transport Layer Security** (**TLS**)
- **Internet Protocol Security** (**IPSec**)

These standard technologies are complemented by Microsoft technologies providing encryption for the following:

- Hard drives (BitLocker)
- Service encryption (Microsoft managed keys/customer-managed keys)

With that, we have covered the features available and the possibilities of encrypting data in the form of an overview. Let's now take a deeper dive into the topics specifically relying on Microsoft technologies to improve our knowledge in this regard.

BitLocker and how it encrypts data at rest

In Microsoft 365, BitLocker is used to encrypt disk drives containing customer data at the volume level, making sure that all data at rest is encrypted and only available to authorized individuals.

The feature consists of several encryption processes, including **Advanced Encryption Standard** (**AES**) 256-bit encryption on the disks containing customer data, and disk sectors encrypted with **Full Volume Encryption Key** (**FVEK**), which itself is encrypted with a **Volume Master Key** (**VMK**), which is bound to the Trusted Platform Module in the server itself. This can be visualized in the following diagram:

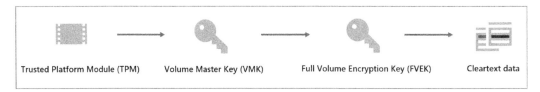

Figure 6.1 – Describing the encryption flow using BitLocker on Microsoft 365 servers

With that, we have covered the basics of how BitLocker is used to encrypt data at rest in Microsoft 365. Let's now move on to our next topic, which will provide insights into how service encryption works.

Service encryption

In addition to BitLocker for encrypting at the volume level, Microsoft 365 employs service encryption for encryption of customer data at the application layer. There are two key management options provided for the use of service encryption:

- **Microsoft** Managed Keys: In a default implementation of Microsoft 365, Microsoft manages all cryptographic keys providing service encryption, and can be visualized in the following diagram:

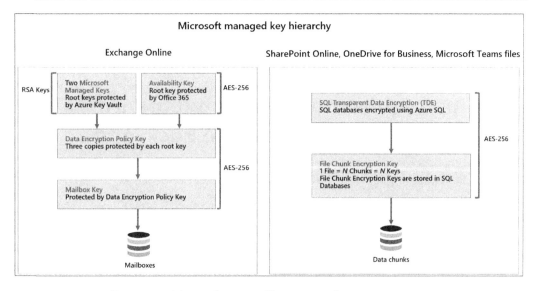

Figure 6.2 – Microsoft managed key option of service encryption

- **Customer managed key**: This option provides the possibility for customers to use their own root keys to encrypt data. These keys are uploaded to, or created within, Azure Key Vault, allowing customers to have a greater impact on the ability of Microsoft services such as Exchange Online, OneDrive for Business, and SharePoint Online to process and decrypt data:

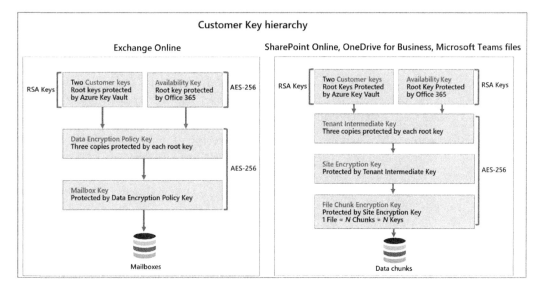

Figure 6.3 – Customer managed key option of service encryption

This concludes the first topic of the chapter, in which we have covered an introduction to encryption in Microsoft 365, and the following section will focus on defining requirements for Office 365 Advanced Message Encryption.

Defining requirements for implementing Office 365 Advanced Message Encryption

After deciding how to manage encryption in your Microsoft 365 tenant, it is time to start looking at how to use these encryption settings in other services, such as Exchange Online.

Before implementing **Office 365 Advanced Message Encryption** (**OME**), you will need to do a quick check to see that the information rights management features in your tenant are working as expected. To perform this verification, follow the outlined steps shown next:

1. You need to have Exchange Service Administrator permissions or higher to configure tenant-wide settings.

2. Install the Exchange Online PowerShell module, `ExchangeOnlineManagement`, by starting your PowerShell prompt as an administrator and entering the following text: `cmdlet: Install-Module -Name ExchangeOnlineManagement`.

3. Connect to Exchange Online using the `cmdlet` command: `Connect-ExchangeOnline -UserPrincipalName <UPN@domain.com>`.

4. Use the following `cmdlet` command to validate the information rights management configuration in your tenant: `Get-IRMConfiguration | Format-List AzureRMSLicensingEnabled`.

5. If the `AzureRMSLicensingEnabled` parameter returns the value of `$false`, you can activate the Office 365 Message Encryption capabilities by issuing the following `cmdlet` command: `Set-IRMConfiguration -AzureRMSLicensingEnabled:$true AzureRMSLicensingEnabled`.

6. To test whether IRM data can be obtained for a recipient inside your organization, run the following `cmdlet` command: `Test-IRMConfiguration -Sender UPN@domain.com`.

7. The output of the `cmdlet` run in *step 5* will display the results of multiple tests and an overall result. The result should be PASS.

8. If any of the tests performed in *step 5* show the result FAIL, you will not able to fetch the RMS templates for the specified recipient, or there may be an issue with the encryption keys used.

Now that we have verified the functionality of IRM in our tenant, we need to discuss the business requirements for using the product, as it contains several branding features to more easily identify the fact that the email is specifically sent from your organization rather than spoofing as your organization.

> **Note**
>
> If your tenant only has Microsoft 365 E3 licenses available, you can only manage the default OME template. There is no possibility to create a new template or add other Office 365 Advanced Message Encryption settings.

Customizing the branding templates for your company allows you to control the way your organization sends email messages and the portal for encryption. There are two `cmdlets` that come into play when it comes to customization or modifications of the templates or the email messages. These are `Get-OMEConfiguration` and `Set-OMEConfiguration`.

The parts of email messages and templates that you can customize consist of the following:

- The introductory text
- The disclaimer text
- The URL for the privacy statement of your organization
- The text displayed in the OME portal
- The background color in the email messages and the OME portal
- The logo or brand that is on display in the email message, if one is used

The following diagram gives you an overview of what is customizable in a branding template:

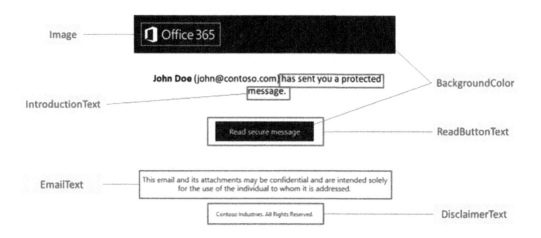

Figure 6.4 – Customizable portions of a branding template in OME

Once we have gathered the required information to proceed with our deployment of OME within the organization, we can safely proceed with the actual deployment, a topic that we will cover in the following section.

Implementing Office 365 Advanced Message Encryption

Given that we have *ticked all the boxes* when it comes to verifying the technical requirements listed at the beginning of the chapter, the business requirements in the previous section, we are all set to begin implementing these features in our Microsoft 365 tenant.

OME gives us the option to use several templates for email messages and, for example, define an expiration time for protected messages. The templates created can be used to fulfill multiple business use cases, for example:

- Templates for geographical regions or countries

- If you want to have the option to revoke email messages

- If you want email messages sent to external mail addresses to expire after a given number of days

- Separate templates for individual departments in your organization, such as HR, IT, PR, and the Executive Office

> **Note**
> Prior to creating templates, you will need to make sure that you have sufficient permissions in Exchange Online to run the commands.

To list the permission roles required for running the OME `cmdlets`, open PowerShell and run these commands in order:

1. `Connect-ExchangeOnline`

2. `$Permissions = Get-ManagementRole -Cmdlet New-OMEConfiguration`

3. `$Permissions | ForEach {Get-ManagementRoleAssignment -Role $_.Name -Delegating $false | Format-Table -Auto Role,RoleAssigneeType,RoleAssigneeName`

This will give us an output similar to the following screenshot:

```
Role                            RoleAssigneeType  RoleAssigneeName

Data Loss Prevention RoleGroup                    Compliance Management
Data Loss Prevention RoleGroup                    Organization Management



Role                                    RoleAssigneeType  RoleAssigneeName

Information Rights Management RoleGroup                    Compliance Management
Information Rights Management RoleGroup                    Organization Management



Role                     RoleAssigneeType  RoleAssigneeName

Transport Rules RoleGroup                  Compliance Management
Transport Rules RoleGroup                  Organization Management
Transport Rules RoleGroup                  Records Management
```

Figure 6.5 – Output of the Get-ManagementRoleAssignmet cmdlet to show the required permissions needed to run New-OMEConfiguration

Here, the listed `RoleAssigneeName` lists the roles/permissions needed to run the `cmdlet`.

Creating an OME template

To create a new template, we once again turn to PowerShell. The `cmdlet` used for creating a template is `New-OMEConfiguration`, which has the following parameters available:

- `-Identity`
- `-BackgroundColor <String Value>`
- `-DisclaimerText <String Value>`
- `-EmailText <String Value>`
- `-Image <Byte[ ]>`
- `-ExternalMailExpiryInDays <Integer Value between 1-730>`
- `-OTPEnabled <Boolean Value>`
- `-PortalText <String Value>`
- `-PrivacyStatementURL <String Value>`
- `-ReadButtonText <String Value>`
- `-SocialIdSignIn <Boolean Value>`
- `-Confirm`
- `-WhatIf`

Here is an example of how you can create an OME template:

```
New-OMEConfiguration -Identity "Expire in 14 days"
-ExternalMailExpiryInDays 14
```

This will create a branding template with an expiration date of 14 days.

Once we have created an OME template, we need to create a mail flow rule in Exchange Online to apply the template to certain senders or, as in the template we created in the example, to be sent to external addresses as the expiration value only applies to external emails.

Using mail flow rules to apply OME templates

To create a mail flow rule that is designed to use our newly created OME template, we can either go via the **Exchange Online Admin Center (EAC)** or via PowerShell.

Creating a mail flow rule in EAC is realized by following the steps outlined here:

1. Sign in to the EAC, `https://outlook.office365.com/ecp/`, using an account that has been granted the Exchange Service Administrator permissions.

2. In the EAC, go to **mail flow** > **rules** and select **New** > **Apply Office 365 Message Encryption and rights protection to messages**:

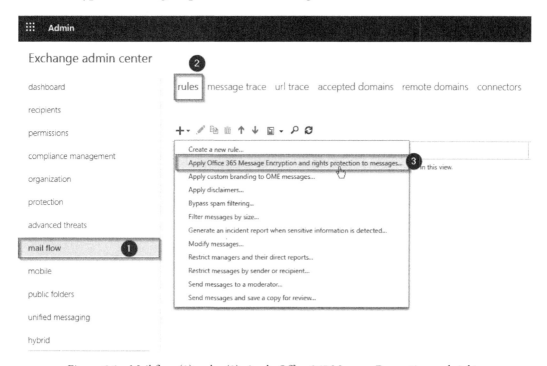

Figure 6.6 – Mail flow (1), rules (2), Apply Office 365 Message Encryption and rights protection to messages (3)

Here we provide the following information to create our mail flow rule:

1. **Name**: A name for the rule, to easily distinguish it in the EAC.

2. **Apply this rule if**: Select the condition **The recipient address includes** and **any of these words** and add a domain that you want to use the rule for:

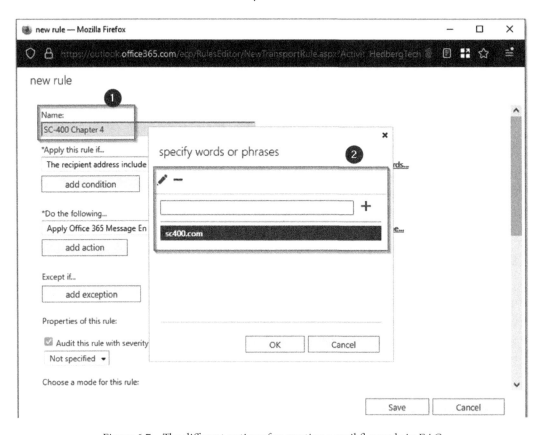

Figure 6.7 – The different options for creating a mail flow rule in EAC

Once we have entered a name for our rule and the external domain for which it is intended, we proceed with selecting an OME encryption template by going through these steps:

1. Click on **Select one** to get a pop-up window displaying the OME templates available for encrypting email messages:

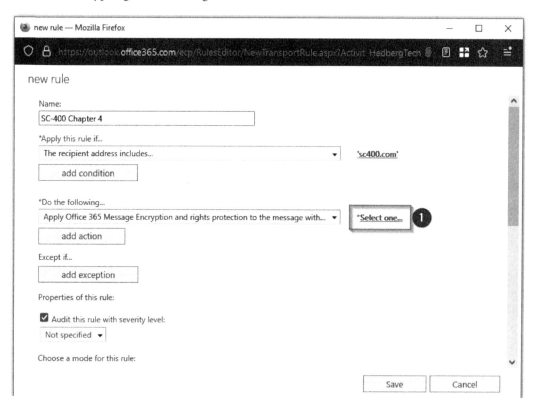

Figure 6.8 – Click on Select one… to display the OME templates available

2. Select the OME template you wish to use for encrypting the emails sent to the domain you specified when you created the rule:

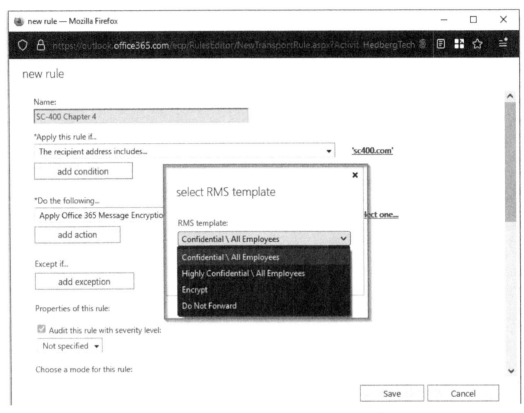

Figure 6.9 – Select the desired OME template in the drop-down menu

3. In the **Choose a mode for this rule:** field, specify whether or not it should be enforced immediately on creation or whether it should run in **Test** mode with policy tips activated or deactivated:

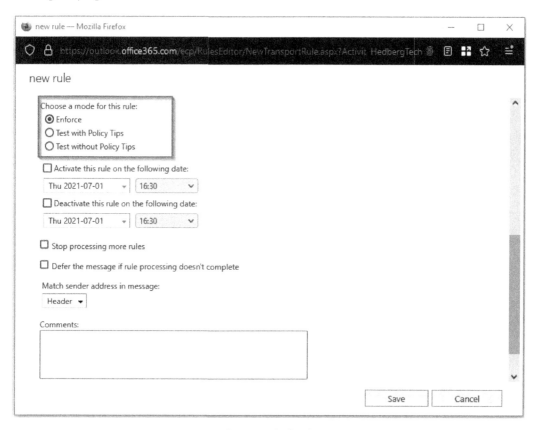

Figure 6.10 – Select a mode for the transport rule

4. We could choose to delay the activation of the rule to a specific date. For instance, if we want our new rule to become active starting on the January 1, 2022, we specify this in the **Activate this rule on the following date field:**

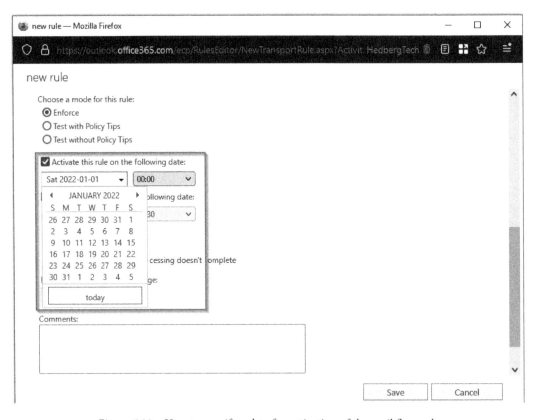

Figure 6.11 – How to specify a date for activation of the mail flow rule

5. Once all options in the creation of the mail flow rule are taken care of, we simply click on **Save** to create our rule in the EAC:

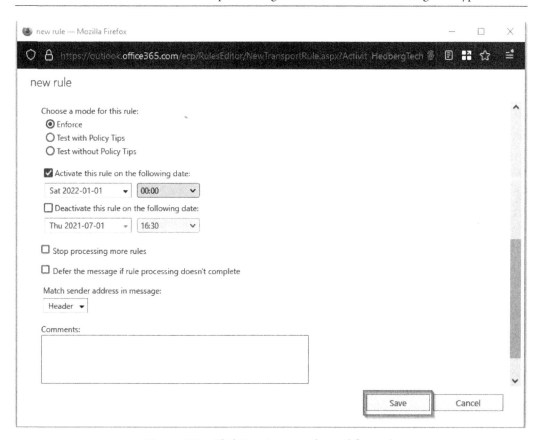

Figure 6.12 – Click Save to create the mail flow rule

6. We have now created a mail flow rule that will encrypt all messages sent to the domain we specified. Well done!

To summarize this section, we have covered the way we create mail flow rules to use in conjunction with our OME templates created in the previous section.

Summary

This chapter has been all about encryption in Microsoft 365 – how it is used to secure our data in the cloud, and how we, as customers, can take advantage of these encryption settings to make sure that our email messages are safe from prying eyes, both at rest and in transit.

Up next, we have a chapter on data loss prevention and how to implement this feature to make sure that no data leakage occurs in our environment.

Section 3: Implementing Data Loss Prevention

This part of the book will focus on implementing data loss prevention within a Microsoft 365 tenant. This will include DLP policies, Microsoft Endpoint data loss prevention, and managing data loss prevention activities.

This section comprises the following chapters:

- *Chapter 7, Creating and Configuring Data Loss Prevention Policies*
- *Chapter 8, Implementing and Monitoring Microsoft Endpoint Data Loss Prevention*
- *Chapter 9, Managing and Monitoring Data Loss Prevention Policies and Activities*

7
Creating and Configuring Data Loss Prevention Policies

The previous chapter discussed implementing and managing sensitivity labels from within the Microsoft 365 Compliance and Security Center. We covered a whole range of topics within this scope, including identifying roles and permissions for administering sensitivity labels, creating and managing sensitivity labels and applying sensitivity labels to Microsoft SaaS applications, configuring automatic labeling policies and monitoring label usages, applying bulk classification to on-premises data and managing protection settings, and applying and managing protections and restrictions.

In this chapter, we're going to cover the following main topics, which will allow you to understand data loss prevention and how it can integrate various Microsoft 365 SaaS applications:

- Configuring data loss prevention for policy precedence
- Configuring policies for Exchange Online, SharePoint Sites, OneDrive, and Microsoft Teams
- Integrating **Microsoft Defender for Cloud Apps** with information protection and configuring policies in Microsoft Defender for Cloud Apps
- Implementing data loss prevention policies in test mode

Technical requirements

In this chapter, we will continue to explore configuring Information Protection within Microsoft 365. There will be an exercise where you will need access to *Microsoft 365* with Global Administration rights. If you have followed the exercises in the previous chapter, you should now have the relevant trial licenses. However, if you have not created this for Microsoft 365 yet, please follow the instructions in *Chapter 1*, *Preparing for Your Microsoft Exam and SC-400 Exam Objectives*.

Configuring data loss prevention for policy precedence

When data loss prevention policies and rules contained within a policy are processed, that process is referred to as **policy precedence**. The order in which the rule is evaluated can be manually configured, with the lowest priority number being processed first. The default rule is that the first rule is configured as priority 0, while the one after that is configured as priority 1; this continues in sequence.

Although only one DLP policy is enforced, all potential policy matches are in the logs, and you can also see this information in reports.

Specific condition matches can have configured actions that contradict each other. An example of this is that you can configure a DLP policy that blocks personal data from being shared externally, without an override allowed. You can then have another policy for financial data, which does allow end users to perform overrides. In this scenario, if only the final matching policy is applied rather than the priority of a policy, then the user could potentially hide personal data within an email that also has financial data in it and choose the override encoded into a financial data policy block action. In this case, however, the personal data policy will have a higher priority, so it will be applied instead.

Now, let's look at how we can change the priority rule to give a different policy a higher precedence.

Amending rule priority

In the financial data example we provided earlier, the priority was ordered so that the rule for a high volume of matches was given priority below the rule that had a lower number of matches. Although a high number of matches is more restrictive, a user can still potentially choose the override option that is enabled in the low matches' rule.

Both actions are logged in this scenario, but it could potentially be a long time until an admin checks logs and takes the required action.

The following steps outline how to change the order in which the DLP rules within a policy are given priority. To make these changes, you will need the **DLP Compliance Management role**:

1. From within **Microsoft Purview Compliance Portal**, navigate to **Policies**.

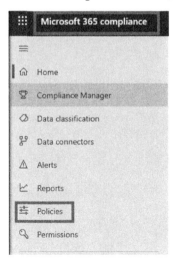

Figure 7.1 – Policies

2. From within the **Policies** section, navigate to **Data** and then click on **Data loss prevention**.

Figure 7.2 – Data loss prevention option

3. Select the **Policies** tab, highlight the policy you want to amend, and then click on the edit button (which looks like a pencil).

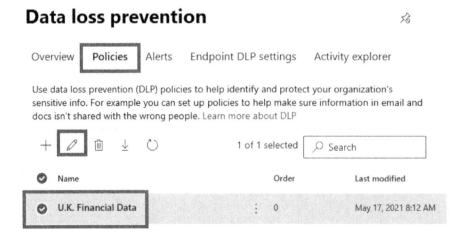

Figure 7.3 – Editing the DLP policy

4.   Click on **Next** two times to navigate to the **Customize Advanced DLP Rules** section.

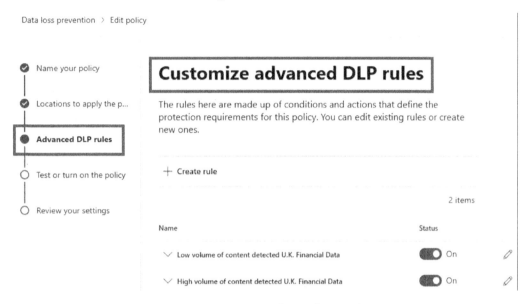

Figure 7.4 – Customize advanced DLP rules

5.   Click on **Edit** behind the low volume rule you wish to change:

Customize advanced DLP rules

The rules here are made up of conditions and actions that define the protection requirements for this policy. You can edit existing rules or create new ones.

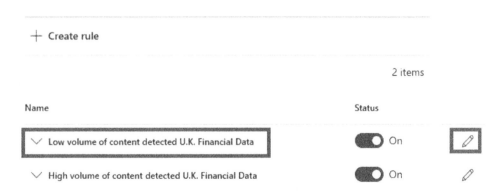

Figure 7.5 – Editing the Low volume rule

6. Click on the drop-down list in **Additional Options** and select the new priority for this policy. For the highest priority, select 0.

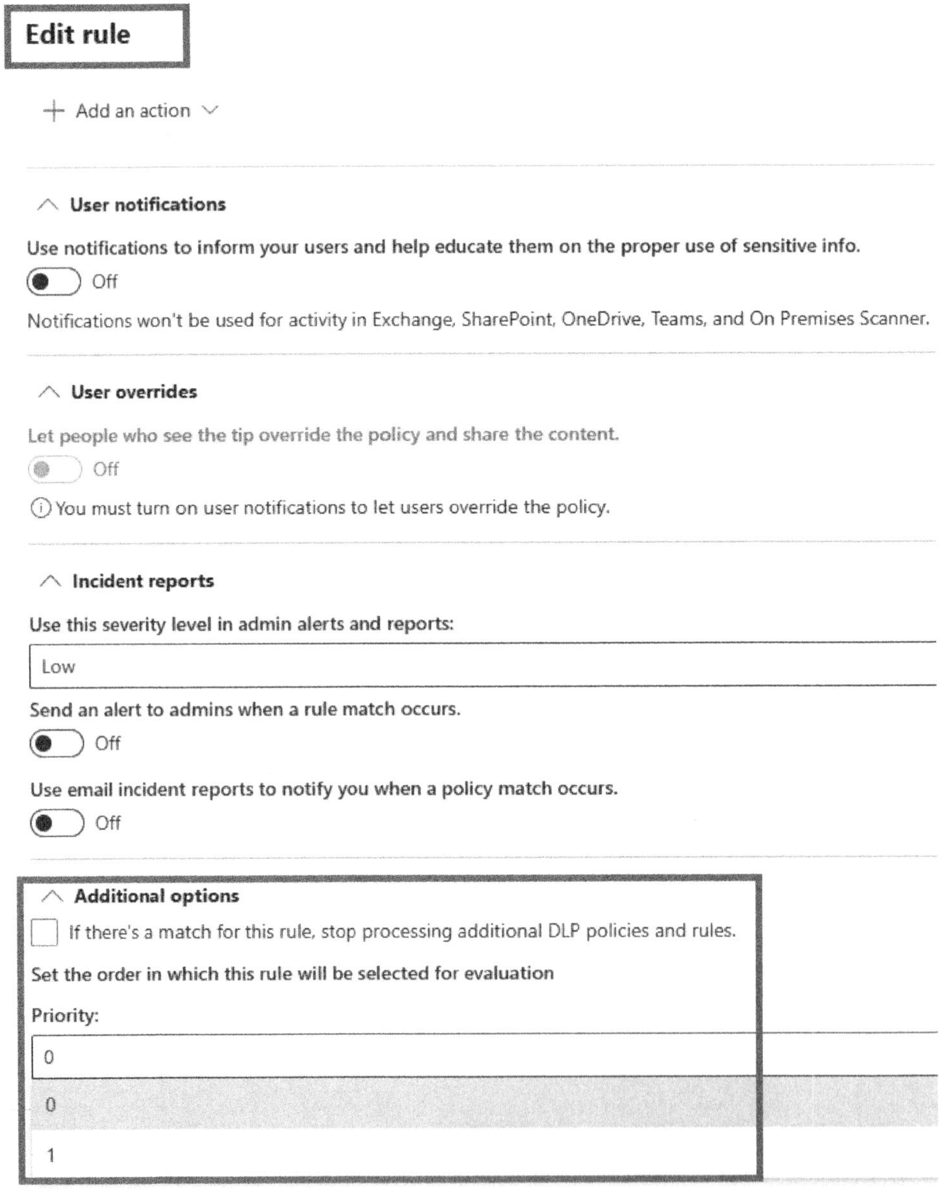

Edit rule

＋ Add an action ∨

∧ **User notifications**

Use notifications to inform your users and help educate them on the proper use of sensitive info.

(●⃝) Off

Notifications won't be used for activity in Exchange, SharePoint, OneDrive, Teams, and On Premises Scanner.

∧ **User overrides**

Let people who see the tip override the policy and share the content.

(●⃝) Off

ⓘ You must turn on user notifications to let users override the policy.

∧ **Incident reports**

Use this severity level in admin alerts and reports:

Low

Send an alert to admins when a rule match occurs.

(●⃝) Off

Use email incident reports to notify you when a policy match occurs.

(●⃝) Off

∧ **Additional options**

☐ If there's a match for this rule, stop processing additional DLP policies and rules.

Set the order in which this rule will be selected for evaluation

Priority:

0
0
1

Figure 7.6 – Changing rule priority

The preceding instructions show how to make the changes from within the Microsoft Purview Compliance Portal. However, you can make these changes via PowerShell as well. The following `cmdlet` can be run within PowerShell to change the priority of the `Low Volume of Financial Data` DLP rule to the highest value:

```
Set-DLPComplianceRule -Identity "Low Volume of Financial Data"
 -Priority 0
```

With that, we have changed the rule's priority. In the next section, we will look at changing the policy's priority.

Amending policy priority

In the scenario where you have configured more than a single DLP policy, you can change the priority/order. An example of this is if you have a personal data DLP policy and a different financial data DLP policy. In our scenario, you would like the personal data DLP policy to have higher precedence than the financial data DLP policy. To configure this, we would need to complete the following steps:

1. From within **Microsoft Purview Compliance Portal**, click on **Policies** > **Data loss prevention**.

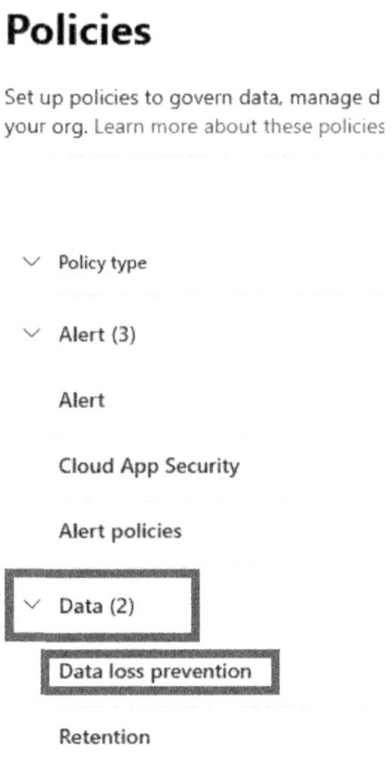

Figure 7.7 – Data loss prevention option

2. Click on the three vertical dots at the end of the policy's name.

Figure 7.8 – Choosing the option to move policy priority

3. After clicking the three vertical dots, you will see the option to **Move down** or **Move to the bottom**. Select **Move down** to give this policy lower precedence.

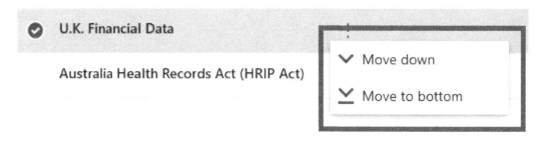

Figure 7.9 – Moving the policy's precedence

The preceding instructions show how to make the necessary changes from within **Microsoft 365 Compliance Centre**. However, you can make these changes via PowerShell as well. The following `cmdlet` can be run within PowerShell to change the priority of the `EU Financial Data Policy` DLP policy to the value 1:

```
Set-DLPCompliancePolicy -Identity "EU Financial Data Policy"
-Priority 1
```

It is good practice to prioritize policies with less constricting actions underneath policies that are more constrictive. In addition to this good practice regarding policy precedence, it is also good practice to prioritize rules with less constrictive actions below rules with more constrictive ones. This helps stop the less restrictive rules from overwriting any block actions of the more constrictive rules and policies.

You should now have an understanding of the recommended data loss prevention policies for different organizations, as well as how to configure and change policy precedence. In the next part of this chapter, we will look at configuring DLP policies for *Microsoft 365* SaaS services, including *Exchange Online*, *SharePoint sites*, *OneDrive*, and *Microsoft Teams*.

Configuring policies for Exchange Online, SharePoint sites, OneDrive, and Microsoft Teams

There are many SaaS applications within the *Microsoft 365* family, and it is always recommended to add an extra layer of protection where possible. In this section, we will take a closer look at how DLP policies can protect *Exchange Online*, *SharePoint sites*, *OneDrive*, and *Microsoft Teams*.

Custom DLP policy in Exchange Online

As we already know, a custom DLP policy enables you to configure conditions, rules, and actions that can assist you in meeting specific requirements for your organization. For DLP policies within Exchange Online, the possible rule conditions that are at your disposal include the standard mail flow rules (these were formerly known as transport rules), as well as the information types that can be found at the following Microsoft doc link: `https://docs.microsoft.com/en-us/exchange/policy-and-compliance/data-loss-prevention/sensitive-information-types?view=exchserver-2019`.

Before configuring DLP policies within *Exchange Online*, ensure you have assigned the relevant permissions to your admin account, which in this scenario will be the *Organization Management Compliance Management* permissions. The following steps will walk through how to create a custom DLP policy for Exchange Online:

1. From within **Microsoft Purview Compliance Portal**, navigate to **Policies** > **Data** > **Data loss prevention**. Please see the *Amending rule priority* section of this chapter for images for these individual steps.

2. On the **Data loss prevention** pane, select **Policies** and then click on **+Create policy**.

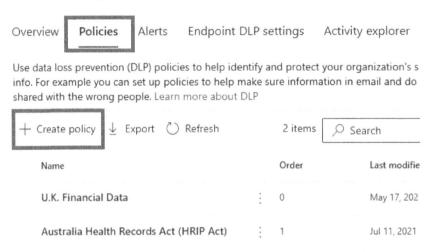

Figure 7.10 – Creating a new DLP policy

3. On the **Start with a template or create a custom policy** page, select one of the existing templates or create a custom policy if you require one. For our example, we will create a custom policy. Click on **Custom policy** and then **Next**.

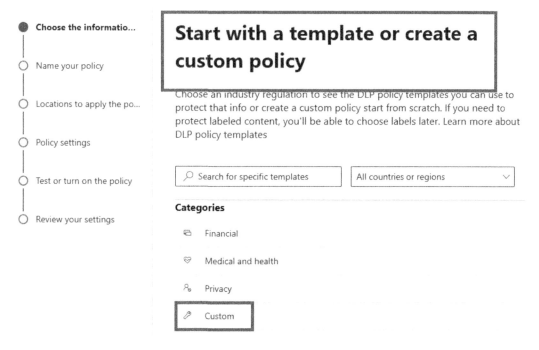

Figure 7.11 – Custom policy

4. On the **Name your DLP policy** page, enter a relevant name for the policy and a description and click on **Next**. In the following screenshot, you can see that I have named the policy **Exchange Online – Test Policy** and entered a relevant description.

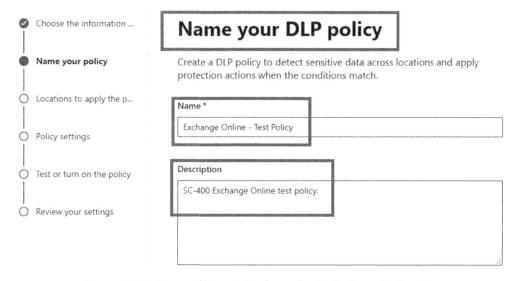

Figure 7.12 – Name and Description boxes for the Exchange DLP policy

5. On the **Choose locations to apply the policy** page, ensure that only the **Exchange email** location status is set to **On**, as shown in the following screenshot:

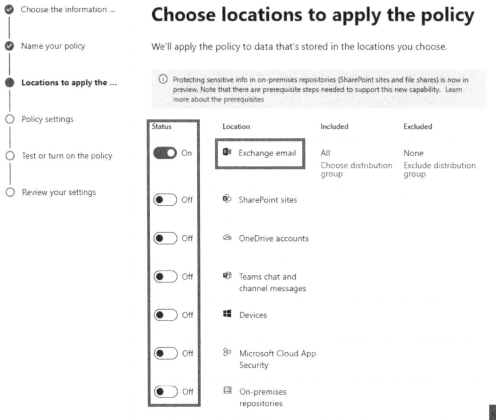

Figure 7.13 – Choosing Exchange Online as the location

6. You have the option to include or exclude specific email distribution groups if your requirement needs this. Click on **Next**.

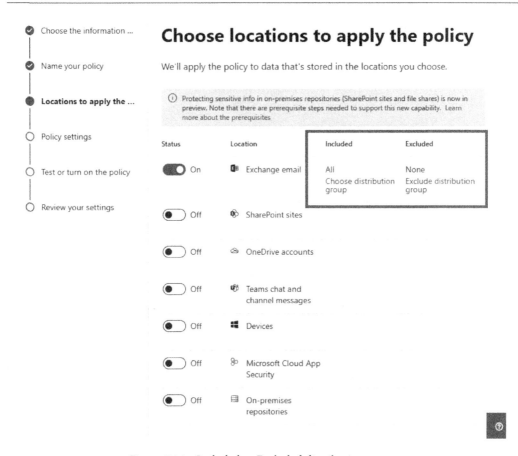

Figure 7.14 – Included or Excluded distribution groups

7. On the **Define policy settings** page, select **Create or customize advanced DLP rules** and click on **Next**.

Figure 7.15 – Define policy settings

8.   On the **Customize advanced DLP rules** page, click on **+Create rule**.

9.   On the **Create rule** page, enter an appropriate **Name** and **Description** for the rule. Under **Condition**, click on the **Add condition** dropdown and select the appropriate condition for this rule. For our example, I am adding a sender domain that the policy will apply.

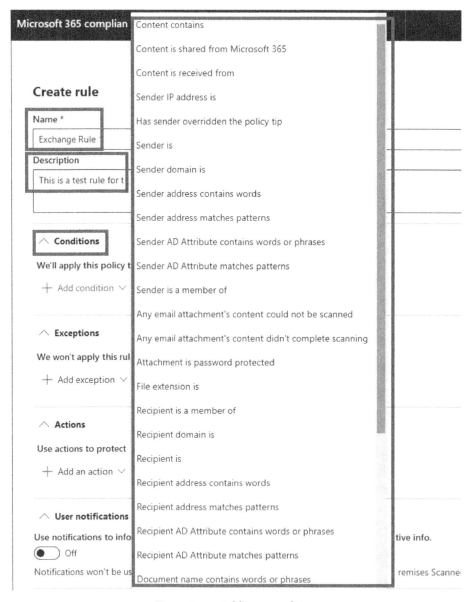

Figure 7.16 – Adding a condition

10. To add an exception to the rule, under **Exceptions**, click on **+Add exception**.

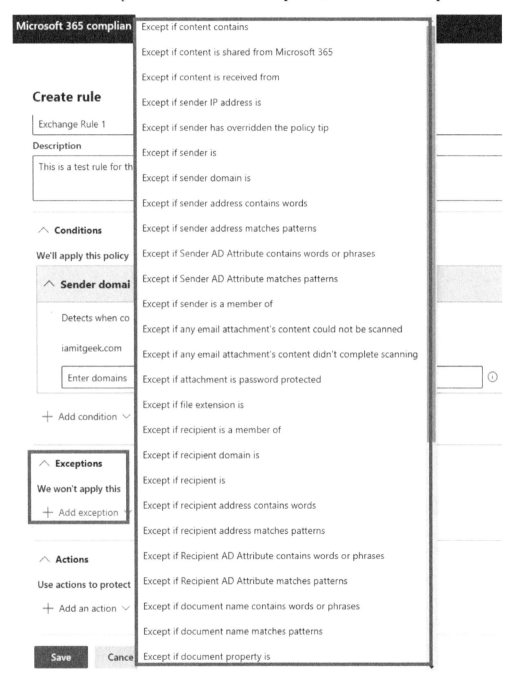

Figure 7.17 – Adding an exception to the rule

11. In the same way you added a **Condition** and an **Exception**, you can also add an **Action**, **User notification**, **User overrides**, **Incident reports**, and **Additional options**:

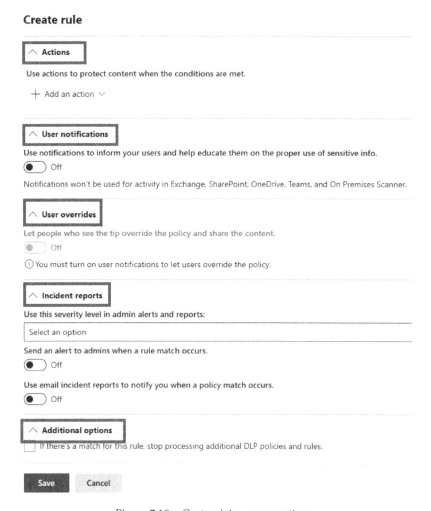

Figure 7.18 – Customizing more settings

12. Once you have completed all the configurations, you need to click on **Save**. On the **Customize advanced DLP rules** page, click on **Next**.

13. On the **Test or turn on the policy** page, you can choose from one of the following three options:

- **Test it out**: This allows you to review alerts to assess the policy's impact. Any restrictions that are configured will not be enforced.

- **Turn it on right away**: Once the policy has been enabled, it can take up to an hour for its effects to kick in.

- **Keep it off**: You can either test it or turn it on at a later date.

14. Click on **Next** to review the policy and click on **Submit** to complete the DLP policy for Exchange.

Now that we have configured a custom DLP policy in Exchange Online, we will take a look at custom policies with SharePoint sites.

Custom DLP policy with SharePoint sites, OneDrive, and Microsoft Teams

You can create DLP policies for SharePoint sites, OneDrive, and Microsoft Teams in the same way you can create custom policies for Exchange Online. As shown in the following screenshot, you can select the appropriate option from the **Choose locations to apply the policy** page, depending on your requirements:

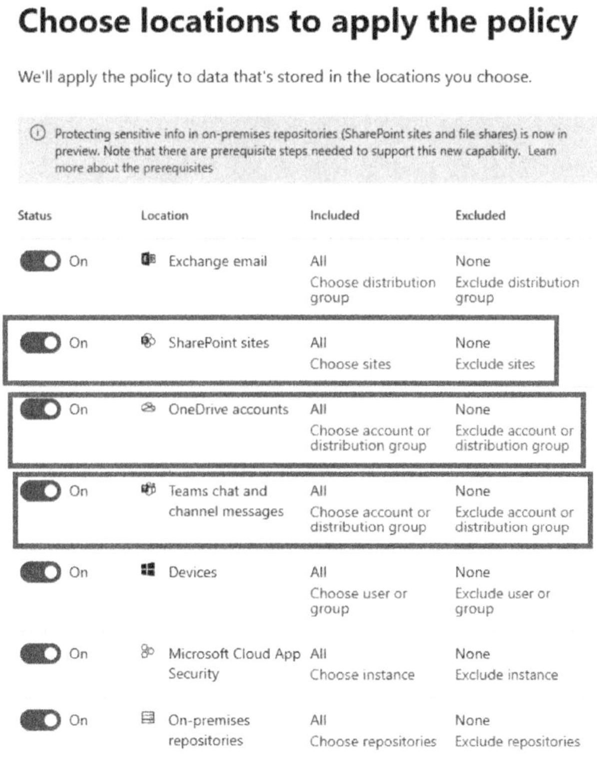

Figure 7.19 – Choosing a Microsoft 365 SaaS application

So far, we have covered the recommend **data loss prevention policy** solutions for an organization, configuring data loss prevention for policy precedence, and configuring policies for *Exchange Online, SharePoint Sites, OneDrive,* and *Microsoft Teams.* In the next section, we will look at integrating **Microsoft Defender for Cloud Apps** with information protection and configuring policies with Microsoft Defender for Cloud Apps.

Integrating Information Protection with, and configuring policies in Microsoft Defender for Cloud Apps

It is possible to use DLP policies for non-Microsoft cloud apps as part of the *Microsoft 365 DLP* suite of features. This feature is traditionally used to monitor and detect situations where sensitive data is being used or shared via non-Microsoft cloud applications.

There are two ways in which you can create DLP policies for non-Microsoft cloud applications:

- Create file policies in the cloud app security portal.
- Create DLP policies in the Microsoft Purview Compliance Portal and select Microsoft Defender for Cloud Apps as the location.

You can control actions with file policies when executing them in Microsoft Defender for Cloud Apps and a policy match is made. However, you can gain even more control over non-Microsoft cloud apps with DLP policies.

Before creating file policies, you will potentially need to activate file monitoring from within Microsoft Defender for Cloud Apps. Perform the following steps to enable Microsoft Defender for Cloud Apps to see files in the SaaS apps:

1. Go to the *Cloud App Security* portal at `https://portal.cloudappsecurity.com`.

2. Click on the **Settings** cog in the top-right corner of the portal.

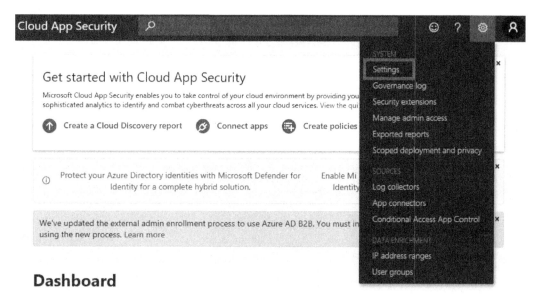

Figure 7.20 – Settings within the Microsoft Defender for Cloud Apps portal

3. Navigate to the **Information Protection** section and select the **Files** option.

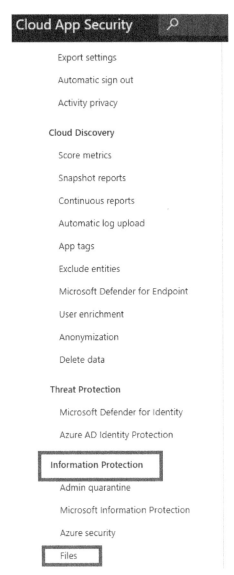

Figure 7.21 – Information Protection settings

4. To enable file monitoring, ensure that the **Enable file monitoring** option is checked and click on **Save**.

Files

ecurity to see files in your SaaS apps.

You must disable all file and malware detection policies if you wish to disable file monitoring
If you want to monitor Office 365 files you need to enable it in the Office 365 connector.

We secure your data as described in our privacy statement and online service terms.

Figure 7.22 – Enable file monitoring option

Once this setting has been configured, you can create file policies in Microsoft Defender for Cloud Apps. To utilize all the features of the Compliance Center to monitor non-Microsoft cloud applications, you must connect these applications to *Microsoft Defender for Cloud Apps*. Only then will they be available to you in the Microsoft Defender for Cloud Apps location of your DLP policies. You must complete this requirement to finish integrating Microsoft Defender for Cloud Apps into data loss prevention.

The policy will apply to all connected applications if you do not specifically select an instance for the policy. You can restrict non-Microsoft applications when you are creating a DLP policy by choosing **Restrict Third-Party Apps**. This allows you to select from various actions for every supported non-Microsoft cloud application. Different actions depend on the cloud app API.

In this section, you will learn about how to apply DLP policies to non-Microsoft applications and how to enable file monitoring in Microsoft Defender for Cloud Apps. In the next section, we will configure file policies in Microsoft Defender for Cloud Apps.

Configuring file policies in Microsoft Defender for Cloud Apps

The built-in engine for Microsoft Defender for Cloud Apps runs content inspections by removing text from all familiar file types, such as compressed files, Open Office, Office, and several rich text formats, such as XML and HTML.

There are three parts within every policy:

- A content scan built on top of preset templates or custom expressions
- Context filters, which include user roles, file metadata, sharing level, organizational group integration, collaboration context, and additional customizable attributes
- Automated actions for governance and remediation

Once you've enabled this, the policy will constantly scan the full cloud tenant, recognize files that match the content and context filters, and then apply the required automated actions. All violations for at-rest content are fully detected and remediated in these policies, including any new information that is created. Policies are monitored by utilizing real-time alerts or by using reports.

An additional option is to utilize the **Data Classification** service, which is used by the DLP policies in the Compliance Center. This option will allow you to have a uniform experience with every configured DLP policy.

The following exercise, which you can also complete, will focus on creating a new file policy within the Microsoft Defender for Cloud Apps portal:

1. Navigate to the **Cloud App Security** portal (`https://portal.cloudappsecurity.com`). From here, click on **Control** and then **Policies**.

Figure 7.23 – Navigating to Policies

2. Click on **Create Policy** and choose **File Policy**.

Figure 7.24 – Creating a File policy

3. Enter a relevant name and description.

4. Here, you will need to specify **Policy severity**. This level is utilized to establish whether the policy matches a trigger notification in the scenario where you have set Cloud App Security to send notifications on policy matches.

Figure 7.25 – Policy severity

5. In the **Category** panel, join the policy to the most relevant risk type. This field will assist you in looking for certain policies and alerts at a later date, depending on its risk type.

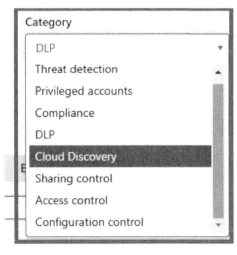

Figure 7.26 – Category

6. To set which discovered apps trigger this specific policy, you will be required to select the **Create a filter for the files this policy will act on** option. It is recommended that you be as restrictive as possible to avoid false positives.

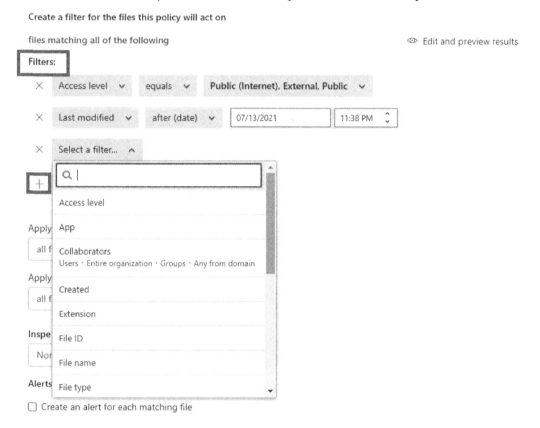

Figure 7.27 – Filters

7. Beneath the first **Apply to** filter, choose **all files excluding selected folders** or **selected folders** for *Box*, *SharePoint*, *Dropbox*, and *OneDrive*. Here, you can impose your file policy on all the files on the app or certain folders.

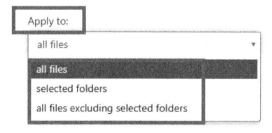

Figure 7.28 – Apply to options

8. Beneath the second **Apply to** filter, choose **all file owners, file owners from selected user groups** or **all file owners excluding selected user groups**. You must then choose the specific user groups to ascertain which users and groups should be in the policy.

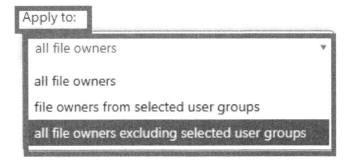

Figure 7.29 – Apply to options – continued

9. Choose the content **Inspection method**. You have the choice of **Built-in DLP** or **Data Classification Service**.

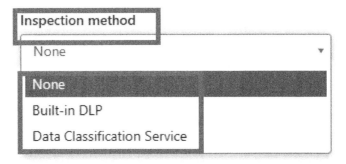

Figure 7.30 – Inspection method

10. Select the **Governance** action you require **Cloud App Security** to have when a match is detected. Then, choose **Create policy**.

To view all the files that are believed to have violated a policy, complete the following steps:

1. Choose **Control** and then **Policies**.

2. Look for the relevant **File Policy** you want to review.

3. Click on the three dots (…) on the right-side of the policy and choose **View all matches**.

4. You should now see a list of files that have been recognized by the file policy to match the chosen filters. You may utilize this to review the impact the policy has had before you amend it to apply any **Governance** actions.

In this section, we learned how to configure file policies within the *Microsoft Defender for Cloud Apps Admin Center* and create file policy matches. In the next section, we will discuss how to implement DLP prevention policies in test mode.

Implementing data loss prevention policies in test mode

When you are configuring data loss prevention policies, it can be hard to understand the full effect on users. Test mode is there so that administrators can make new DLP policies and monitor the effect and usefulness of the policy for users. You will receive an email with the results that contain incident reports, where a rule within the policy matches data in the specific locations. Reviewing these reports will assist you in determining whether the policy is working as it should be or whether you need to amend the policy before turning it on.

A good example of this is when you configure a policy that protects UK driving license numbers from being shared but when checking the data classification specs, you see that the internal product numbers the organization uses are almost identical to the pattern of the license numbers you are trying to protect. Here, you want to test the impact this policy would potentially have on users before activating it, and creating a policy in test mode can accomplish this.

To configure a policy in test mode, you need to follow the standard procedure of creating a policy. The next step is to decide whether you want to communicate with users that they are about to share sensitive content. Test mode can be implemented to be hidden or to show policy tips and send emails to users. Users can view their sensitive content if you do decide to inform them. This allows the user to report false positives if they occur. These can happen when information matches a pattern it is not meant to match with. This user feedback can be used to increase the value of a DLP policy.

In our UK driving license example, the license number and a phone number may have different patterns, but they can still have a string of numerical values that match both patterns. The DLP policy can both match the pattern and require other specific configurations to identify whether the value is a driving license number or a telephone number. In the case where a user is sending a client their mobile number, the policy will recognize that the driver's license pattern is in proximity to a driver's license identifier, which will result in the user being able to view a policy tip for the driver license policy.

Now that you understand the scenarios and real-life use cases in which you can implement a DLP policy in test mode, the following section will walk through how to enable test mode for an existing DLP policy.

Enabling test mode in an existing DLP policy

To allow test mode for your DLP policy, you are required to manage the DLP policy and go to the **Test or turn on the policy** page, and then follow these steps:

1. Click on **I'd like to test it out first**.

2. If you would like to show policy tips to users, then you should select **Show policy tips in test mode**. However, if this is not the case, then do not select this option.

3. Click on **Next** and look at the policy summary.

4. Click on **Submit** once you have reviewed the policy.

5. You can review the information the policy matches by using the **Reports** dashboard.

6. From within the *Compliance Center*, click on **Reports** and then click on **DLP policy matches**.

7. From the **Reports** page, filter the policy you created and look at the results.

At this stage, you have reviewed the effect that a policy has on users from the **Reports** dashboard. You can amend the policy to change its sensitivity and add specific exceptions if you highlight words that continuously trigger false positives. In the next section, we will take a closer look at user notifications.

DLP rule – user notifications

You can notify users when a policy has been triggered. By allowing these notifications, users should be able to report false positives, which will allow you, as the admin, to adjust the policy's sensitivity. The following steps outline how to enable user notifications for DLP rules:

1. Modify the **DLP policy** and navigate to the **Customize advanced DLP rules** section.

2. Click **Edit** on the DLP rule you wish to amend.

3. From within the **Edit rule** window, navigate to the **User Notifications** section. Click **On** underneath the **Use notifications to inform your users and help educate them on the proper use of sensitive info** option.

You should now understand how user notifications work, where to enable them on existing policies, and the benefit they give to end users. In the final section of this chapter, we will discuss incident reports.

DLP rule – incident reports

When enabling test mode on an existing policy, you need to be updated about matches so that you can amend the sensitivity if the matches are causing a high percentage of false positives. In this scenario, we will be monitoring every rule within the policy for itself but not the overall policy match.

Follow these steps to configure incident reports within the DLP policy:

1. While creating the DLP rules, in the **Edit rule** section, within the **Incident reports** section, under **Use this severity level in admin alerts and reports**, choose **Low/Medium/High** as the severity level.

2. If you would like to receive a notification email, choose **Send alert to admins when a rule match occurs** and choose your email address, and then choose **Send an alert every time an activity matches the rule**.

3. Determine the other parameters that have been offered to fine-tune the incident report.

You should now understand how to enable incident reports for an existing DLP policy. Now, let's look back at what we have covered and what you should know now that you've completed this chapter.

Summary

In this chapter, we covered several different topics, including configuring data loss prevention for policy precedence, configuring policies for Exchange Online, SharePoint Sites, OneDrive, and Microsoft Teams, integrating **Microsoft Defender for Cloud Apps** with Information Protection and configuring policies in Microsoft Defender for Cloud Apps, and implementing data loss prevention policies in test mode.

In this chapter, you completed multiple lab exercises, but if you have not followed any of these, I strongly recommend that you do so before moving on to the next chapter.

The next chapter will focus on implementing and monitoring Microsoft Endpoint data loss prevention.

8

Implementing and Monitoring Microsoft Endpoint Data Loss Prevention

Following the last chapter, which guided us through how to implement **data loss prevention (DLP)**, which covers our modern workplace workloads such as *Exchange* for email, *SharePoint* for collaboration, and *Teams* for collaboration and chats, we are now going to take a deep dive into how we implement this feature on Windows 10 at the operating system level. The main topics we are going to cover in this chapter are the following:

- Onboarding devices to Endpoint DLP
- Configuring Endpoint DLP settings

- Configuring policies for endpoints
- Monitoring endpoint activities

Technical requirements

As always, there are some technical requirements for running Endpoint DLP in your Microsoft environment. These are basically the same as before, but as a reminder we will go through them once more.

Microsoft Endpoint DLP is available in the following license subscriptions:

- **Microsoft 365 E5**
- **Microsoft 365 A5**
- **Microsoft 365 E5 Compliance**
- **Microsoft 365 A5 Compliance**
- **Microsoft 365 E5 Information Protection and Governance**
- **Microsoft 365 A5 Information Protection and Governance**

Furthermore, the licensing bit is not all the requirements, as usual. You also need to have a supported Windows 10 installation on your computers for the feature to work. The supported Windows 10 versions are **Windows 10 x64 build 1809 or later**.

Beyond the operating system being on the supported level, you also need to have a supported version of the Windows built-in antimalware client. The supported levels of antimalware client are **Antimalware Client Version 4.18.2009.7 or more recent releases**.

> **Note**
> There is no requirement for the Windows Security components, such as *Credential Guard, Tamper Protection*, and so on, to be in active mode in order to run Endpoint DLP. You can run it independently of the Windows Security status; however, *Real-time protection* and *Behavior monitor* must be enabled.

There are some Windows updates that are not specifically a requirement for onboarding a device to Endpoint DLP; however, as they contain important fixes for issues, they should be installed prior to using the product:

- **Windows 10 1809** – KB4559003, KB4577069, KB4580390
- **Windows 10 1903 or 1909** – KB4559004, KB4577062, KB4580386
- **Windows 10 2004** – KB4568831, KB4577063
- **For devices running Office 2016** – KB4577063

The devices must be in in one of these states when it comes to Azure Active Directory:

- Azure Active Directory joined
- Hybrid Azure Active Directory joined
- Azure Active Directory registered

Now, with the requirements all figured out, we will proceed with our first topic of the chapter, which will guide us through how to configure policies for endpoints.

Onboarding devices to Endpoint DLP

To start using **Endpoint DLP**, we must onboard our devices to the solution to see them in the compliance center and get alerts if they are in breach of a DLP policy, a topic we will cover next!

For starters, we must onboard our devices to Endpoint DLP using one of the following methods:

- Local script (this option is meant for **proof of concept** (**PoC**) scenarios or demos)
- Group policy
- Microsoft Endpoint Configuration Manager
- Mobile Device Management/Microsoft Intune
- VDI onboarding scripts for non-persistent machines

Given how your environment is configured, you should choose the method that aligns best with how you currently deploy software.

> **Note**
> We need to have local administrator privileges on the device that we are going
> to onboard to Endpoint DLP.

The following steps will guide you through how to onboard a device to **Endpoint DLP**
using a local script; if you are interested in guidance for the other deployment methods
listed, please refer to `https://docs.microsoft.com/en-us/microsoft-365/`
`security/defender-endpoint/configure-endpoints?view=o365-`
`worldwide`:

1. Sign in to the **Microsoft compliance center**.

2. On the left-hand side of your screen, navigate to the **Settings** area and select **Device onboarding**:

Figure 8.1 – The location of the Device onboarding settings in the Microsoft compliance center

3. Select the method you want to use for onboarding devices to Endpoint DLP under
    Onboarding and **Deployment method**:

Device onboarding

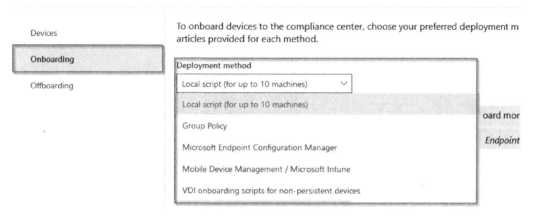

Figure 8.2 – The available deployment methods as presented in the Microsoft compliance center

4. As stated in the introduction to these steps, we are going to choose **Local script** as the deployment method in this case. Select it and click **Download package**, which will start a download of a .zip file containing a .cmd script called DeviceComplianceLocalOnboardingScript.cmd:

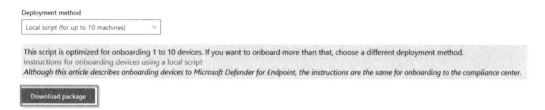

Figure 8.3 – Clicking on Download package to download the onboarding script

Once download starts, we will choose the location to save the `.zip` file as usual with downloads:

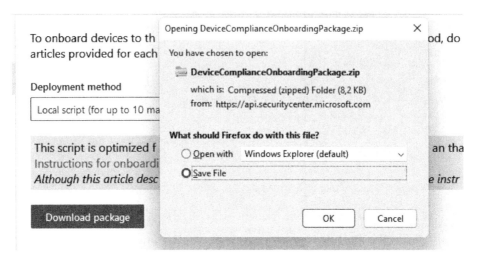

Figure 8.4 – Once download is initiated, you can see the .zip file as mentioned in step 4 and choose a location to save it

5.   The callout in the compliance center can be discarded in this scenario as we are only onboarding a single computer to our **Endpoint DLP** solution. But, as stated, the same deployment scenarios are in use here as for Microsoft Defender for Endpoint, and the guidance is the same for onboarding to the compliance center solutions.

6.   Once we have saved our `.zip` file to our computer hard drive, we need to extract the content and run the script provided:

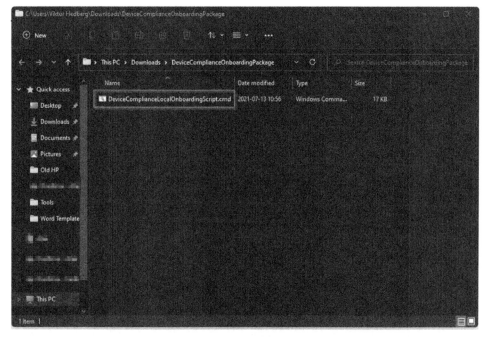

Figure 8.5 – The .cmd script downloaded from the compliance center, ready to be used!

7.   I find the easiest way to start the script is to start an elevated Command Prompt, navigate to the folder where the script is located, and execute the script:

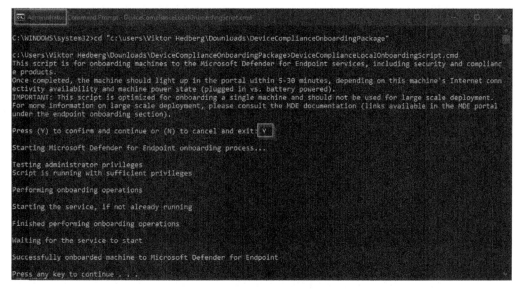

Figure 8.6 – Using an elevated Command Prompt to execute the script, to make sure that you are running it as administrator

8. And we have successfully onboarded our device to the **Endpoint DLP** solution. Please note that although the script states it has been onboarded to **Microsoft Defender for Endpoint**, this is not the case. This is simply a typo from Microsoft in this case.

9. If we head back to the **Devices** portion of the **Device onboarding** page, we should see our device in the list:

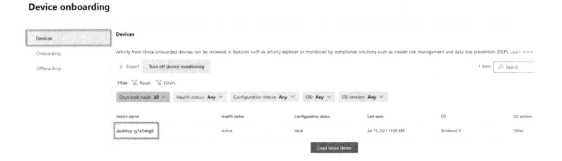

Figure 8.7 – The Devices list shows us all of the onboarded devices in Endpoint DLP

This concludes the topic of onboarding devices to **Endpoint DLP** using the **Local script** method. Up next, we will take a deeper look at what settings we can configure in Endpoint DLP.

Configuring Endpoint DLP settings

Moving back to the general DLP settings in the **Microsoft compliance center**, we will now cover the specific settings that are available for **Endpoint DLP**. The solution enables you to audit and act on several activities users take on sensitive items. The activities available for monitoring are as follows:

- **Upload to cloud service, or access by unallowed browser**: Detects when an individual tries to upload a protected item to a restricted service domain or access the item through an unallowed browser.

- **Copy to other app**: Detects when an individual tries to copy sensitive information from a protected item and then paste it into another application, item, or process.

- **Copy to USB removable media**: Detects when an individual tries to copy information or an item to a USB device or other removable media.

- **Copy to a network share**: Detects when an individual tries to copy an item to a mapped network share.

- **Print a document**: Detects printing attempts of sensitive information.

- **Copy to a remote session**: Detects attempts to copy sensitive information to a remote desktop session.

- **Copy to a Bluetooth device**: Detects copy attempts to unallowed Bluetooth apps (as defined in the general settings for Endpoint DLP for **Unallowed Bluetooth apps**).

- **Create an item**: Detects when a user creates an item. This setting is only auditable.

- **Rename an item**: Detects when a user renames an item. This setting is only auditable.

The following screenshot from a DLP policy highlights the specific **Endpoint DLP** settings:

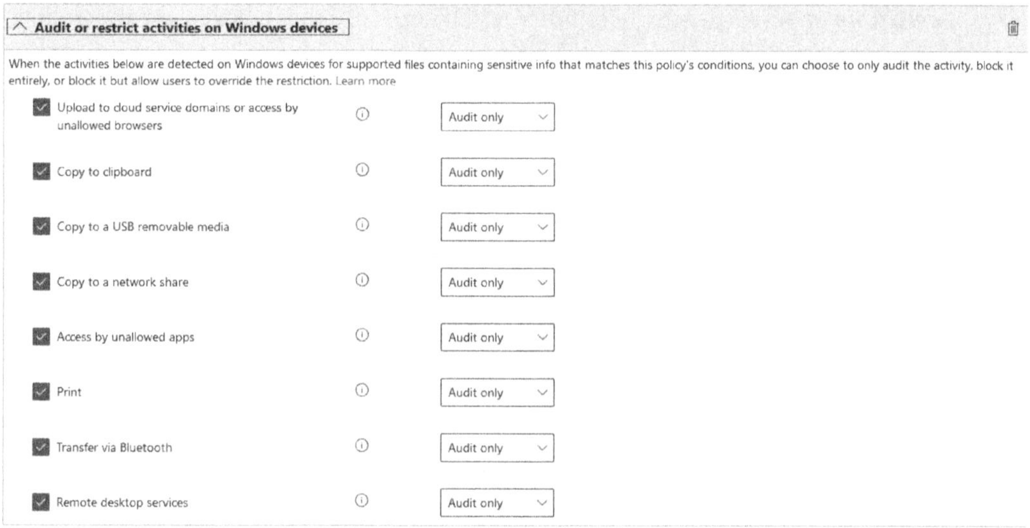

Figure 8.8 – Overview of Endpoint DLP settings in a DLP policy

There are several settings available for the feature as well; these apply to all onboarded devices, as the previous settings shown in *Figure 8.8* only apply to the specific policy for which it is enabled.

The global **Endpoint DLP** settings are as follows:

- **File path exclusions**: Files in these Windows device locations will not be monitored by DLP policies.

- **Unallowed apps**: Prevents specific apps from accessing files protected by a DLP policy.

- **Unallowed Bluetooth apps**: Prevents transfer via Bluetooth for files protected by your policies.

- **Browser and domain restrictions to sensitive data**: Restricts the usage of unallowed browsers when handling sensitive information or prevents the uploading of said information to unallowed service domains.

- **Additional settings for Endpoint DLP**: Controls how your users interact with the *justification* pop-up windows that appear if the policy is set to **Block with override**, with the following options: **Show default options with custom text box**, **Only show default options**, and **Only show custom text box**.

- **Always audit file activity for devices**: The default setting here is **Active** and when devices are onboarded, activity for Office, PDF, and CSV files is automatically audited.

If you are interested in learning even more about these settings, refer to `https://docs.microsoft.com/en-us/microsoft-365/compliance/endpoint-dlp-using?view=o365-worldwide#dlp-settings`.

Let's dive in to how we create a DLP policy meant for endpoints, where we will use the settings we just covered in practice.

Configuring policies for endpoints

Now that we are familiar with the different settings available in Endpoint DLP, let's use this knowledge and configure some DLP policies for endpoints. As usual, we will start by heading over to the compliance center at `https://compliance.microsoft.com`.

As we covered this in the previous chapter, you should now be accustomed to creating a DLP policy, but as we are looking to scope this for our endpoints, we need to add some settings to our policies.

Heading to our overview of DLP policies in the tenant, we will select the one that we are going to configure these **Endpoint DLP** settings for. In my example, I am using the **U.K. Financial Data** DLP policy as listed here:

Figure 8.9 – The table listing all of the DLP policies present in the Microsoft 365 tenant

Follow the steps shown next for configuring policies for endpoints:

1. Click on the policy you wish to alter these settings for and select **Edit policy** at the top of the table listing your policies:

Figure 8.10 – Selecting the policy you wish to edit and clicking the Edit policy button

2. This will take us to the editing mode of our DLP policy. Unless you wish to edit the description of the policy, click **Next** to select the locations to apply the policy:

Figure 8.11 – The only editable thing here is the description of the policy; the name cannot be edited

3. Here, we will toggle the **Devices** switch to **On**, meaning that this policy will from now on also cover the devices onboarded to **Endpoint DLP**. We are given the option to scope which devices this policy would apply to, and which ones, if any, to exclude from the policy:

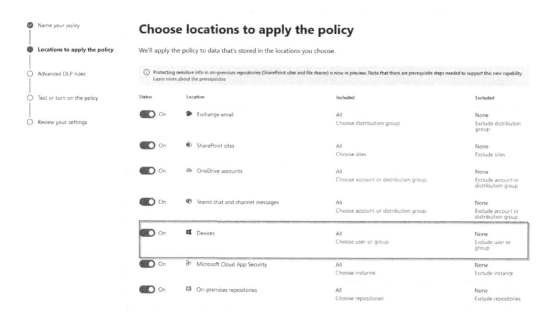

Figure 8.12 – Toggling the Devices switch to On

4. On the next page, **Advanced DLP rules**, expand either **Low volume of content detected U.K. Financial Data** or **High volume of content detected U.K. Financial Data** and click on the **Edit** button, which is visually present as a pen in the portal:

Figure 8.13 – Click on the pen to edit the rules for the DLP policy

5.   Scroll down to **Actions** and select **Audit or restrict activities on Windows devices** from the **Add an action** drop-down list. Here, we can adjust the settings for **Endpoint DLP**, in audit, block, or block with override mode:

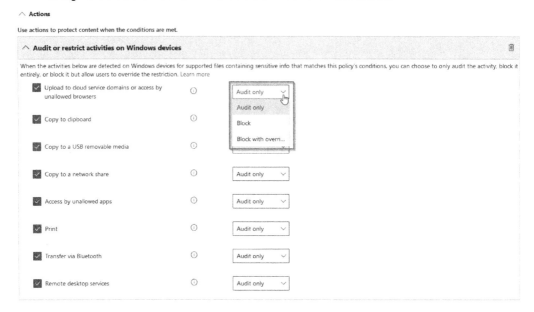

Figure 8.14 – Showing the possible enforcement for each setting for Endpoint DLP

6.   Let's change these settings as shown in *Figure 8.15*:

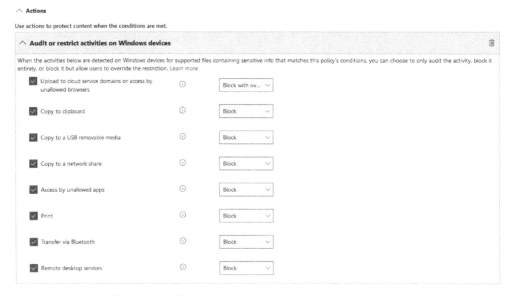

Figure 8.15 – The settings altered to meet our requirements

7. Once we have saved these settings, we can verify them by looking at the **Customize advanced DLP rules** page, which we are returned to after pressing **Save**, as the **Actions** portion now lists **Audit or restrict activities on Windows devices**:

Customize advanced DLP rules

The rules here are made up of conditions and actions that define the protection requirements for this policy. You can edit existing rules or create new ones.

+ Create rule

2 items

Name	Status			
∨ Low volume of content detected U.K. Financial Data	🔘 On	✎	↓	🗑
∧ High volume of content detected U.K. Financial Data	🔘 On	✎	↑	🗑

Conditions
Content contains any of these sensitive info types:
   Credit Card Number
   EU Debit Card Number
   SWIFT Code

Actions
Notify users with email and policy tips
Audit or restrict activities on Windows devices
Send incident reports to Administrator
Send alerts to Administrator

Figure 8.16 – Showing Audit or restrict activities on Windows devices

8. We go forward through the edit guide and keep the policy in the **Test** mode so as not to interfere with our users' daily work. We can now try to create an item containing any of the information types the DLP policy is looking for and try to copy it to a USB device. As the policy is in **Test**, no enforcements are in place, but we should be able to see it in the activity explorer:

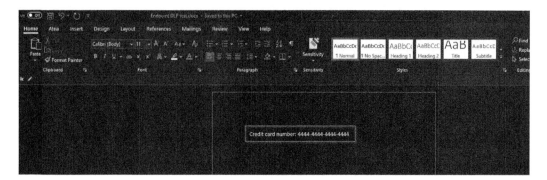

Figure 8.17 – A dummy document created with a credit card number within

9. In the activity explorer in the compliance center, we can now see that the document was created, and when we try to copy it to a USB device, this will also be audited and logged for us:

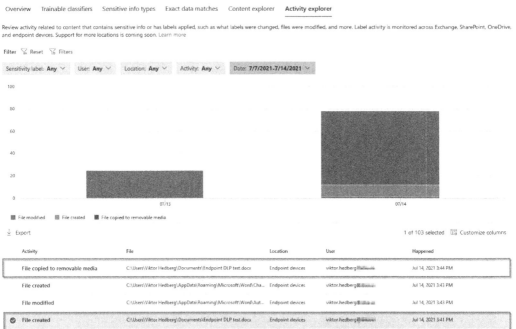

Figure 8.18 – Showing the auditing in the activity explorer for our dummy document

10. If we expand the **File copied to removable media** log entry, we can see the file hash and file path, along with other relevant information:

File copied to removable media

Activity details

Activity	Happened
File copied to removable media	Jul 14, 2021 3:44 PM
Client IP	Enforcement mode
▓▓ ▓▓▓ ▓▓ ▓▓	Audit
Target file path	
D:\Endpoint DLP test.docx	

About this item

File	User
Endpoint DLP test.docx	viktor.hedberg▓▓ ▓▓▓▓
File extension	File size
docx	14 KB

Sensitive info type

Sha1
a2090aa0f1fbbfcfdcbc1186fe29827f1c7b06f4

Sha256
8b8a8f2c892e2f95646d99070f331f18399f783b90f76211297328d8ddbf1893

Previous file name
Endpoint DLP test.docx

Location details

Location
Endpoint devices

Parent
C:\Users\Viktor Hedberg\Documents

File path
C:\Users\Viktor Hedberg\Documents\Endpoint DLP test.docx

Source location type	**Destination location type**
Local	Removable
Platform	**Application**
Windows	explorer.exe

Device name
desktop-g7e5mg6

MDATP device ID
3070faf5e46f85c4c96741b773a746b59db5efbf

Removable media device manufacturer	**Removable media device model**
Kingston	DataTraveler 3.0

Figure 8.19 – Showing the file information on an audit log event

And with that, we have edited our DLP policy to accommodate the **Endpoint DLP** settings as well.

Up next, we will look at to how to monitor endpoint activities using the compliance center.

Monitoring endpoint activities

There are several built-in reports available for DLP in the compliance center (`https://compliance.microsoft.com`), which will be covered in *Chapter 9, Managing and Monitoring Data Loss Prevention Policies and Activities*.

To monitor the endpoint activities, we will instead use the activity explorer in the compliance center. Navigate to either one of the following places:

- **Data classification | Activity explorer**
- **Data loss prevention | Activity explorer**

Using the **activity explorer**, we can see exactly what our onboarded devices are doing when it comes to creating items, editing items, moving items, and/or sharing them. The information is collected from the Microsoft 365 unified audit logs, transformed, and made available in the activity explorer interface:

Figure 8.20 – The activity explorer shows us all activities performed on endpoints

You can use the activity explorer to drill down into specific events, as described in *Figure 8.20*, and make sure that your classified or sensitive information is taken care of in the correct manner according to the information security policy in your organization.

This concludes the section about monitoring endpoint activities.

Summary

To summarize, we have taken a deep dive into the wonders of Endpoint DLP in Microsoft 365. This feature will no doubt help guarantee that your information does not leave the organization in any way, shape, or form.

Up next, we have a chapter on how to manage and monitor DLP policies and activities.

9
Managing and Monitoring Data Loss Prevention Policies and Activities

In the previous chapter, we discussed implementing and monitoring Microsoft Endpoint **Data Loss Prevention** (**DLP**), including configuring policies for endpoints, configuring endpoint DLP settings, and monitoring endpoint activities. In this chapter, we will take a closer look at managing and monitoring DLP policies and activities. This chapter will include practical labs, which you should follow as they will help you understand how the policies work and the different settings that are available.

In this chapter, we are going to cover the following main topics:

- Managing and responding to DLP policy violations
- Reviewing and analyzing DLP reports
- Managing permissions for DLP reports
- Managing DLP violations in **Microsoft Defender for Cloud Apps**

Technical requirements

In this chapter, we'll continue to explore configuring Information Protection within Microsoft 365. There will be an exercise that will require access to **Microsoft 365** with *Global Administrator* rights. If you have followed the exercises from the previous chapter, you should now have the relevant trial licenses; however, if you have not yet created these for Microsoft 365, please follow the instructions from *Chapter 1, Preparing for Your Microsoft Exam and SC-400 Exam Objectives*.

Managing and responding to DLP policy violations

In the case where a DLP policy alerts an admin that a DLP policy violation has occurred, it can have multiple meanings. It does not always mean that data loss has occurred or has been stopped. You will get alerted if a policy violation has been observed; however, the policy will not take any action based on the reason for trying to share the data that is protected. Escalating any violation to the organization's security team is a reactive action you can take, and you would work with them and key stakeholders to investigate the issue.

A good example is if you are working for an organization that protects highly sensitive information (financial data is a common example) to stop any sharing of client data with third parties. You get several alerts at the end of the month that there have been violations of the specific policy in place for this. When you look at the reports, you see a high level of emails from a department within the organization that includes customer-specific information (in our example, let's assume it is billing information). Now, the policy does not take context into account and reacts accordingly, but this is where the compliance administrator comes in as it is their job to assess and appraise policy violations and make the correct decisions on how to proceed. In this scenario, we have to accept the fact that at the latter part of the month, alerts will be set off due to the policy correctly recognizing protected data and it updates you about this.

DLP reports can assist admins in recognizing users who have a high number of matches. There are a number of reasons a user may match; however, as a compliance admin, it is your job to assess whether those incident matches require further investigation.

You can additionally utilize reports to enable users to assist you with improving DLP policies. You will find a report called *DLP False reports and overrides report*. In the scenario in which you enable users to override by using a relevant justification, you not only make them accountable by selecting to override, but this also allows you to investigate the reason and recognize business processes that justify a change to the existing policy.

We will now do a lab exercise in which we need to amend the *U.K. Financial Data* DLP policy to exclude instances where your finance data matches the custom sensitive information type for UK driving licenses.

Implementing DLP rule exclusion

The following exercise will amend the U.K. Financial Data DLP policy:

1. From within the Microsoft Purview Compliance Portal, navigate to the **Policies** page | **Data** and then select **Data loss prevention**:

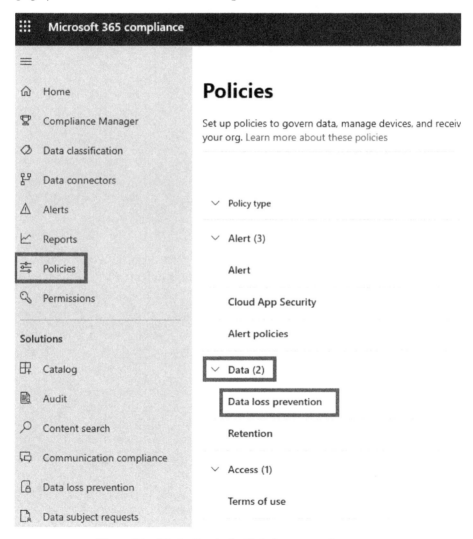

Figure 9.1 – Navigating to the Data loss prevention menu

2. Click on the **Policies** tab and check the **U.K Financial Data** policy. Select the edit button:

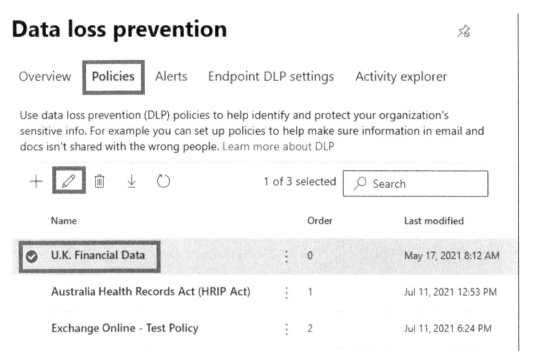

Figure 9.2 – Editing a policy

3. Click on **Next** until you arrive at the **Customize advanced DLP rules** page. Click on the edit button next to **High volume of content detected U.K. Financial Data**:

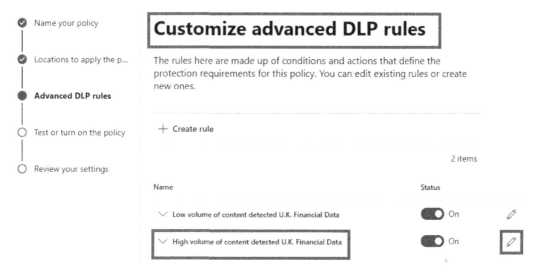

Figure 9.3 – Editing customized advanced DLP rules

4. Navigate to **Exceptions** and then click **Add exception**:

Figure 9.4 – Add exception

5.   Click on **Except if content contains** from the drop-down menu:

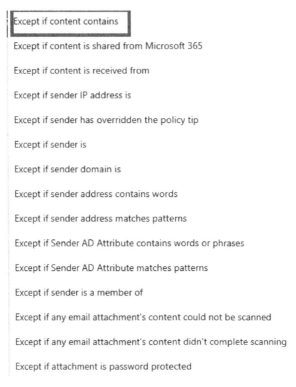

Figure 9.5 – Except if content contains

6.   Click on **Add** and choose **Sensitive info types**:

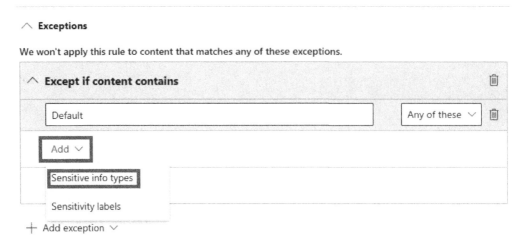

Figure 9.6 – Selecting Sensitive info types

7. A pop-up window will appear. Click the **U.K. Driver's License Number** type and click on **Add**:

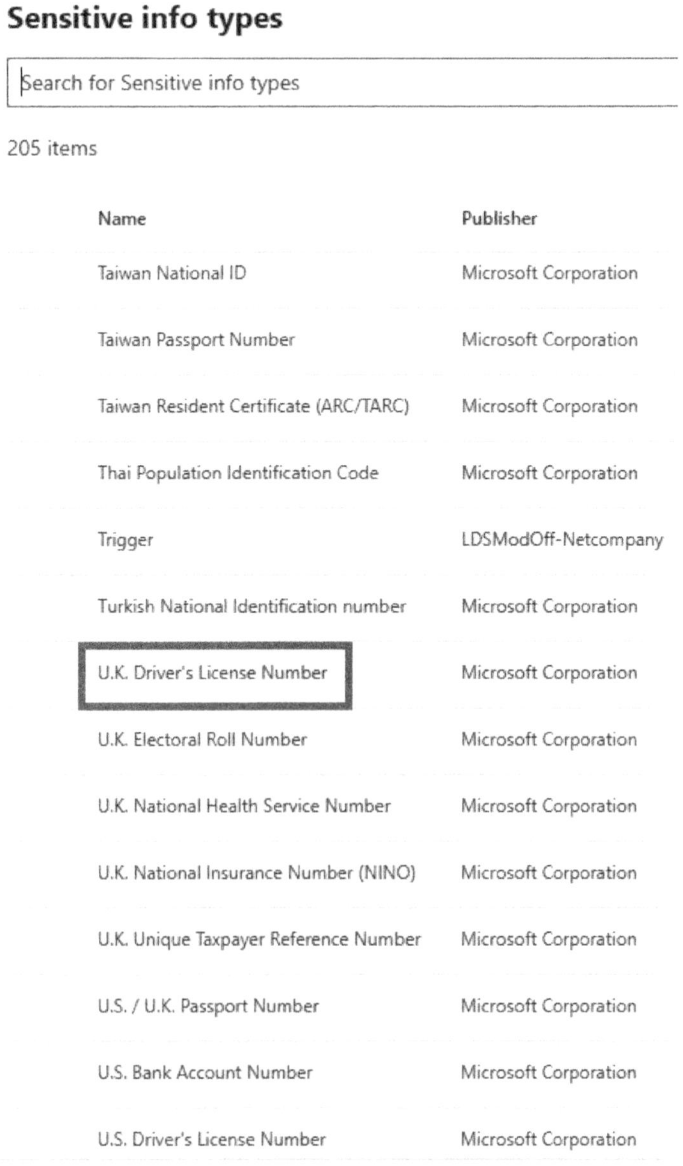

Sensitive info types

| Search for Sensitive info types |

205 items

Name	Publisher
Taiwan National ID	Microsoft Corporation
Taiwan Passport Number	Microsoft Corporation
Taiwan Resident Certificate (ARC/TARC)	Microsoft Corporation
Thai Population Identification Code	Microsoft Corporation
Trigger	LDSModOff-Netcompany
Turkish National Identification number	Microsoft Corporation
U.K. Driver's License Number	Microsoft Corporation
U.K. Electoral Roll Number	Microsoft Corporation
U.K. National Health Service Number	Microsoft Corporation
U.K. National Insurance Number (NINO)	Microsoft Corporation
U.K. Unique Taxpayer Reference Number	Microsoft Corporation
U.S. / U.K. Passport Number	Microsoft Corporation
U.S. Bank Account Number	Microsoft Corporation
U.S. Driver's License Number	Microsoft Corporation

Figure 9.7 – U.K. Driver's License Number type

8. Click on **Save**.

9. Click on **Next** until you get to the review page, and then click on **Submit**.

This type of implementation will lower the number of false positives of the policy as it will not apply when it recognizes UK driver's licenses within any shared content.

In this section, we have looked at how to manage and respond to DLP policy violations. In the next section of this chapter, we will look at reviewing and analyzing DLP reports.

Reviewing and analyzing DLP reports

With both the DLP Policy Matches report and the **DLP Incidents report** page, there is a chart and a table you will be able to view that display information based on their corresponding events.

When analyzing both these reports, you have the ability to break down the charts and separate them by either of the following:

- **Affected service**
- **Enforced action**
- **Applied policy**

You will need to familiarize yourself with the existing filters of DLP that will aid you in fine-tuning the policies and limit the false positives and overrides.

Reviewing DLP policy matches

When you are utilizing DLP policy match reports, it is recommended to use filters to reduce the report to particular policies. This will aid in lowering the number of matches that are viewable and concentrate on the effect of the specific policies in your tenant.

Imagine a scenario in which you created a new policy to protect financial content a week ago and it is currently in test mode. In this case, you need to set the start date within the filter to be close to the start date of the policy to prevent whitespace in the report from before the policy creation date. The following steps will outline how you can accomplish this:

1. Navigate to the **DLP Policy Matches** page and click on **Filter** (in the right corner).
2. Choose a start date close to the date you created the policy.
3. Underneath **Services**, ensure all services are chosen.
4. Underneath **Policies**, choose the DLP policy you wish to review in the drop-down menu.
5. Underneath **Rules**, choose all the rules, and then click on **Apply**.

6. You can utilize the drop-down menu at the top of the page to amend the breakdown of the chart. This will help you get a better insight into how and where the policy is affecting users.

7. Click on **Chart breakdown by Services**.

8. From within the drop-down menu, click on **Chart breakdown by Action**.

9. Choose an option from the legend to filter the results even further.

10. Utilize the table to review which rule matched as well as the sensitive information that is responsible for the match.

11. Alternate between the breakdown choices and amend the filters to find peaks in specific services and ties that may indicate a requirement to amend the policy.

Following on from the previous lab exercise, imagine a spike in the exchange service for bank account number details. This may suggest a leak; however, it may also suggest a legitimate business practice that is conflicting with the new policy. It is recommended to investigate the reason behind this conflict before amending the policy.

In this section, we looked at reviewing DLP policy matches. Now, we will look at reviewing DLP incidents.

Reviewing DLP incidents

You can use the DLP Incidents report to get an overview of which objects create more matches than others. When utilizing this overview, you should not constrain the report to specific policies. By doing this, it will enable you to identify items that come under the scope of several policies and review which action is applied in the end. When utilizing the DLP Incidents report, you should try to keep the timeframe wide-ranging and drill down if you find any peaks at specific times.

Imagine a scenario where you have created a new set of DLP policies and put them in order according to your organization's DLP strategy. If you wish to review whether or not the priority you chose matches the reality of sensitive data in the organization, you should open the **DLP Incidents report** page and follow these measures:

1. Click on **Filter** in the right corner.

2. Choose a start date and an end date.

3. Underneath **Services**, ensure all services are chosen.

4. Click on **All Policies** in the drop-down menu.

5. Click on **Apply**.

Not only can you utilize DLP incident reports to see items that conflict with the policy priority, but you can also use them as a tool to find objects that create high-volume matches. This data enables you to think of additional protective methods for these items for the DLP policies.

Imagine a scenario in which you notice documents with five times as many policy matches as the next highest match count. Although the protective action stops these files from being shared, you may want to consider saving them at a more secure location.

After completing this section of the chapter, you should be able to understand how to review DLP incidents. Now, we will take a closer look at reviewing DLP false positives and overrides.

Reviewing DLP false positives and overrides

With this particular report, all the false positives and overrides you see come from your organization's users. It is important to train users to ensure they understand how to report false positives correctly, which ensures the information in this report is accurate.

Imagine a scenario in which you create a new financial data policy that is currently in test mode. A few days ago, you enabled policy tips and allowed overrides of the policy. If you utilize the reports to tune a new policy to match only when it is meant to match, you need to select a start date that is shortly before the time you enabled the policy tips settings and reduce the scope to show false positives.

The following steps will explain how to do this:

1. Click on **Filter** (in the right corner).
2. Choose a start date.
3. Underneath **Services**, ensure all services are chosen.
4. Choose the financial data policy you would like to analyze and click on **Apply**.
5. Uncheck **DLP policy override** from the legend of the chart.

In this view, you can see all of the reports with false positives for your financial data policy and utilize this to detect the sensitive information that it is falsely matching with.

Overrides are able to assist with detecting business processes that are contradicting your policy. A high volume of overrides on a policy means you should take a closer look at those business processes. In this case, you need to decide whether you can make a modification to the policy without having an adverse effect on its protective functions. You can do this by completing the following steps:

1. From within the legend of the chart, select **DLP overrides** and untick **DLP false positives**.

2. Choose an item from the table and look at the **Justification** section of the popup.

Overrides are able to help with auditing as the user is responsible and accountable for the override and it enables you to investigate whether valid reasons require the DLP policy override. Overrides are not negative.

You have now completed the reviewing and analyzing DLP reports section of this chapter and have completed multiple labs as part of it. The next section will focus on managing permissions for DLP reports.

Managing permissions for DLP reports

As with all services in Microsoft 365, you need specific permissions to be able to review DLP reports in the compliance center. The following table outlines the required permissions and their purpose:

Role	Role assigned to the role group	Purpose
Security Reader (Exchange)	Security Reader, Organization Management	Grants the user the same permissions as assigning users to the Security & Compliance Center Security Reader role
View-Only DLP Compliance Management	Security Reader, Compliance Administrator, Security Administrator, Organization Management	Grants read-only access to the DLP Reports in the Security & Compliance Centre

Table 9.1 – Required permissions

Users within your IT admin team, or members of the compliance team who review DLP reports, require the correct permissions to the compliance center. The default permissions for your admin tenant are that they will have access to this area, therefore they are able to give the relevant team members access to the Microsoft Purview Compliance Portal without granting access to the entire tenant. Follow the next steps to do this:

1. In Azure AD, create a group and add the members of your team that are compliance officers to it.

2. On the **Permissions & roles** page, create a role group under **Compliance center**:

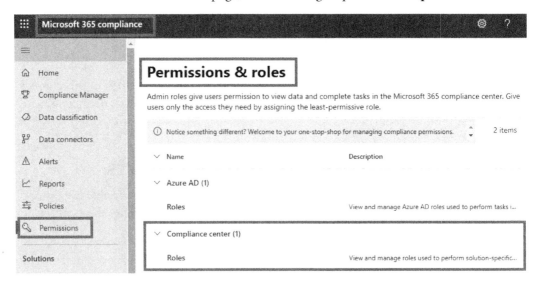

Figure 9.8 – Compliance center permissions and roles

3. During the role group creation process, you can use the **Choose roles** options to add the relevant role to the role group. In our example, we will add the **View-Only DLP Compliance Management** role:

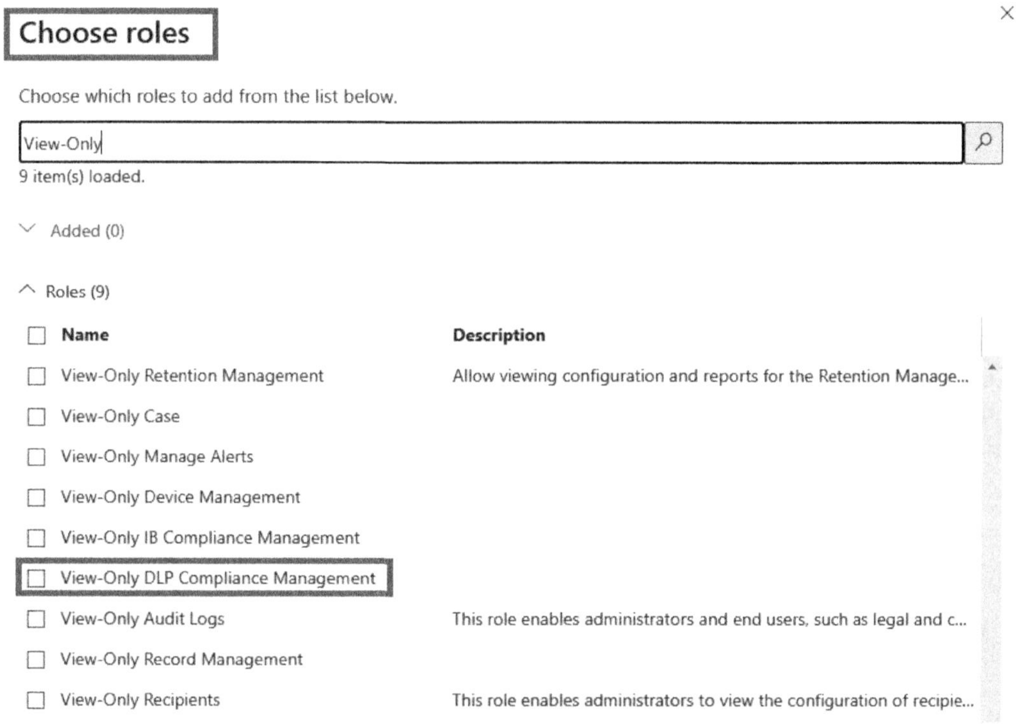

Figure 9.9 – Adding the View-Only DLP Compliance Management role

4.   You can then add the AD group that was created in the earlier step in the **Choose members** section.

You are also able to assign an existing role group in the compliance center under **Permissions**. Assign the **Security Reader** role to any users you want to have read-only access to the existing reports page.

You should now understand how to manage permissions for DLP reports. In the next section, we will discuss how to manage DLP violations in Microsoft Defender for Cloud Apps.

Managing DLP violations in Microsoft Defender for Cloud Apps

If you configure the location of the DLP policy as Microsoft Defender for Cloud Apps in the compliance center, then the matches will show in the standard DLP report.

If you configure a file policy in Microsoft Defender for Cloud Apps, the matched conditions and actions will be logged in Microsoft Defender for Cloud Apps rather than in the DLP report.

Let's use an example in which you have configured a file policy in Microsoft Defender for Cloud Apps to detect files that include tax ID numbers that are shared with users outside your organization from either OneDrive or SharePoint Online. The file policy is also configured to automatically move them into the trash and block external access.

To review any matches for this policy, you will need to open the Microsoft Defender for Cloud Apps portal, `https://portal.cloudappsecurity.com`, and complete these steps:

1. Underneath the **Control** setting, click on **Policies**:

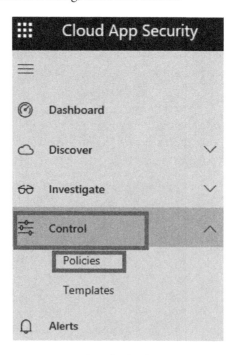

Figure 9.10 – Microsoft Defender for Cloud Apps policies

2. Look for the policy you want to evaluate:

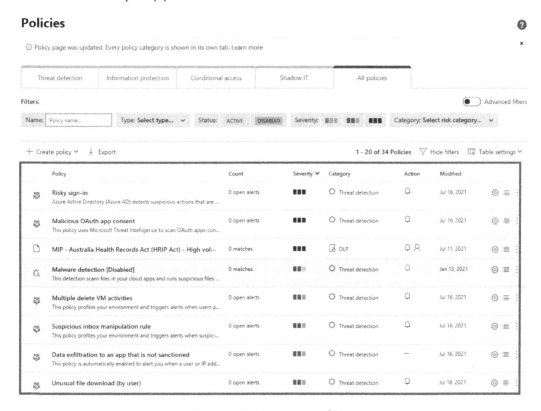

Policies

ⓘ Policy page was updated. Every policy category is shown in its own tab. Learn more

| Threat detection | Information protection | Conditional access | Shadow IT | All policies |

Filters: ⬤ Advanced filters

Name: [Policy name...]   Type: **Select type...** ⌄   Status: ACTIVE DISABLED   Severity: ▰▯▯ ▰▰▯ ▰▰▰   Category: **Select risk category...** ⌄

\+ Create policy ⌄   ↓ Export   1 - 20 of 34 Policies   ▽ Hide filters   ⊞ Table settings ⌄

	Policy	Count	Severity ⌄	Category	Action	Modified		
🖼	**Risky sign-in** Azure Active Directory (Azure AD) detects suspicious actions that are ...	0 open alerts	▰▰▰	◌ Threat detection	⏻	Jul 16, 2021	⚙ ≡	⋮
🖼	**Malicious OAuth app consent** This policy uses Microsoft Threat Intelligence to scan OAuth apps con...	0 open alerts	▰▰▰	◌ Threat detection	⏻	Jul 16, 2021	⚙ ≡	⋮
🗋	**MIP - Australia Health Records Act (HRIP Act) - High vol···**	0 matches	▰▰▰	⊡ DLP	⏻ 👤	Jul 11, 2021	⚙ ≡	⋮
⚠	**Malware detection [Disabled]** This detection scans files in your cloud apps and runs suspicious files ...	0 matches	▰▰▯	◌ Threat detection	⏻	Jan 13, 2021	⚙ ≡	⋮
🖼	**Multiple delete VM activities** This policy profiles your environment and triggers alerts when users p...	0 open alerts	▰▰▯	◌ Threat detection	⏻	Jul 16, 2021	⚙ ≡	⋮
🖼	**Suspicious inbox manipulation rule** This policy profiles your environment and triggers alerts when suspici...	0 open alerts	▰▰▯	◌ Threat detection	⏻	Jul 16, 2021	⚙ ≡	⋮
🖼	**Data exfiltration to an app that is not sanctioned** This policy is automatically enabled to alert you when a user or IP add...	0 open alerts	▰▰▯	◌ Threat detection	—	Jul 16, 2021	⚙ ≡	⋮
🖼	**Unusual file download (by user)**	0 open alerts	▰▰▯	◌ Threat detection	⏻	Jul 16, 2021	⚙ ≡	⋮

Figure 9.11 – Reviewing policies

3. Click on **Open matches** from the **Count** column on the policy you want to evaluate.

4. You should notice that there are three tabs at top of the page:

- **Matching now** enables you to view current matches for the file policy. You can then utilize the filters at the top to enhance the results.

- **Quarantined** enables you to view files that have been quarantined due to a file policy governance action.

- **History** enables you to view historical matches to the policy that were resolved due to a change to either the file or the policy:

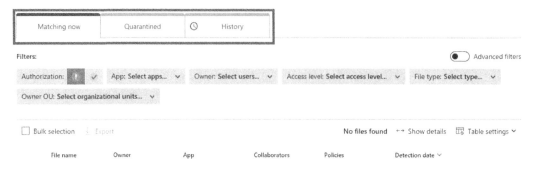

Figure 9.12 – Matching now, Quarantined, and History tabs

It is recommended to utilize this page to find patterns in the match and decide on whether or not to act. Imagine a scenario where you notice an increased number of matches, however, they all come from one user. You can inspect the matches and discover whether the user has a legitimate business reason for creating these matches.

You should now understand how to manage DLP violations in Microsoft Defender for Cloud Apps. This brings an end to this chapter; now, let's finish off by summarizing what we have covered in this chapter.

Summary

Within this chapter, we have covered a number of different topics, including managing and responding to DLP policy violations, reviewing and analyzing DLP reports, managing permissions for DLP reports, and managing DLP violations in Microsoft Defender for Cloud Apps. By the end of this chapter, you have completed multiple lab exercises; if you have not followed any of these, I strongly recommend that you do so before moving on to the next chapter.

The next chapter will focus on configuring retention policies and labels.

Section 4: Implementing Information Governance

This part of the book will focus on how to plan and implement information governance solutions in Microsoft 365.

This section comprises the following chapters:

- *Chapter 10, Configuring Retention Policies and Labels*
- *Chapter 11, Managing Data Retention in Microsoft 365*
- *Chapter 12, Implementing Records Management in Microsoft 365*

10
Configuring Retention Policies and Labels

Information governance aids in managing the end-to-end life cycle of all content across your organization's digital estate, regardless of whether it is kept in Microsoft 365, third-party cloud services, or hybrid deployments. This chapter will discuss the planning and implementation of retention labels and retention policies, which is broken down into these main topics:

- Creating and applying retention label policies
- Creating and applying retention labels
- Configuring and publishing auto-apply label policies

Technical requirements

As with previous chapters in this book, there are requirements when it comes to implementing retention labels and policies as well. To keep it streamlined with the other chapters and with the exam as well, the license we are going to use in the demonstrations and guides is **Microsoft 365 E5**.

Licensing is always a jungle to navigate, as retention labels are present in licensing subscriptions other than E5. Microsoft has a well-documented description of this at the following link: `https://docs.microsoft.com/en-us/office365/servicedescriptions/microsoft-365-service-descriptions/microsoft-365-tenantlevel-services-licensing-guidance/microsoft-365-security-compliance-licensing-guidance#which-licenses-provide-the-rights-for-a-user-to-benefit-from-the-service-8`.

Creating and applying retention label policies

Before we jump into creating and applying retention label policies, we must cover the principles of retentions policies, which are described in the following diagram:

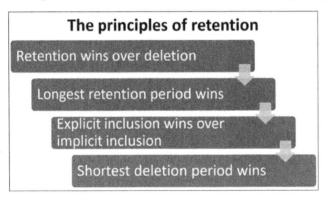

Figure 10.1 – The principles of retention in Microsoft 365

- **Retention always wins over deletion**: Suppose that one retention policy states that Exchange emails are to be deleted after 3 years, but another policy states that Exchange emails are to be retained for 5 years and then deleted. Under these circumstances, any content that reaches 3 years of age will be deleted and hidden from the user, but still retained in the `Recoverable Items` folder until the content reaches the 5-year retention period. After 5 years, the item would be permanently deleted. Content retained by one policy cannot be permanently deleted by another policy.

- **Longest retention period wins**: If any content is subject to multiple policies as regards the retention of said content, it will be retained until the end of the longest retention period.

- **Explicit inclusion wins over implicit inclusion**: If a label with retention settings is manually assigned by a user to an item (known as an explicit label), that label takes precedence over a policy assigned at the site or mailbox level. Suppose that an explicit label says to retain an item for 10 years, but the policy assigned to the item says to retain it for 5 years, then the label would take precedence. Auto-applied labels are considered implicit because they are applied automatically by **Microsoft 365**.

- **Shortest deletion period wins**: If content is subject to multiple policies that delete it with no retention, it will be deleted at the end of the shortest retention period.

With the principles of retention in Microsoft 365, we can start to create and apply retention label policies.

Configuring retention policies

The creation of a retention policy consists of the following steps:

1. Naming the policy

2. Locations to cover with the policy

3. Retention settings for the policy

4. Reviewing the settings of the policy

These are described in the following diagram:

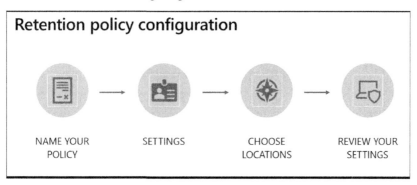

Figure 10.2 – Retention policy configuration

To create a retention policy, we will head back into the **Microsoft Purview Compliance Portal**, under **Information Governance and Retention** policies, as described by the following screenshot:

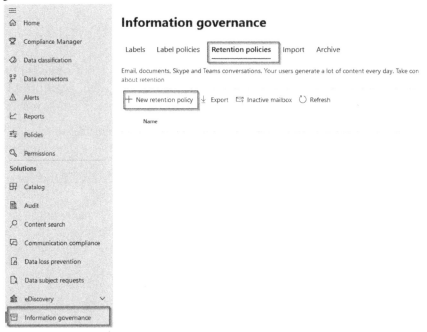

Figure 10.3 – The location of retention policies in the Microsoft Purview Compliance Portal

Now follow the steps shown next to create a retention policy:

1. **Naming the policy**: Enter a friendly name for the policy and an admin description for the policy:

Figure 10.4 – Naming the retention policy

2. On the next page, we will select the locations we will cover with this retention policy. To select a location, simply toggle the switch to **On** for the desired location. Here, we are also given the option to specify explicitly which users, sites, OneDrive accounts, and Microsoft 365 groups to include in the policy or exclude from it:

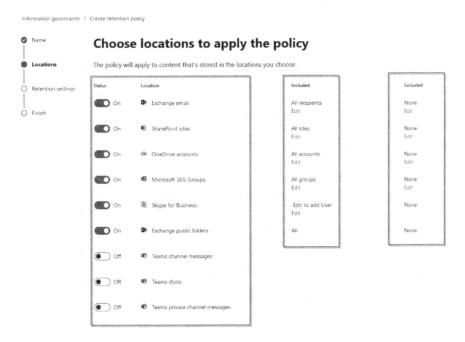

Figure 10.5 – Choosing the location to apply the retention policy

> **Note**
>
> To create a retention policy for Microsoft Teams content, you will need to create a policy for Teams channel messages and Teams chats explicitly turned on, with everything else turned off. If you want to create a policy for Teams private channel messages, you will need to create a policy with that location explicitly turned on, with everything else turned off.

3. On the next screen, we will configure **Retention settings** for the policy. We will have to configure the following items for the policy:

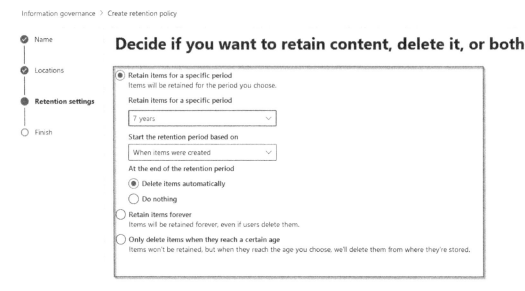

Figure 10.6 – The retention settings for a policy

4. The **Retain items for a specific period** field has a number of options – **5 years, 7 years (default), 10 years**, and **Custom,** as described in *Figure 10.7*:

Figure 10.7 – Showing the options for the Retain items for a specific period setting

5. The same goes for the **Start the retention period based on** field, which has the options **When items were created** and **When items were last modified**, as described in *Figure 10.8*:

Figure 10.8 – Showing the options for the Start the retention period based on setting

6. Two other options are available, which are **Retain items forever** and **Only delete items when they reach a certain age**, where the latter gives us basically the same options as with the **Retain items for a specific period** option mentioned in step 5. But instead of choosing the retention period, we will choose an expiry age on items, after which they will be permanently deleted:

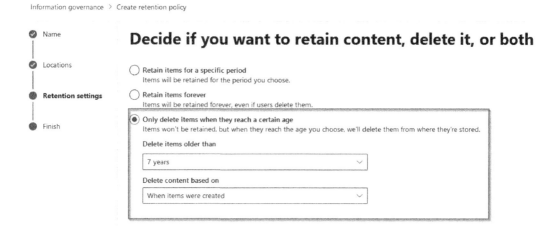

Figure 10.9 – Showing the options for the Only delete items when they reach a certain age setting

7. On the last page of the creation of a retention policy, we get to review our settings for the policy before creating said policy in our tenant. Please note the callout at the bottom, stating that items currently older than the time range specified in the policy will be deleted permanently in your tenant:

Figure 10.10 – Showing the Review and finish page

8. After creating the policy, we are taken back to the page in the Microsoft Purview Compliance Portal showing us our newly created retention policy listed:

Figure 10.11 – Showing the retention policies available in the tenant

That covers how to create and configure a retention policy. Up next, we will delve deeper into how to create and configure retention labels.

Creating and applying retention labels

Retention labels will appear in users' applications such as Outlook, SharePoint, and OneDrive when published. When a label gets applied to an item, either automatically or manually by the user, the content is retained based on the settings configured on the label.

There are some important things to note prior to creating retention labels, as listed next:

- *Retention label creation is the first step in a two-step process to making them available. You must also publish or auto-apply the label.*
- *Retention label names cannot be changed after they are created.*
- *Only one retention label can be assigned to content (such as an email or document) at a time.*
- *Auto-applied retention labels can be replaced by a manually assigned retention label.*
- *Retention labels do not take effect immediately after publishing or being auto-applied.*
- *Exchange public folders do not support labels.*
- *Retention label policies can trigger a disposition review at the end of a retention period. Retention policies cannot.*

The process of creating a retention label consists of three steps:

1. Naming the label
2. Configuring settings for the label
3. Reviewing the label's settings

This is described visually by means of *Figure 10.12*:

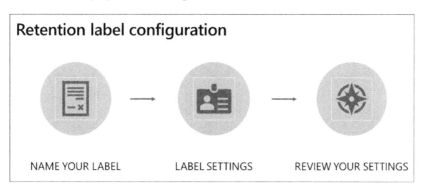

Figure 10.12 – Describing the process of creating a retention label

Follow the next steps to create a retention label:

1. To start the creation process, navigate to the Microsoft Purview Compliance Portal, head to **Information governance**, and select **Labels**, as presented in *Figure 10.13*:

Figure 10.13 – The location of retention labels in the Microsoft Purview Compliance Portal

2. Name the policy and then add an explanatory description for end users and a description for administrators:

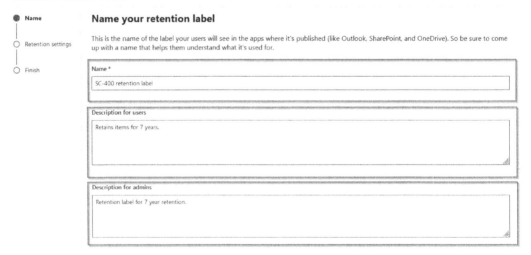

Figure 10.14 – The settings for a retention label name and descriptions

3. The options given here are like the ones on creating a retention policy, with some minor differences, as described in *Figure 10.15*. This is called **Trigger a disposition review**, which means that we have the option to review the item once the retention period is up and reviewers can then decide whether it can be deleted safely. More information about disposition review can be found at the following URL:
`https://docs.microsoft.com/en-us/microsoft-365/compliance/disposition?view=o365-worldwide#disposition-reviews:`

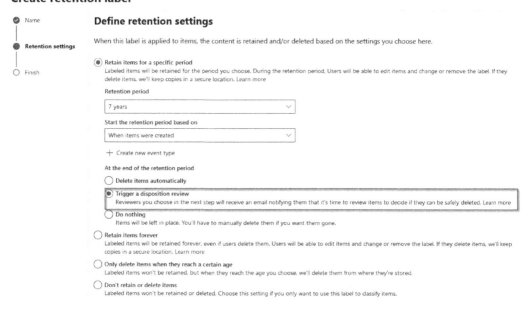

Figure 10.15 – Showing the Trigger a disposition review setting

4. We also have more options regarding the **Start the retention period based on** setting, as listed next and presented in *Figure 10.16*:

a. When it was created

b. When it was last modified

c. When it was labeled

d. An event:

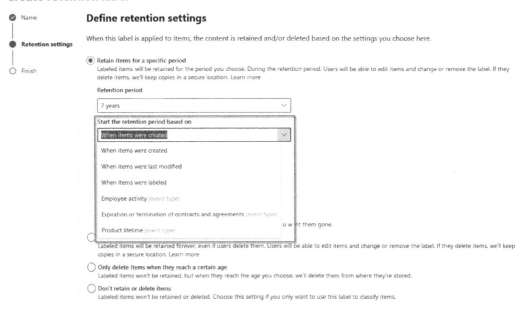

Figure 10.16 – Showing the Start the retention period based on setting for retention labels

5. If we choose one of the options a, b, or c under step 4, the content in email messages will be retained or deleted based on when the message was sent or received, and documents when they were created or last modified. Basing the label on an event (option d) means the content will be retained indefinitely until the event trigger is started. Event-driven retention will be covered in more depth in *Chapter 12, Implementing Microsoft Purview Records Management*.

6. Once we have selected our settings for the retention label, we are brought to the **Review and finish** screen, just as with retention policies:

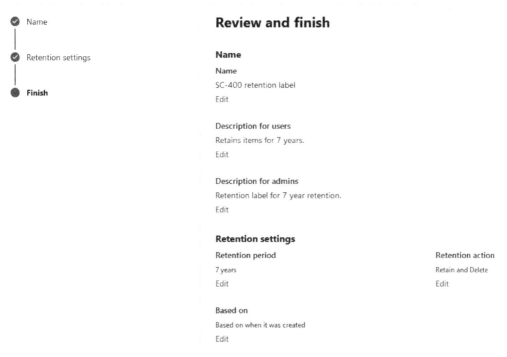

Figure 10.17 – Showing the review screen of the newly created retention label

7. The final step involves publishing the label. Here we are given three choices on what to do with the label we have just created, as described in *Figure 10.18* and in the following list:

a. **Publish this label to Microsoft 365 locations**

b. **Auto-apply this label to a specific type of content**

c. **Do Nothing**:

✅ Your retention label is created

Setting up the label is just the first step. Now it's time to make it available in your organization so it can be used to classify and retain content. You can do this by publishing or auto-applying it.

Next steps

◉ **Publish this label to Microsoft 365 locations**
You'll create a label policy to make this label available in locations like Exchange and OneDrive. When published, users can manually apply it to their content or set it as the default label for content containers (such as SharePoint document libraries or email folders).

○ **Auto-apply this label to a specific type of content**
You'll create an auto-labeling policy to apply the label to content matching certain conditions, such as content containing specific sensitive info.

○ **Do Nothing**
You can publish or auto-apply it to content later.

Figure 10.18 – Showing the publishing options for a retention label

8. Selecting the **Publish this label to Microsoft 365 locations** option takes us to another screen, allowing us to choose the users and groups for which the label is to be published as well as which locations in **Microsoft 365** to cover with the label:

Publish labels so users can apply them to their content.

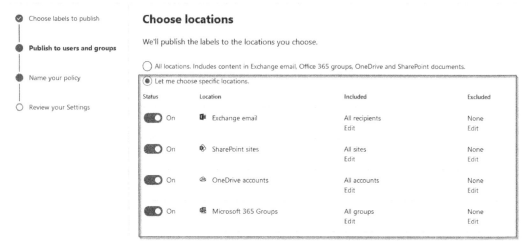

Figure 10.19 – Showing the Publish this label to Microsoft 365 locations options

9. On the next screen, we are asked to give the policy we are publishing the label to a name and a description:

Publish labels so users can apply them to their content.

Figure 10.20 – Showing the Name your policy screen when publishing a new label

10. Lastly in this process, we are taken to another **Review your Settings** screen, which shows us the settings we have configured for this new retention label policy:

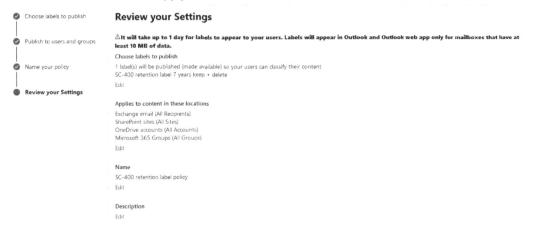

Figure 10.21 – Showing the review settings screen for a retention label policy

> **Note**
>
> As *Figure 10.21* states, it will take up to 1 day for labels to appear for your users. Labels will appear in Outlook and Outlook web apps only for mailboxes that have at least 10 MB of data.

11. Once completed, the retention label policy will appear in the **Microsoft Purview Compliance Portal** under **Label policies**:

Figure 10.22 – Showing the location of the retention label policy in the Microsoft Purview Compliance Portal

That completes this segment of the chapter, which has guided us through the process of creating retention labels, which settings are available, and how to configure them. Up next, we will look at configuring and publishing auto-apply label policies.

Configuring and publishing auto-apply label policies

The final type of retention policy we will be covering in this chapter is the auto-label policy. Much like the label policy covered in the last topic, this is created by issuing a label where we define our retention settings, but instead of publishing the label to our users, we let the policy look for sensitive data in our **Microsoft 365** tenant and auto-apply the label to said information.

Looking back at the creation of a retention label from *step 7*, we will see *Figure 10.23* in front of us:

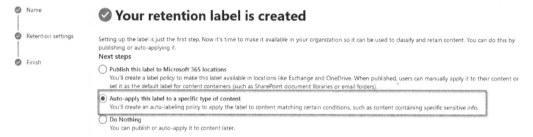

Create retention label

Figure 10.23 – Selecting the Auto-apply this label to a specific type of content option to create your auto-label policy

To get started, we need to follow the steps provided in the last walk-through from 1 to 7, where we will make a different choice to create our auto-label policy:

1. Select the **Auto-apply this label to a specific type of content** option, where we can select a sensitive information type created in *Chapter 3, Creating and Managing Sensitive Information Types.*

2. This will bring us to *Figure 10.24*, where we will fill in the basic information regarding our auto-labeling policy:

Auto-labeling > Create auto-labeling policy

○ **Name**

○ Info to label

○ Locations

○ Label

○ Finish

Name your auto-labeling policy

Name *

SC-400 auto-label policy

Description

SC-400 auto-label policy

Figure 10.24 – The basic information relating to the auto-labeling policy

3. On the next page, we can choose what we want our auto-labeling policy to apply to. We have covered these earlier in the book, where we have created or worked with sensitive information types, regular expressions, or trainable classifiers:

a. **Apply label to content that contains sensitive info**

b. **Apply label to content that contains specific words or phrases, or properties**

c. **Apply label to content that matches a trainable classifier**:

Auto-labeling > Create auto-labeling policy

✓ Name

● **Info to label**

○ Locations

○ Label

○ Finish

Choose the type of content you want to apply this label to

◉ Apply label to content that contains sensitive info

○ Apply label to content that contains specific words or phrases, or properties

○ Apply label to content that matches a trainable classifier

Figure 10.25 – Showing the options in terms of content to apply the auto-labeling policy to

4. To keep it somewhat streamlined to what we looked at in the chapters about *data loss prevention* (DLP) and endpoint DLP, we are going to choose the **Financial** category and the **U.K. Financial Data** sensitive information type:

Figure 10.26 – Showing the options for sensitive information types on the auto-labeling policy

5. The next page allows us to adjust the confidence and instance count of each sensitive information type in U.K. Financial Data. We are not going to alter these in this demonstration, but if you were to change this, it would be able to identify with granularity, just as the chapter on data loss prevention described.

6. When it comes to location, the same settings apply as with other retention labels, sensitive information types and trainable classifiers, and others. We simply choose which workload this auto-labeling policy will be applied to. If necessary, we could alter this policy to include specified individuals, sites, or accounts, or exclude specified individuals, sites, or accounts. The choices are as follows:

   a. **Exchange email**

   b. **SharePoint sites**

   c. **OneDrive accounts**

   d. **Microsoft 365 Groups**

7. The second to last page allows us to choose which label we are going to publish for this policy. Given that we only have the one in the demo environment, the choice is rather straightforward:

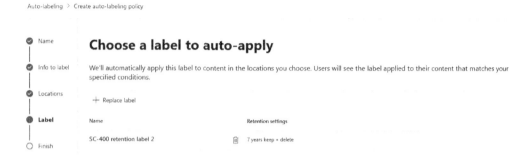

Figure 10.27 – Choosing the label for which we are going to issue an auto-labeling policy

8. On the last page, as with the other labels or policies we have created, we have an option to review our settings and finally submit the changes to our **Microsoft 365** tenant:

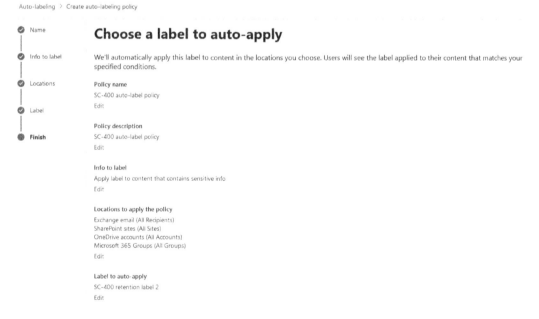

Figure 10.28 – Lastly, reviewing the settings for the auto-labeling policy prior to creation

9. And with that, we have successfully created a retention policy, a retention label policy, and an auto-labeling policy in our tenant, making sure that no sensitive information accidentally or maliciously gets deleted:

Information governance

Labels   Label policies   Retention policies   Import   Archive

When published, retention labels appear in your users' apps, such as Outlook, SharePoint, and OneDrive. Whe settings you chose. For example, you can create labels that retain content for a certain time or ones that simpl

\+ Create a label   📮 Publish labels   ⬆ Import   ⬇ Export   ◯ Refresh

Name

SC-400 retention label

SC-400 retention label 2

Information governance

Labels   **Label policies**   Retention policies   Import   Archive

Create retention label policies to either publish or auto-apply labels. When you publish labels to locations such apply labels, users will see the labels automatically applied to content that matches your conditions (such as co

📮 Publish labels   🔏 Auto-apply a label   ◯ Refresh

Information governance

Labels   Label policies   **Retention policies**   Import   Archive

Email, documents, Skype and Teams conversations. Your users generate a lot of content about retention

\+ New retention policy   ⬇ Export   ✉ Inactive mailbox   ◯ Refresh

Name

SC-400 Retention Policy

Figure 10.29 – Showing the progress of the labels and policies created

This section has been about auto-labeling policies, the last topic of this chapter.

Summary

This chapter has been all about retention labels and the different retention policies available in the **Microsoft 365 tenant**. We learned about creating and applying retention labels, configuring and publishing auto-apply label policies, and creating and applying retention label policies. In the following chapter, we will investigate the topic of managing data retention in Microsoft 365.

11
Managing Data Retention in Microsoft 365

The previous chapter looked at configuring retention policies and labels, including creating and applying retention labels, creating and applying retention label policies, and configuring and publishing auto-apply label policies. In this chapter, we will take a deeper look at managing data retention in Microsoft 365, including the following topics:

- Creating and applying policies in **Microsoft SharePoint** and **OneDrive**
- Creating and applying retention policies in **Microsoft Teams**
- Recovering content in **Microsoft Teams**, **SharePoint**, and **OneDrive**
- Implementing retention policies and tags in **Microsoft Exchange**
- Applying mailbox holds in **Microsoft Exchange**
- Implementing **Microsoft Exchange Online** archiving policies.

Technical requirements

In this chapter, we continue to explore configuring Information Protection within Microsoft 365. There will be an exercise that will require access to **Microsoft 365** with Global Administration rights. If you have followed the exercises from the previous chapter, you should now have the relevant trial licenses; however, if you have not yet created this for Microsoft 365, please follow the instructions from *Chapter 1, Preparing for Your Microsoft Exam and SC-400 Exam Objectives.*

Creating and applying retention policies in Microsoft SharePoint and OneDrive

Dedicated libraries for items and versions to hold called Preservation Hold libraries are utilized to apply retention in **SharePoint Online** and **OneDrive for Business**. This works the same for both **OneDrive for Business** and **SharePoint Online** as they are both implemented with personal site collection. Preservation Hold libraries are only observable to site administrators as they are stored on the top level of sites.

A validation is made on content if you try to make any changes or delete a document that has retention settings applied to it regardless of whether content has been amended since the retention settings were applied. When the first modification since the retention settings were applied is made, the data is duplicated to the Preservation Hold library. This then enables the individual to amend or delete the original data that is stored in the original document library.

Preservation Hold libraries are cleaned up by a timer job. All data in the Preservation Hold library is compared during the job to all the queries that are utilized by the retention settings for that data. Any content that is older than the retention period that has been configured is deleted from the Preservation Hold library; however, the initial location is not deleted and can still be accessed. It can take up to 7 days for the content to be deleted, which is due to the timer job running every 7 days.

You get this type of conduct on content that exists when the retention settings were originally applied, as well as for retention policies for new data that is added to the site collection when it is incorporated in the policy, and means that information will be retained once deleted. New data, on the other hand, is not copied to the Preservation Hold library when it is initially modified, but it is once it has been deleted. If you wish to keep all versions of a file separate from the retention settings, then you can utilize the *versioning* feature.

If a user attempts to delete a list, library, folder, or site that is part of a retention policy then they will get an error. They can get around this when trying to delete a folder if they move or delete the files that are stored in the folder that are part of the retention policy first. It is at this stage that the Preservation Hold library is created, rather than when the retention policy is created or when the label is applied.

So far in this section of the chapter, we have introduced the concept of retention policies in **Microsoft SharePoint** and **OneDrive**. We will now discuss Preservation Hold Library functionality and how this interacts with retention policies.

Preservation Hold Library functionality

In *Figure 11.1*, you can see how files are treated in SharePoint Online libraries if Preservation hold libraries are utilized:

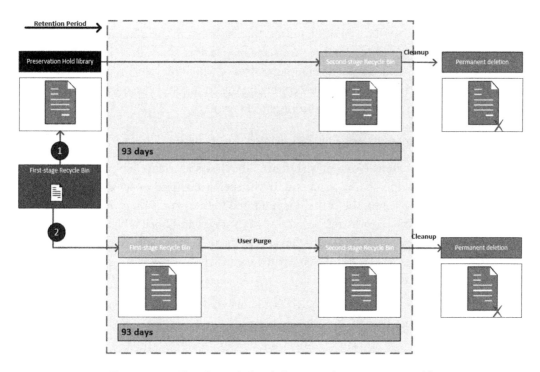

Figure 11.1 – SharePoint Online behavior with Preservation Hold

The preceding diagram shows the process flow with both *first-stage* and *second-stage* recycle bins through to permanent deletion as well as the retention periods, which allows you to see how long the process roughly takes.

There are two different process flows indicated by the ① and the ② in the diagram:

- ① When content is amended or deleted *during the retention period*:

  a. **Retain and delete**: The original data is copied in the state it was in when the retention policy was designated and is created in the **Preservation Hold library**. Data is identified by the *timer job* where, when its retention period has expired, it is transferred to the *second-stage recycle bin*, where it is permanently deleted.

  b. **Retain-only**: The original data is duplicated and created in the **Preservation Hold library**, where it is then held up to the end of the retention period. At this point, the duplicate content is then shifted to the *second-stage recycle bin*, where it is permanently deleted once the 93 days has passed.

  c. **Delete-only**: The content is shifted to the *first-stage recycle bin*. If the recycle bin is emptied, the content is then migrated to the *second-stage recycle bin*. It is important to note that the 93-day retention period that is shown in the diagram stretches across both the *first-stage* and *second-stage recycle bins*. Once the 93 days has passed, the content is permanently deleted regardless of which recycle bin it resides in. In the scenario where the data is edited during the configured period, it will adhere to the same deletion path after the configured period.

- ② When content is not edited or deleted *during the retention period*:

  a. **Retain and delete**: Content is shifted to the first-stage recycle bin once the retention period has come to an end. In the scenario where a user deletes data or purges the recycle bin, the content is migrated to the *second-stage recycle bin*. The 93-day retention period stretches across both stages and once it has passed, the data is permanently deleted from whichever recycle bin it currently lives in. Please note that the recycle bin is not indexed, which means you cannot run a search for data that resides in either stage.

  b. **Retain-only**: The document stays in the original location before and after the retention period. Essentially, nothing happens.

c. **Delete-only**: When the retention policy's configured period has passed, the content is shifted to the *first-stage recycle bin*. If a user deletes content or purges the recycle bin, that content is shifted to the *second-stage recycle bin*. At the end of the 93-day retention period (which stretches across both stages), the content is deleted permanently from wherever it currently resides. Please note that the recycle bin is not indexed, which means you cannot run a search for data that resides in either stage.

You should understand **Preservation Hold libraries** and how these interact with retention policies. We will now take a look at how retention with document versioning works.

Retention with document versioning – how it works

One of the main features of SharePoint and OneDrive lists and libraries is versioning. Five hundred major versions are retained by default with versioning; however, this can be expanded. In the scenario where content has versioning enabled and retention settings are set to keep content, the versions that are moved to the **Preservation Hold library** are stored as individual elements.

If you have a case where the retention period is built on when the data is created, every version will have the same expiry date as the original data, therefore all will have the same expiry date.

If you have a scenario in which the retention period is built on when the data was last edited, all versions have their own expiry date, which is dependent on when the original data was edited to create that specific version. This means that the original data and its versions expire at different times.

Configuring a retention policy for SharePoint Online and OneDrive for Business

The following lab exercise will walk through the steps to create and configure a retention policy for **SharePoint Online** and **OneDrive for Business**:

1. Log in to the Microsoft 365 Compliance portal at `https://compliance.microsoft.com` with an Administrator account that has Global Administrator privileges.

2.   Navigate to **Policies** > **Retention policies** and click on **New retention policy**:

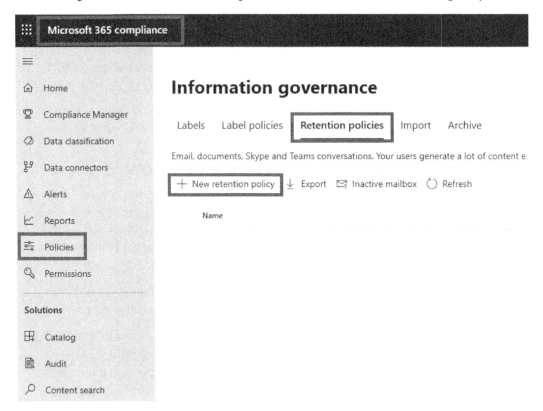

Figure 11.2 – Navigate to New retention policy

3.   On the **Name** page, give the policy a sensible name and description and then click on **Next**.

4.   On the **Locations** page, select **SharePoint sites** and **OneDrive accounts**. Depending on your use case, you may want to select only one of these or both. Click **Next**:

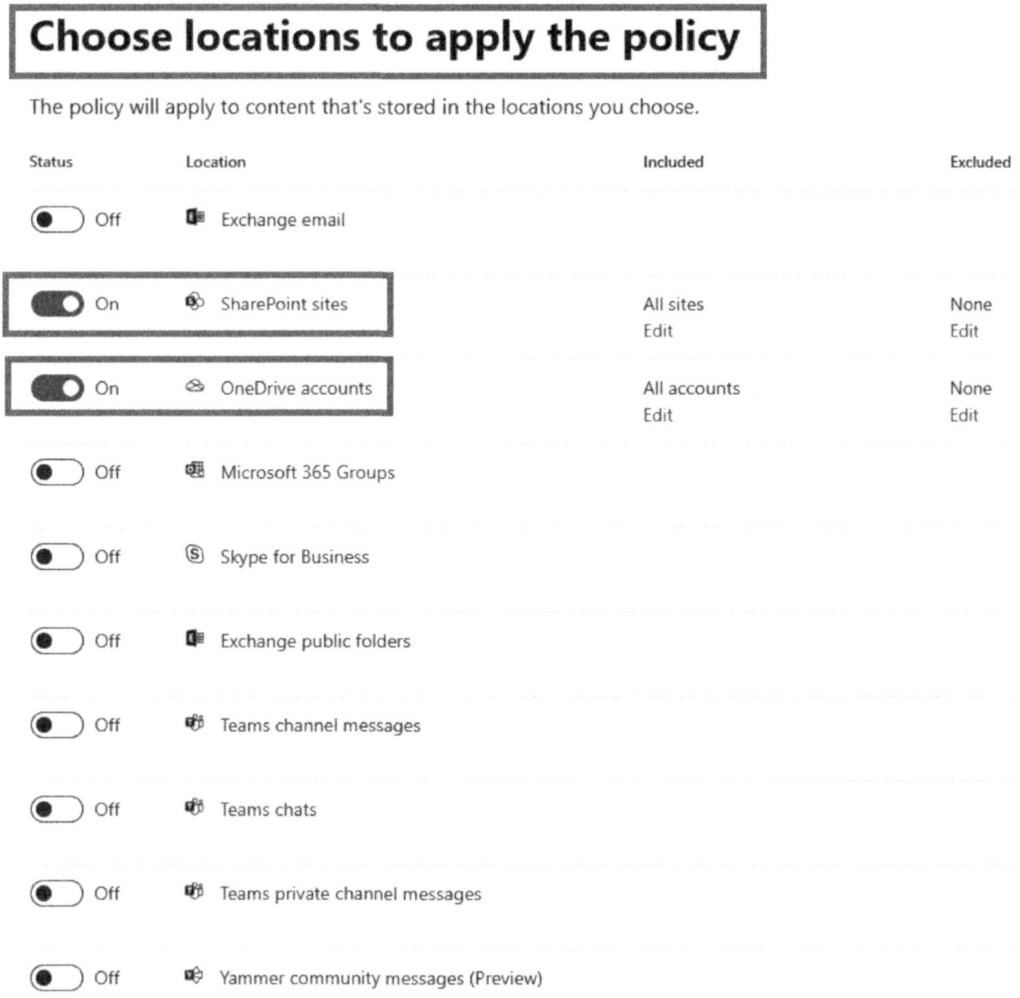

Choose locations to apply the policy

The policy will apply to content that's stored in the locations you choose.

Status	Location	Included	Excluded
Off	Exchange email		
On	SharePoint sites	All sites Edit	None Edit
On	OneDrive accounts	All accounts Edit	None Edit
Off	Microsoft 365 Groups		
Off	Skype for Business		
Off	Exchange public folders		
Off	Teams channel messages		
Off	Teams chats		
Off	Teams private channel messages		
Off	Yammer community messages (Preview)		

Figure 11.3 – Locations to apply the policy

5. On the **Retention settings** page, you can configure the following:

    a. Retain items for a specific period, which can be 5, 7, or 10 years. You can then customize this setting if you want to be more granular and select a certain number of months and days as well.

    b. Start the retention based on either when the item was created, or when the item was last modified.

Click on **Next** once you are finished configuring your retention settings:

Figure 11.4 – Retention settings

6.   Review the policy and click **Submit**.

We have now covered all aspects of creating and applying retention policies in **SharePoint Online** and **OneDrive for Business**. In the following section, we will move on to creating and applying retention policies in **Microsoft Teams**.

Creating and applying retention policies in Microsoft Teams

Microsoft Teams stores data throughout the various Microsoft 365 services and Azure ecosystem. This means that the behavior of the retention policies depends on the type of data you wish to keep or delete.

Data can be kept or deleted by utilizing retention policies for Microsoft Teams. Single chat and channel messages, including embedded images, links, and tables as well as links to other messages and files can all be included as part of the policy. With individual chat messages, it includes all names of the users within the chat, and with channels it includes the team's name and the title of the message. Private channel Teams messages are not included, nor are emoticons.

Any document or emails that are utilized with Microsoft Teams are not included in retention policies. This content needs a different retention policy that has Exchange locations configured to protect group mailboxes.

Chats and channels are kept when a retention policy has Teams as a location, which is consumed from the Azure Cosmos DB storage location into a concealed folder in the group mailbox.

Retention functionality with Teams

A timer job from the Exchange service continually assesses chat and channels after a retention policy is configured. The timer job can take up to 7 days to initially run. The content is shifted to the `SubstrateHolds` folder once the content's retention period has expired. This concealed folder exists in every user or group mailbox and is utilized as a *soft-delete* location before permanent deletion.

The process flow taken by the retention policies for chat and channel messages depends on whether the policy is set to *retain and then delete*, *retain only*, or *delete only*. The following diagram shows the process flow for Teams chat and channel messages:

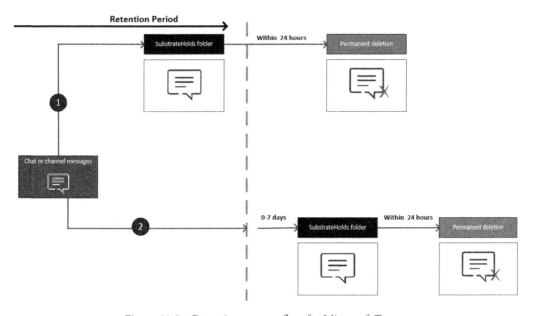

Figure 11.5 – Retention process flow for Microsoft Teams

There are two different process flows indicated by the ① and the ② in the diagram:

- ① In the case where a channel or chat message is modified or purged by the user during the retention period we can do the following:

  a. **Retain and delete**: In this scenario, the initial message is copied (if modified) or shifted (if purged) to the `SubstrateHolds` location within 21 days. Once the retention period expires, the message is then purged within 2 hours.

  b. **Retain-only**: A duplicate of the initial message is made in the `SubstrateHolds` folder within 21 days. Once the retention period expires, the message is purged within 24 hours.

  c. **Delete-only**: Once the retention period has finished, the message is shifted to the `SubstratHolds` folder. This takes 7 days from the expiry date, after which the message is then purged.

- ② In the case where a channel or chat message is not deleted during the retention period we can do the following:

  a. **Retain and delete**: After the retention period has expired, the deleted message is moved to the **SubstrateHolds** folder. This can take up to 7 days after the expiry date and then, after 24 hours, it is deleted.

  b. **Retain-only**: The message will stay where it was originally located, and no actions take place before or after the retention period has expired.

  c. **Delete-only**: The message is moved to the **SubstrateHolds** folder within 21 days and, after another 24 hours, it is deleted.

  Due to **Microsoft Teams** storage being complicated, we need to consider multiple points when configuring Microsoft Teams retention policies:

- A Teams channel message's location is required for retention of channel meeting messages, which are stored using the same method.

- A Teams chat location is required for retention of impromptu meeting messages, which are stored in the same way as group chat messages.

- A shadow mailbox exists in the tenant for guest users in a meeting that your organization hosts. This mailbox can be subject to a retention policy and all messages from the meeting are stored in the shadow mailbox and the user's mailbox.

- Your retention policies cannot delete messages for an external user who is joining by using an account from a different Microsoft 365 organization as those messages are stored in that specific user's mailbox in the other tenant.

You will also need to be aware of what happens to content for users when they leave the org:

- **Documents and files**: With Microsoft Teams, these have the same conduct as SharePoint Online and OneDrive for Business due to them being stored in the same location.

- **Chat messages**: These are stored in an inactive mailbox for users who leave the organization whose account is deleted and when the chat messages are subject to retention. The same retention policies that were placed on the user before they were deleted are still in place and the data can be viewed by utilizing an eDiscovery search.

- **Channel messages**: An Azure database and the mailbox of the team is used for the storage of channel messages posted by a user. This content stays unaffected when that user leaves the organization.

In this section, we have looked at retention policies in **Microsoft Teams**. You can use the same method for creating a retention policy as shown in the *Configuring a retention policy for SharePoint Online and OneDrive for Business* section of this chapter, with the only difference being that you select the relevant option in the **Locations** window. In the next section, we will take a closer look at recovering data in **Microsoft 365**, including **Teams**, **SharePoint**, and **OneDrive**.

Recovering content in SharePoint and OneDrive

Documents and files that are retained allow users to restore them from a specific time period as and when they are needed. In this section, we will complete small lab exercises and take a look at recovery options for OneDrive for Business, SharePoint Online, and Microsoft Teams.

OneDrive for Business

You can restore a file in OneDrive as a standard user by completing the following steps:

1. Go to **OneDrive** for Business.

2. Choose **Recycle bin** on the left-hand side:

Figure 11.6 – OneDrive for Business recycle bin

3. Click on the checkbox that is to the left of the item you want to restore and click on **Restore** from the top menu pane.

4. You can now access the item in its original location as it has been successfully restored.

SharePoint Online

The steps to restore from **SharePoint Online** are very similar to the steps used for **OneDrive for Business**; however, the following lab exercise explains how to restore an item from a SharePoint Online document library:

1. Browse to SharePoint Online for your Microsoft 365 account.

2. Choose the site collection that has the files you wish to restore.

3. Click on **Recycle bin** on the left-hand side menu:

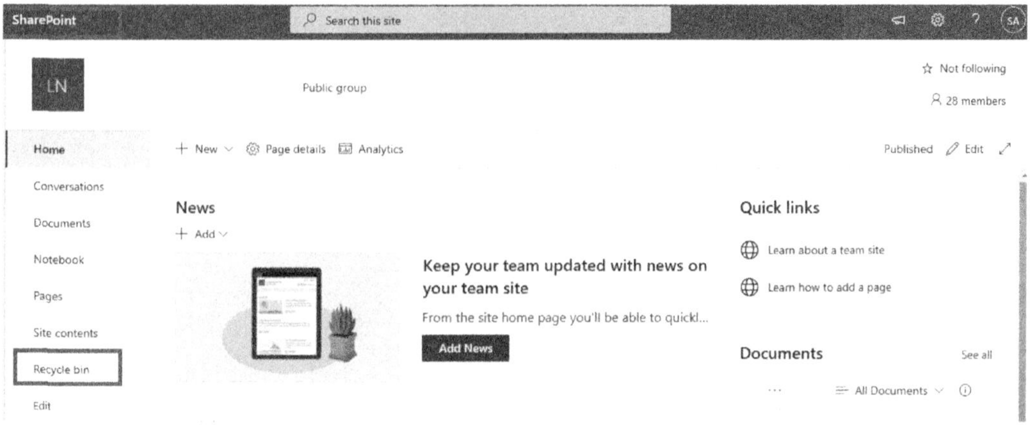

Figure 11.7 – SharePoint Online recycle bin

4. Click on the checkbox that is to the left of the item you want to restore and click on **Restore** from the top menu pane.

5. The file will now be accessible from its original location.

Previous versions

As well as restoring files that have been deleted, you also have the option of restoring previous versions of existing files from both **SharePoint Online** and **OneDrive for Business** from either the portal or from the online apps.

Restoring from SharePoint Online

In the following lab exercise, we will walk through the steps to restore a previous version of a file from the **SharePoint Online** portal:

1. Browse to the **SharePoint Online** portal in your tenant.

2. Choose the site collection that contains the file you wish to restore a previous version of.

3. Browse to the location of the file in the document library.

4. Click on the three dots (…) to the right of the file and select **Version history**:

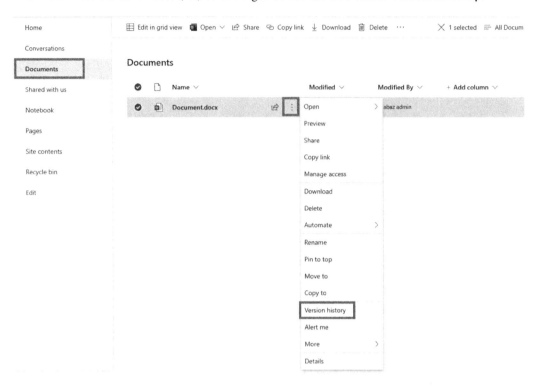

Figure 11.8 – SharePoint Online Version history

5. Put your mouse over the **Modified** date of the version you wish to recover and click on the down arrow:

Figure 11.9 – Version options

6. Click on **Restore** to migrate the file back to the previous version.

7. Confirm the replacement of the document by selecting **OK**.

The file has now successfully been restored and the last version has been overwritten.

Restoring from OneDrive for Business

A standard user can reinstate their full **OneDrive for Business** structure to a previous date and revert all changes. The following lab exercise will walk through how to complete this task in the Microsoft 365 portal:

1. Browse to your **OneDrive for Business** site.

2. Click on the cogwheel in the top-right corner and click on **Restore your OneDrive**:

Figure 11.10 – Restore entire OneDrive

3. Click on the date to which **OneDrive** should be restored.

4. Click on **Restore** to set all changes.

In this section, we have discussed recovering content in **SharePoint Online** and **OneDrive for Business**, as well as restoring to previous versions of files and entire folder structures. In the next section of the chapter, we will look at implementing retention policies and tags in **Microsoft Exchange**.

Implementing retention policies and tags in Microsoft Exchange

Messaging records management (**MRM**) includes retention tags and retention policies in Exchange Server and Exchange Online. These have traditionally been used to manage the life cycle of emails stored in mailboxes.

The following features are part of MRM:

- **Retention policies**: These are utilized to apply sets of retention tags to standard user mailboxes.

- **Retention policy tags** (**RPTs**): These are utilized on default folders, for example, `Deleted Items`, which have a standard setting of **30 days delete**.

- **Default policy tags** (**DPTs**): These manage the retention of all untagged items in a mailbox, for example, the **Default 2-year move to archive setting**.

- **Personal tags**: These manage custom folders and separate items that are assigned by standard users.

All mailboxes are assigned an MRM retention policy, which is named **Default MRM Policy** as standard.

How to create a new retention tag

Administrators can use the **Exchange admin center** or **Exchange Online PowerShell** to create tags, amend existing policies, and assign them to mailboxes.

The following lab exercise will go through the steps to create a new retention tag in the **Exchange Admin Center** (**EAC**):

1. Browse to the **Exchange Admin Center** at `https://outlook.office365.com/ecp` and sign in with an account that has **Exchange Administrator** permissions.

2. Click on **compliance management** and then **retention tags** from the top windowpane:

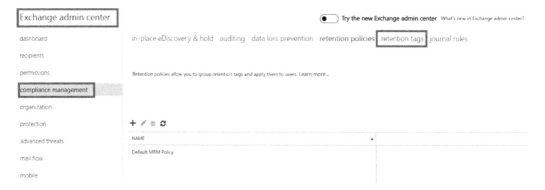

Figure 11.11 – Exchange Admin Center retention tags

3. Click on the + button and then choose one of the following three options:

- **Applied automatically to entire mailbox (default)**

- **Applied automatically to default folder**

- **Applied by users to items and folders (personal)**

In our example, we will click on **Applied automatically to entire mailbox (default)**:

1. Type in a **Name** for the new tag and select the relevant **Retention action** and **Retention period**:

Figure 11.12 – New retention tag

2. Click on **Save** when all the relevant information has been inserted into the retention tag.

3. Click **OK** in the **Information** window.

Enter the following **cmdlet** in an elevated **Exchange Online PowerShell** window to perform the same actions:

```
New-RetentionPolicyTag <tag name> -Type Personal -Comment <tag
comment> -RetentionEnabled $true -AgeLimitForRetention 2556
-RetentionAction PermanentlyDelete
```

`<tag name>` should be the name you want to give the retention tag and `<tag comment>` should be any relevant comment you wish to have on the retention tag. As you can see in the cmdlet, this will create a new policy tag that users can utilize for tagging emails that are removed after 2,556 days (7 years) from the mailbox.

Modifying the default retention policy

Administrators can use both the **Exchange Admin Center** and **Exchange Online PowerShell module** to amend existing retention policies.

The following lab exercise we will modify the **Default MRM** policy from within the **Exchange Admin Center**:

1. Browse to the **Exchange Admin Center** at `https://outlook.office365.com/ecp` and sign in with an account that has **Exchange Administrator** permissions.

2. Click on **Compliance management** and then **Retention policies** from the top windowpane.

3. Choose **Default MRM Policy** and then click on the edit button (pencil icon).

4. Utilize the + and - (plus and minus) buttons to add or delete retention tags to the policy. Click on **Save** when finished:

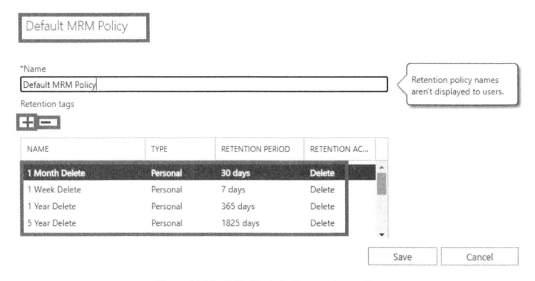

Figure 11.13 - Edit the default retention policy

All users who have the retention policy assigned automatically get these updates. As mentioned earlier in this section, you also have the option of changing the default retention policy using the **Exchange Online PowerShell module**. This can be achieved by utilizing the following `cmdlets`:

1. To show the existing default retention policy, use the following `cmdlet`:

```
Get-RetentionPolicy -Identity "Default MRM Policy"
```

2. To get an overview of all the retention tags that are linked to the default policy, use the following `cmdlet`:

```
(Get-RetentionPolicy -Identity "Default MRM Policy").
RetentionPolicyTagLinks
```

3. If you want to assign specific retention tags to the policy, utilize the following `cmdlet`:

```
Set-RetentionPolicy -Identity "Default MRM Policy"
-RetentionPolicyTagLinks "1 Year Delete","5 Year
Delete","Recoverable Items 14 days move to archive"
```

In this section, we have discussed implementing retention policies and tags in Microsoft Exchange. There were multiple exercises in this section, and it is strongly recommended that you follow these and complete them.

In the next section, we will take a look at applying mailbox holds in **Microsoft Exchange**.

Applying mailbox holds in Microsoft Exchange

There are multiple ways in which organizations can prevent data in mailboxes from being deleted in **Microsoft 365**. **Exchange Online** provides a feature called **holds** that enables this functionality, as well as retention policies and labels that we have already discussed in the *Implementing retention policies and tags in Microsoft Exchange* section of this chapter.

Exchange Online has two different type of mailbox holds:

- **Litigation hold**: This prevents any content that is stored in the mailbox from being deleted and is set on a mailbox level.

- **eDiscovery hold**: This prevents mailbox data that matches a specific search criterion from being purged or modified and it is created in an eDiscovery case.

Applying a litigation hold

In this section, we will run through an exercise to apply a litigation hold on a mailbox from the **Exchange Admin Center** and **Exchange Online PowerShell module**:

1. Browse to the **Exchange Admin Center** at `https://outlook.office365.com/ecp` and sign in with an account that has *Exchange Administrator* permissions.

2. Click on **recipients** > **mailboxes** in the left-hand pane:

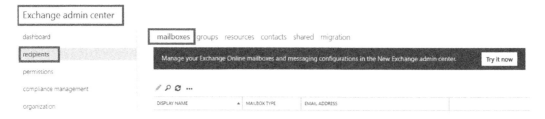

Figure 11.14 – Recipients > mailboxes

3. Choose the mailbox you wish to set litigation on and then click on **Edit** (the pencil icon).

4. On the **Properties** page of the mailbox, click on **mailbox features**.

5. Browse to **Litigation hold: Disabled** and click on **Enable** to set a litigation hold on this mailbox:

Figure 11.15 – Enabling a litigation hold

To complete the same task via the **Exchange Online PowerShell module**, use the following `cmdlet`:

```
Set-Mailbox <username> -LitigationHoldEnabled $true
```

To amend the number of days to put mailbox data on hold for, utilize the following cmdlet:

```
Set-Mailbox <username> -LitigationHoldEnabled $true
 -LitigationHoldDuration <number of days>
```

Please note, `<username>` should be the user's **Microsoft 365** FQDN and `<number of days>` is the numerical value of days you want to set for the litigation hold duration.

In the next section, we will look at how to implement archiving policies for **Microsoft Exchange Online** mailboxes.

Implementing Microsoft Exchange Online archiving policies

Administrators can utilize the **Exchange Admin Center** and **Exchange Online PowerShell module** to enable an archive mailbox for users in addition to their existing user mailbox. The following exercise will enable an archive mailbox for a standard user utilizing both admin locations:

1. Browse to the **Exchange Admin Center** and sign in with an account that has **Exchange administrator** permissions.

2. Choose **recipients** and click on the user mailbox you want to enable.

3. On the right-hand side of the window, under **In-Place Archive**, click on **Enable**:

Figure 11.16 – Enable archive mailbox

The same task can be completed by using the following cmdlet in the **Exchange Online PowerShell module**:

```
Enable-Mailbox -Identity <username> -Archive
```

In this example, <username> is the FQDN of the user's **Microsoft 365** account.

Once archiving is enabled on a mailbox, you can then create policies for archiving and deletion that automatically move a user's archive mailbox and purge content from it by creating the custom retention tags and policies that have been discussed earlier in this chapter in the *Implementing retention policies and tags in Microsoft Exchange* section.

Summary

In this chapter, we covered managing data retention in Microsoft 365, including creating and applying policies in Microsoft SharePoint and OneDrive, creating and applying retention policies in Microsoft Teams, recovering content in Microsoft Teams, SharePoint, and OneDrive, implementing retention policies and tags in Microsoft Exchange, applying mailbox holds in Microsoft Exchange, and implementing Microsoft Exchange Online archiving policies. There were multiple lab exercises in this chapter, which should all be completed to ensure you have a full understanding of the topic. In the next chapter, we will discuss implementing Microsoft Purview Records Management.

12
Implementing Microsoft Purview Records Management

In this last chapter of this book, preparing you for the *SC-400 (Information Protection Administrator Associate)* exam, we are going to cover the topic of Microsoft Purview Records Management. We will discuss how to use intelligent classification to automate and simplify the retention schedule for regulatory, legal, and business-critical records in the organization. We are going to cover these topics:

- Configuring labels for records management
- Managing and migrating retention requirements with a file plan
- Configuring automatic retention using file plan descriptors
- Implementing in-place records management in Microsoft SharePoint
- Configuring event-based retention
- Managing the disposition of records

Technical requirements

As always, there are technical requirements for using records management. It is also an E5 feature, available in the following license plans:

- **Microsoft 365 E5/A5/G5**
- **Microsoft 365 E5/A5/G5 Compliance add-on**
- **Microsoft 365 Information Protection and Governance E5/A5/G5 add-on**
- **Office 365 E5/A5/G5**

The **Office 365** plans listed previously allow the usage of records management by declaring items as records or regulatory records, automatically applying retention or record labels, and executing disposition review processes. To use trainable classifiers for automatically applying a retention label, you need to have one of the **Microsoft 365 E5/A5/G5** plans listed previously.

For more information regarding records management licensing requirements, please refer to official documentation such as the following:

```
https://docs.microsoft.com/en-us/microsoft-365/
compliance/get-started-with-records-management?view=o365-
worldwide#subscription-and-licensing-requirements-for-records-
management
```

The licensing is, of course, one part of the requirement, the other being the permissions required for configuring and managing the records management features:

- **Global Administrator**
- **Record Management admin role**

These permissions are required only to create, configure, and apply retention labels that declare records. The person configuring these labels does not require access to the content.

For a more role-based access control of the records management solution, there is a read-only role present to provide viewing rights:

- **View-Only Record Management admin role**

To display the option to mark content as a regulatory record, we need to connect to the **Office 365 Security & Compliance Center PowerShell** and run the following cmdlet:

```
Set-RegulatoryComplianceUI -Enabled $true
```

With the technical requirements covered, we are going to dive into the first topic, which is configuring labels for records management.

Configuring labels for records management

The process of creating and configuring labels for records management is not unlike the topic covered in *Chapter 10, Configuring Retention Policies and Labels.* The process consists of the steps outlined here:

1. Naming your label
2. Configuring label setting
3. Adding file plan descriptors
4. Reviewing settings and creating the label

This process can be visualized with *Figure 12.1*:

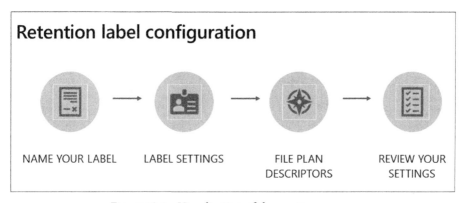

Figure 12.1 – Visualization of the creation process

Heading to the compliance center (`https://compliance.microsoft.com`), we can begin creating and configuring our records management. The features are present on the left-hand side under **Solutions** and **Records management**, as shown in *Figure 12.2*:

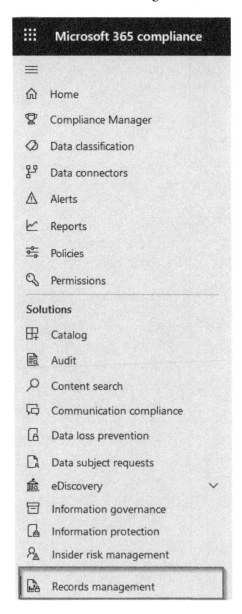

Figure 12.2 – Showing the location of Records management in the Microsoft Purview Compliance Portal

Once we have navigated to the **Records management** segment in the compliance center, let's proceed with creating a label:

1. Select the **File plan (1)** option in the **Records management** pane, as highlighted in *Figure 12.3*:

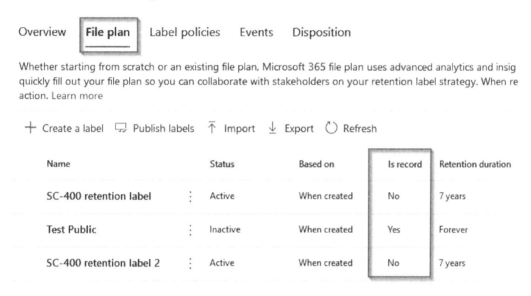

Records management

Overview   **File plan**   Label policies   Events   Disposition

Whether starting from scratch or an existing file plan, Microsoft 365 file plan uses advanced analytics and insig quickly fill out your file plan so you can collaborate with stakeholders on your retention label strategy. When re action. Learn more

+ Create a label   Publish labels   ↑ Import   ↓ Export   ○ Refresh

Name		Status	Based on	Is record	Retention duration
SC-400 retention label	⋮	Active	When created	No	7 years
Test Public	⋮	Inactive	When created	Yes	Forever
SC-400 retention label 2	⋮	Active	When created	No	7 years

Figure 12.3 – Selecting File plan to start configuring Records management

2. Here, we will see the retention labels configured in *Chapter 10, Configuring Retention Policies and Labels*, but as shown in *Figure 12.3*, these labels do not indicate that an item is a record (**2**).

3. Selecting **Create a label** allows us to start the process visualized in *Figure 12.1*, which brings us to the page shown in *Figure 12.4*:

Create retention label

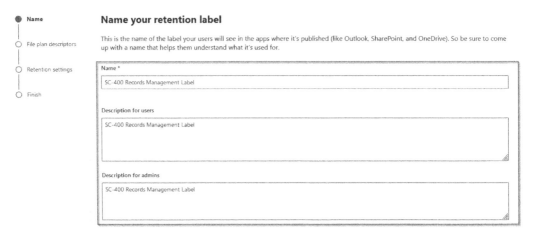

Figure 12.4 – Creating a new retention label, intended for usage in Records management

4. After providing a name for the label, a description for the end users, and a description for administrators, we can proceed to the next step of the process.

5. The next page gives us the opportunity to define the file plan descriptors for this label, where Microsoft provides several predefined options to choose from as well as the possibility to create our own for each option available. The options available for the file plan descriptors are as follows:

   A. **Business function/department**

   B. **Category (Sub category)**

   C. **Authority type**

   D. **Provision/citation**

6. In this case, we are going to create a file plan descriptor, covering the following areas as described in *Figure 12.5*:

   A. **Business function/department**: Human resources

   B. **Category**: Payroll

   C. **Authority type**: Regulatory

   D. **Provision/citation**: Sarbanes-Oxley Act of 2002

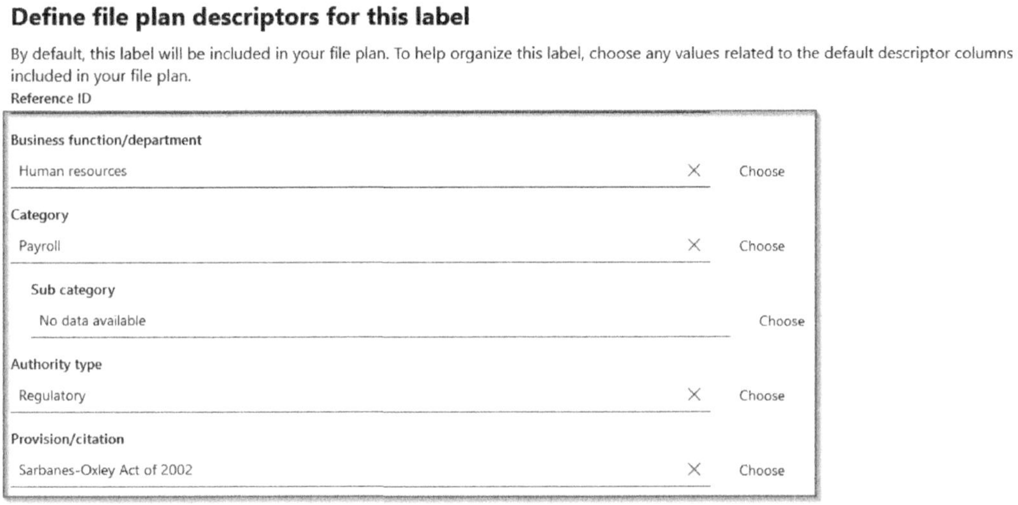

Define file plan descriptors for this label

By default, this label will be included in your file plan. To help organize this label, choose any values related to the default descriptor columns included in your file plan.

Reference ID

Business function/department

Human resources   ✕   Choose

Category

Payroll   ✕   Choose

   Sub category

   No data available   Choose

Authority type

Regulatory   ✕   Choose

Provision/citation

Sarbanes-Oxley Act of 2002   ✕   Choose

Figure 12.5 – Showing the options of a file plan descriptor for a label

7. The next page brings us to a familiar step, where we define the retention settings for this label just like in *Chapter 10, Configuring Retention Policies and Labels*:

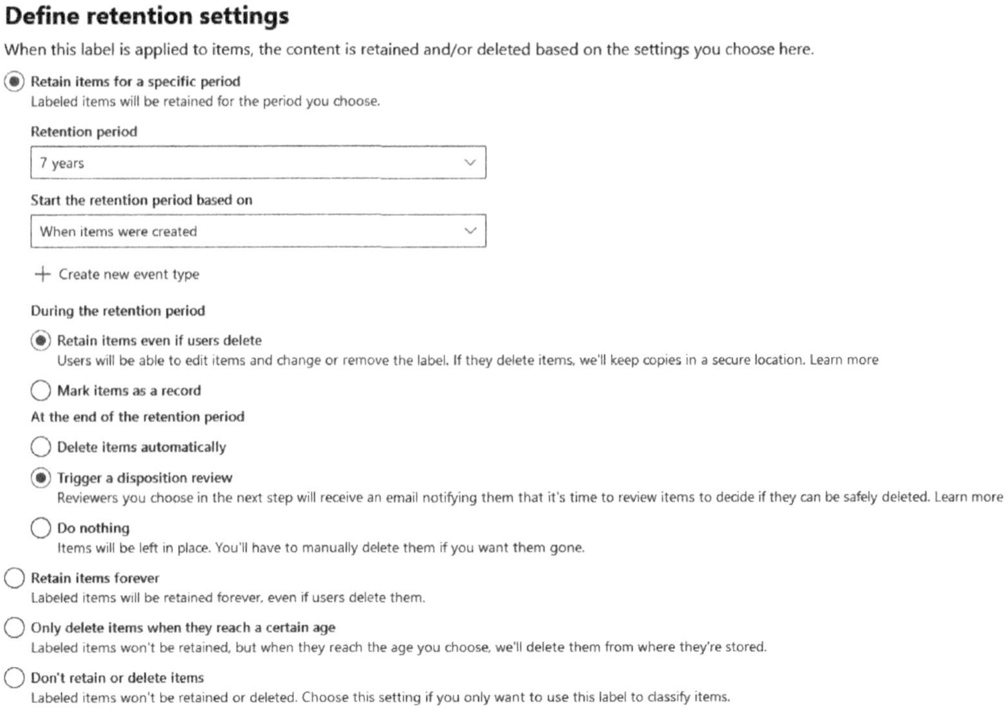

Define retention settings

When this label is applied to items, the content is retained and/or deleted based on the settings you choose here.

◉ **Retain items for a specific period**
Labeled items will be retained for the period you choose.

   Retention period

   7 years   ⌄

   Start the retention period based on

   When items were created   ⌄

   + Create new event type

   During the retention period

   ◉ **Retain items even if users delete**
   Users will be able to edit items and change or remove the label. If they delete items, we'll keep copies in a secure location. Learn more

   ○ **Mark items as a record**
   At the end of the retention period

   ○ **Delete items automatically**

   ◉ **Trigger a disposition review**
   Reviewers you choose in the next step will receive an email notifying them that it's time to review items to decide if they can be safely deleted. Learn more

   ○ **Do nothing**
   Items will be left in place. You'll have to manually delete them if you want them gone.

○ **Retain items forever**
Labeled items will be retained forever, even if users delete them.

○ **Only delete items when they reach a certain age**
Labeled items won't be retained, but when they reach the age you choose, we'll delete them from where they're stored.

○ **Don't retain or delete items**
Labeled items won't be retained or deleted. Choose this setting if you only want to use this label to classify items.

Figure 12.6 – The retention settings for a label meant for records management

8. Having configured the settings regarding retention, we are brought to the settings for disposition reviewers since it was selected in *step 7*. Here, we create (**1**) two stages called **First Stage** (**2**) and **Second Stage** (**3**) and specify reviewers accordingly by entering their email addresses:

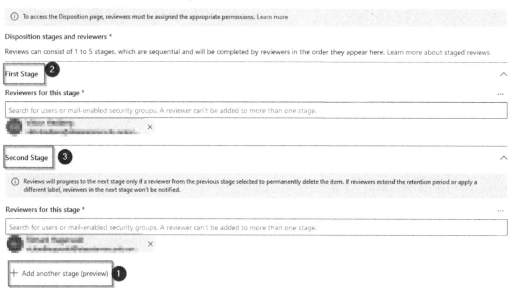

Figure 12.7 – Showing the disposition reviewer settings

9. This brings us to the last step in the creation process, which is the **Review and finish** step, as shown in *Figure 12.8*:

Review and finish

Name

Name

SC-400 Records Management Label

Edit

Description for users

SC-400 Records Management Label

Edit

Description for admins

SC-400 Records Management Label

Edit

File plan descriptors

Business function/department	Category
Human resources	Payroll
Edit	Edit

Authority type	Provision/citation
Regulatory	Sarbanes-Oxley Act of 2002
Edit	Edit

Retention settings

Retention period	Retention action
7 years	Preserve, review and delete
Edit	Edit

Based on	Disposition stages and reviewers
Based on when it was created	Stage 1 name: First Stage
Edit	Stage 1 reviewers:
	Stage 2 name: Second Stage
	Stage 2 reviewers:
	Edit

Figure 12.8 – The Review and finish page of the records management retention label

10. Proceeding from the **Review and finish** page, we are greeted with a familiar page once more. Here, we need to either *publish this label to Microsoft 365 locations*, *auto-apply this label to a specific type of content*, or *do nothing*, exactly as when we created and configured retention labels.

11. In this example, we are going to use the **Auto-apply this label to a specific type of content** option. After adding a name and a description for the policy, we can proceed to the next step and select which sensitive information types we are going to apply this label to:

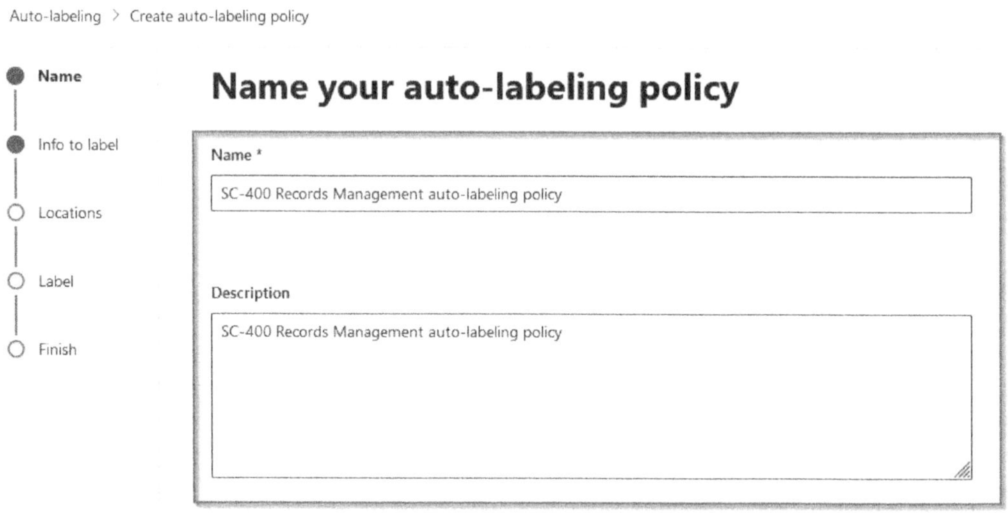

Auto-labeling > Create auto-labeling policy

Name your auto-labeling policy

Name

Info to label

Locations

Label

Finish

Name *

SC-400 Records Management auto-labeling policy

Description

SC-400 Records Management auto-labeling policy

Figure 12.9 – The settings for creating the auto-labeling policy for records management

12. In this example, we are using the US **Gramm-Leach-Bliley Act (GLBA)** to help us detect the presence of information subject to GLBA:

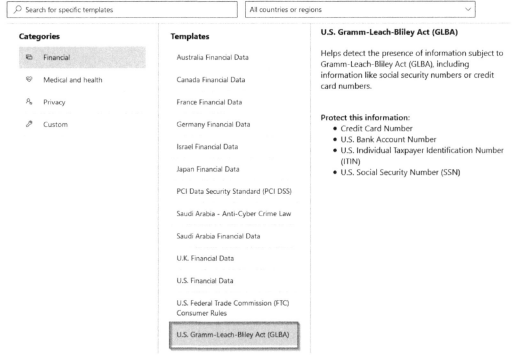

Figure 12.10 – Using the GLBA sensitive information type for this policy

13. Select the locations for which the policy should be used in Microsoft 365:

Choose locations to apply the policy

We'll publish the labels to the locations you choose.

Status	Location	Included	Excluded
On	Exchange email	All recipients Edit	None Edit
On	SharePoint sites	All sites Edit	None Edit
On	OneDrive accounts	All accounts Edit	None Edit
On	Microsoft 365 Groups	All groups Edit	None Edit

Figure 12.11 – Selecting the locations in Microsoft 365 to use the policy

14. Select the newly created records management label and proceed to the last step to create the policy:

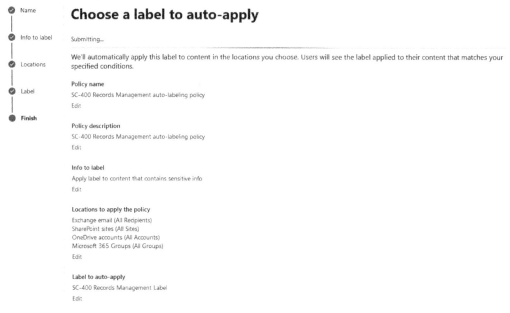

Figure 12.12 – Reviewing the settings and publishing the label

15. Once created, we are brought back to the **File plan** page of **Records management**, where we can spot our new label and its settings:

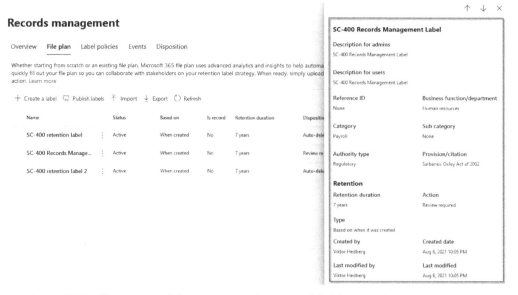

Figure 12.13 – The location of the newly created retention label for records management usage

This concludes the creation process of a retention label meant for records management. Up next, we will investigate the topic of managing and migrating retention requirements with a file plan.

Managing and migrating retention requirements with a file plan

When it comes to records management, a file plan is of the utmost importance to help you identify information of interest outside of the predefined Microsoft file plans. The process consists of these three steps:

1. Download the file plan template.
2. Fill out the file plan.
3. Import the file plan.

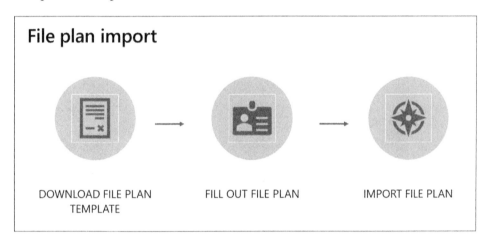

Figure 12.14 – The process for importing a file plan visualized

To get the process started, we once more venture to the Microsoft Purview Compliance Portal (`https://compliance.microsoft.com`), only this time we head toward **Records management**, then over to **File plan**, and select **Import** to obtain the template CSV file provided by Microsoft for creating our own *file plan*.

> **Note**
>
> The file plan template consists of several predefined fields, which may or may not match your organization's existing file plan and/or retention schedule. You will need to determine how to reconcile the differences between the template and your organization.

Here is a list of the fields in the file plan template:

- **LabelName**: This property specifies the name of the retention label and must be unique in your tenant.

- **Comment**: This property can be used to add an admin description of the retention label as it only appears for administrators in the compliance center.

- **Notes**: This property can be used to add an end user description of the retention label. If left blank, a default description is displayed, explaining the label's retention settings.

- **IsRecordLabel**: This property specifies whether the label marks the content as a record.

- **RetentionAction**: This property specifies what actions to take after the value specified by the `RetentionDuration` property expires.

- **RetentionDuration**: This property specifies the number of days to retain the content. The maximum number of days is 24,855, which is 68 years. If you need a longer duration than 68 years, enter **Unlimited** instead.

- **RetentionType**: This property specifies whether the retention duration is calculated from the content creation date, event date, last modified date, or when labeled date.

- **ReviewerEmail**: This property specifies the disposition reviewer email address. It could be an individual user or groups.

- **ReferenceId**: This property specifies the value of the reference ID file plan descriptor.

- **DepartmentName**: This property specifies the value of the function/department file plan descriptor.

- **Category**: This property specifies the value of the category file plan descriptor.

- **SubCategory**: This property specifies the value of the sub-category file plan descriptor.

- **AuthorityType**: This property specifies the value of the authority type file plan descriptor.

- **CitationName**: This property specifies the value of the citation name file plan descriptor, for example, the Sarbanes-Oxley Act of 2002, as used previously.

- **CitationUrl**: This property specifies the value of the URL in the provision/citation file plan descriptor.

- **CitationJurisdiction**: This property specifies the value of the jurisdiction or agency in the provision/citation file plan descriptor, such as the US **Securities and Exchange Commission (SEC)**.

- **Regulatory**: This property specifies whether the label marks the content as a regulatory record.

- **EventType**: This property specifies an event type used for event-based retention.

With these things in order, let's start this process in the same manner as with our records management label policy:

1. Start by selecting the first link in *Figure 12.15* to download a blank template:

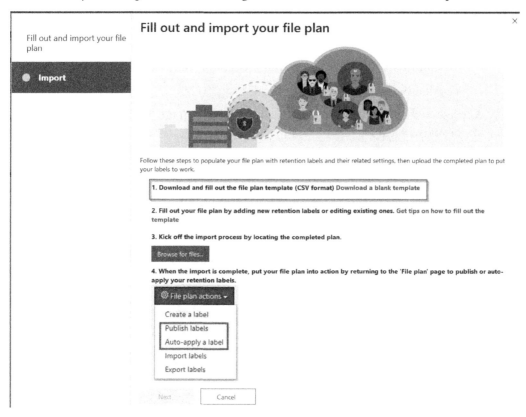

Figure 12.15 – Selecting Download a blank template to download the template for your file plan

2. Fill out the template to add new retention labels or edit existing ones. If you need further tips on how to do this, please refer to the following link from Microsoft: https://aka.ms/Office365-FilePlanManager.

3. To increase the readability of the template, I have used the **Text to Columns** option in Microsoft Excel in this demonstration, as shown in *Figure 12.16*:

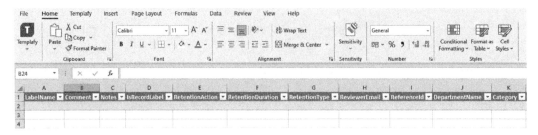

Figure 12.16 – The template in a workable Excel workbook

4. There are some caveats when it comes to filling out the template, as described next:

    A. **LabelName**: Maximum length of 64 characters

    B. **Comment** and **Notes**: Maximum length of 1,024 characters

    C. All other values: Unlimited length

5. As presented in *Figure 12.17*, data has been entered in the template to allow the import of the file plan:

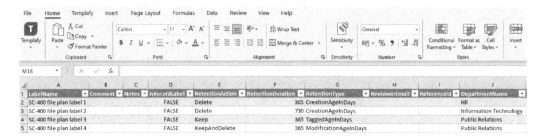

Figure 12.17 – Mock data entered in the template

6. Heading back to the compliance center, we now select the **Browse for files…** option in the **Import** wizard, as highlighted in *Figure 12.18*:

Figure 12.18 – Showing the option to browse your computer for the filled-out .csv template

7. The **Browse for files…** selection brings us to a well-known file import selection pop-up window where we locate the template and click on **Open** to upload the file to the compliance center:

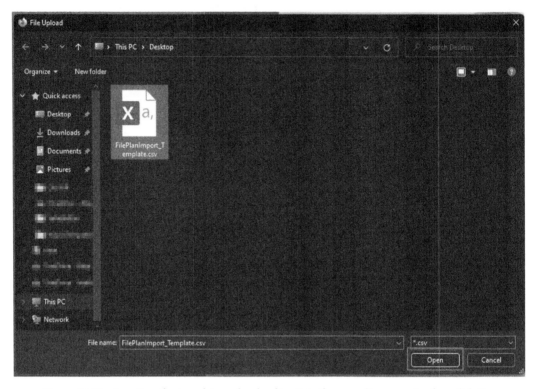

Figure 12.19 – Locating the template and uploading it to the compliance center for validation

8. With the validation of our file plan completed, we are presented with *Figure 12.20* and can review some statistics of the file plan. The **Go Live** button takes us to the process of publishing these labels in our Microsoft 365 tenant:

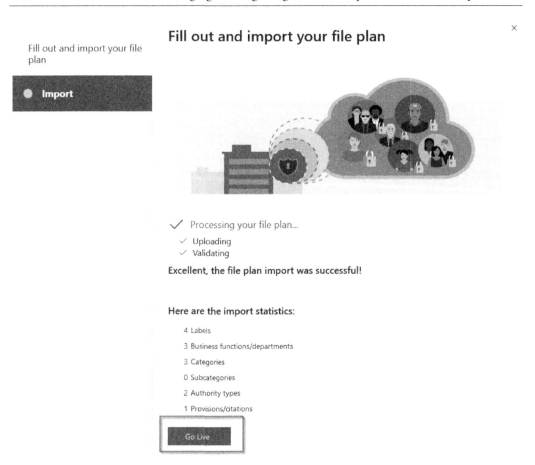

Figure 12.20 – With the validation of the file plan completed, we can now publish our labels

9. With the import completed, our new labels are presented in the view over all retention labels under **File plan** and can be published accordingly following *steps 9-14* in the guide covering **Configuring labels for records management** in this chapter.

And with that, we have covered the process of importing our own file plan, thus bulk creating retention labels to help us govern our information in Microsoft 365. Up next, we will dig into the topic of configuring automatic retention using file plan descriptors.

Configuring automatic retention using file plan descriptors

The configuration of a retention policy using file plan descriptors is more advanced than using any of the other available methods, thus it is more customizable than the others but has its limitations as it is more complex to administer. The query language used is **Keyword Query Language** (**KQL**) in Microsoft SharePoint; for more information on the query language itself, please refer to the following URL: `https://docs.microsoft.com/en-us/sharepoint/dev/general-development/keyword-query-language-kql-syntax-reference`.

The steps outlined in this section will help us construct a query using file plan descriptors for automatic retention:

1. Select the label you wish to use for this scenario and select the **Auto-apply a label** option:

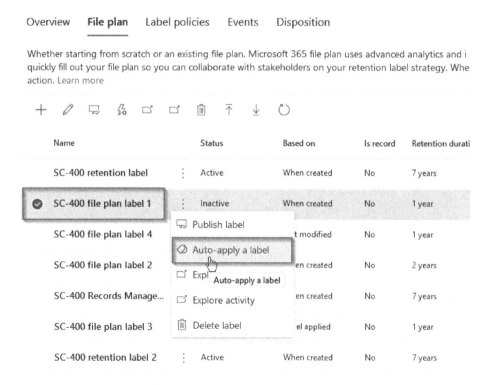

Figure 12.21 – The Auto-apply a label option presented on the label

2. Give the policy a name and an admin description accordingly.

3. On the **Info to label** step, select the **Apply label to content that contains specific words or phrases, or properties** option, as highlighted in *Figure 12.22*:

Choose the type of content you want to apply this label to

○ Apply label to content that contains sensitive info

◉ Apply label to content that contains specific words or phrases, or properties

○ Apply label to content that matches a trainable classifier

Figure 12.22 – The Apply label to content that contains specific words or phrases, or properties option selected

4. This brings us to the KQL editor. The following query contains typical keywords that are usually present in documents or emails for **human resources** (**HR**):

```
(resume AND staff AND employee AND salary AND recruitment
AND candidate)
```

5. Enter your query in the window on the screen, as highlighted in *Figure 12.23*:

Apply label to content matching this query

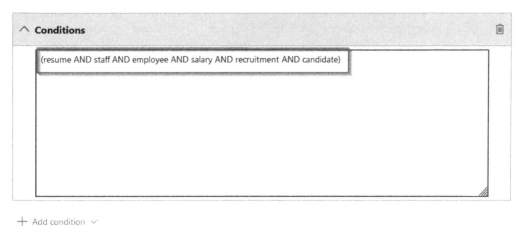

Figure 12.23 – The KQL query in place in the query editor

6. Proceeding with the wizard, we are now on familiar turf once more. Here, we need to select the locations of the information that we are looking for with our query and can explicitly include or exclude individuals from the policy itself:

Choose locations to apply the policy

We'll publish the labels to the locations you choose.

Status	Location	Included	Excluded
On	Exchange email	All recipients Edit	None Edit
On	SharePoint sites	All sites Edit	None Edit
On	OneDrive accounts	All accounts Edit	None Edit
On	Microsoft 365 Groups	All groups Edit	None Edit

Figure 12.24 – Selecting the locations for the retention policy

7. After selecting the label we started with, we can now finish the creation of our policy using KQL:

Choose a label to auto-apply

We'll automatically apply this label to content in the locations you choose. Users will see the label applied to their content that matches your specified conditions.

Policy name
SC-400 KQL Retention Policy
Edit

Policy description
SC-400 KQL Retention Policy
Edit

Info to label
Apply label to content that contains specific words or phrases, or properties
Edit

Locations to apply the policy
Exchange email (All Recipients)
SharePoint sites (All Sites)
OneDrive accounts (All Accounts)
Microsoft 365 Groups (All Groups)
Edit

Label to auto-apply
SC-400 file plan label 1
Edit

Back   Submit

Figure 12.25 – Click Submit to create the KQL-driven policy

And with that, we have configured a policy to look for HR data using KQL. Up next, we will look at how to implement in-place records management in Microsoft SharePoint.

Implementing in-place records management in Microsoft SharePoint

The ability to manage records in SharePoint gives record managers more control over how certain records containing business and legal information with long-term value are handled. Managing records *in place* also provides the opportunity for these records to be a part of a collaborative workspace.

The steps shown next guide us through how to activate records management in SharePoint:

1. Navigate to the top-level site in SharePoint Online.
2. Click **Settings**, and then click **Site Settings**.
3. In a SharePoint group-connected site, click **Settings | Site Contents | Site Settings**.
4. Beneath **Site Collection Administration**, click **Site Collection Features**.
5. In **Site Collection Features**, look after **In Place Records Management** and click on **Activate**.

With those five steps taken, the functionality of in-place records management is now activated for our SharePoint Online instance. Up next, we are going to look at how to configure event-based retention.

Configuring event-based retention

When content is retained, the retention period is more often than not based on the age of the content. For example, you might retain information for 8 years after it is created and then delete it. But when working with retention labels, you can also base a retention period on when an event occurs.

Some examples of event-based retention are as follows:

*   **Employees leaving the organization**: Suppose that employee records must be retained for 5 years from the time employment is terminated. The event that triggers the 5-year retention period is the employee leaving the organization.
*   **Contract expiration**: Suppose that records relating to specific contracts must be retained for 7 years from the time a contract expires. The event in this case is the expiration of the contract.

- **Product lifetime**: The organization might have retention requirements related to the manufacturing date of products. The event in this case would be the last manufacturing date.

Figure 12.26 describes a high-level workflow for event-driven retention:

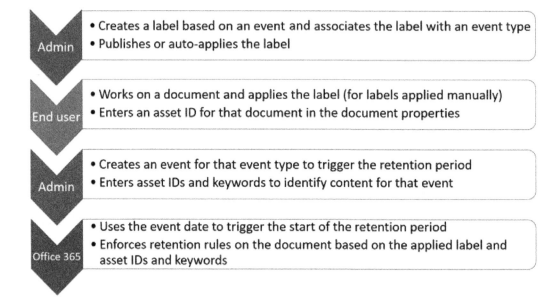

Figure 12.26 – A high-level workflow for event-driven retention

The steps shown next guide us through the process of creating a label whose retention period is based on an event:

1. In the Microsoft Purview Compliance Portal, navigate to the **Information Governance** section and proceed with giving the new retention label a name, end user description, and admin description.

2. Under **Define retention settings** in the wizard, let's now select **Employee activity** as our event:

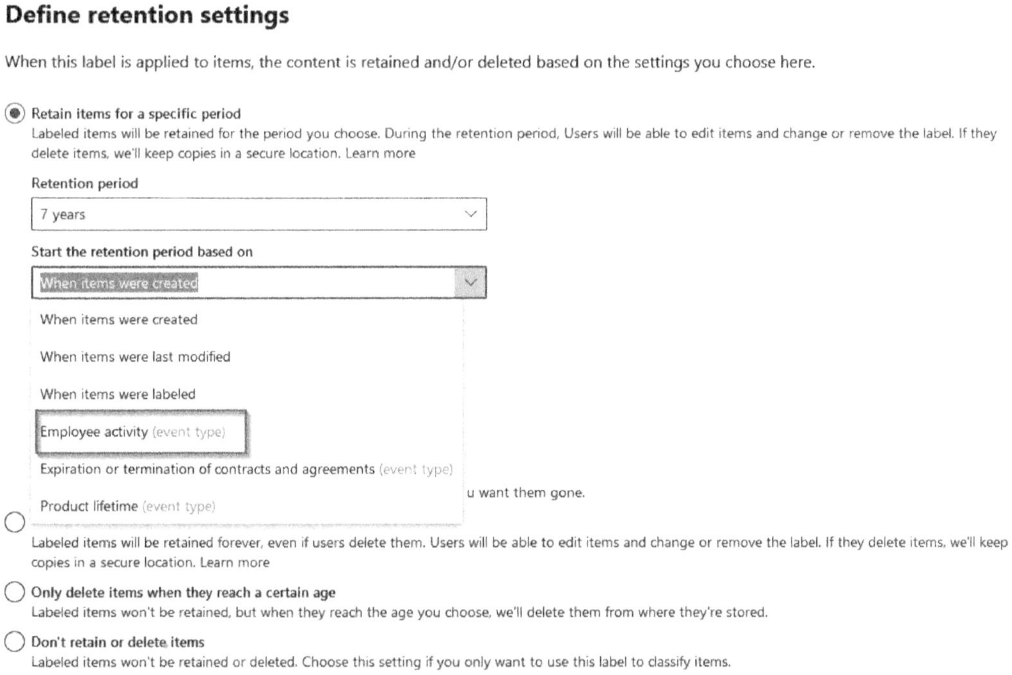

Define retention settings

When this label is applied to items, the content is retained and/or deleted based on the settings you choose here.

● Retain items for a specific period
   Labeled items will be retained for the period you choose. During the retention period, Users will be able to edit items and change or remove the label. If they delete items, we'll keep copies in a secure location. Learn more

   Retention period

   | 7 years | ∨ |

   Start the retention period based on

   | When items were created | ∨ |

   When items were created

   When items were last modified

   When items were labeled

   Employee activity (event type)

   Expiration or termination of contracts and agreements (event type)

   Product lifetime (event type)   u want them gone.

   Labeled items will be retained forever, even if users delete them. Users will be able to edit items and change or remove the label. If they delete items, we'll keep copies in a secure location. Learn more

○ Only delete items when they reach a certain age
   Labeled items won't be retained, but when they reach the age you choose, we'll delete them from where they're stored.

○ Don't retain or delete items
   Labeled items won't be retained or deleted. Choose this setting if you only want to use this label to classify items.

Figure 12.27 – Selecting an event from the drop-down menu or creating a custom event

3. Proceed with creating the retention label as we have done previously.

4. After an event-based label is applied to content, the end user needs to enter an asset ID for each item. In this example, since we are using **Employee activity**, we can use the employee ID for this particular individual:

Figure 12.28 – The location of the asset ID on content

5. Let's create an event to initiate this label. Go to the **Records management** page in the compliance center and select the **Events** tab. Select **+ Create** to create the event. Up to 1 million events are supported per tenant:

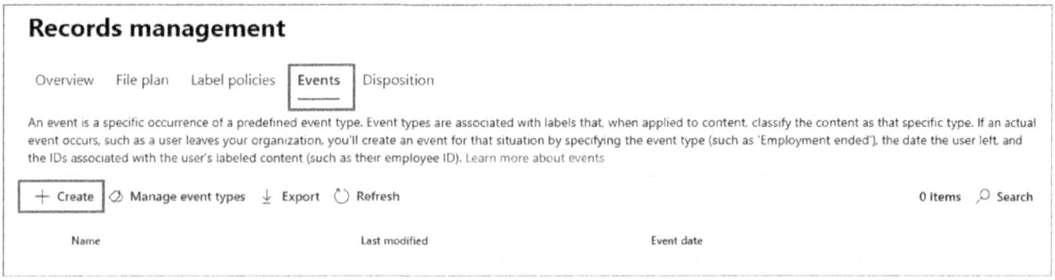

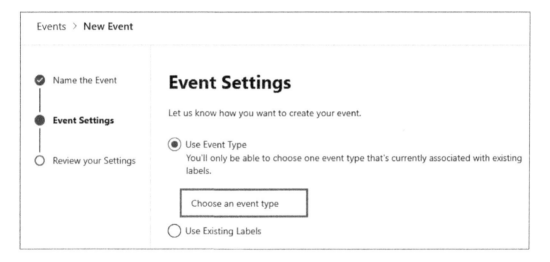

Figure 12.29 – Creating an event

6. Choose the same event type as used by the label we created in *step 2*:

Figure 12.30 – Choosing the same event type as the label was created for

7. Enter keywords or use KQL for querying Exchange and use the asset ID for SharePoint and OneDrive for Business. Since we are focusing on the asset ID in this case, the following property is used: `ComplianceAssetID:<EmployeeID>`:

Event Settings

Identify the items in Exchange, SharePoint and OneDrive that are related to this event. Only items that have labels associated with the event type you chose will be retained.

Keywords for items in Exchange

Asset IDs for items in SharePoint and OneDrive

When did this event occur?

Tue Sep 01 2020

Figure 12.31 – Entering ComplianceAssetID:<EmployeeID> in the highlighted box

8. After creating the event, the retention settings specified take effect for the content that is already labeled and indexed.

9. You can automate events by using PowerShell. If this is of interest, please refer to the following URL for guidance on the topic: `https://docs.microsoft.com/en-us/microsoft-365/compliance/event-driven-retention?view=o365-worldwide#automate-events-by-using-powershell`.

This concludes the section on event-based retention labels. Up next, we will cover the last topic of this chapter, which will guide us through how to manage the disposition of records.

Managing the disposition of records

When information reaches the end of the retention period assigned, there are multiple reasons as to why you might want to review the information prior to deletion. For example, instead of permanently deleting the information, you might want to do the following:

- Suspend deletion of specific content for litigation reasons.
- Assign a different retention period for the information.
- Move the information from its existing location to an archive due to historical value.

This is where disposition review comes into play, allowing you to select one or more reviewers at the end of the retention period to make sure that the information is safe to be deleted or take another action on.

We briefly discussed the possibility to use disposition reviews in retention labels in the *Configuring labels for records management* section of this chapter in steps *7* and *8*.

Figure 12.32 gives us the workflow for a disposition review:

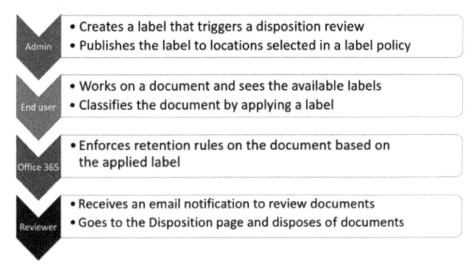

Figure 12.32 – The workflow of a disposition review

> **Note**
>
> Remember to grant reviewers the correct permissions in the compliance center. The role in question is the Disposition Management role. More information on the permissions required and new features regarding permissions can be found on the following page: `https://docs.microsoft.com/en-us/` `microsoft-365/compliance/disposition?view=o365-` `worldwide#permissions-for-disposition`.

There is not much else to the configuration of the workflow outside of the steps taken in the previously mentioned steps 7 and 8 of the *Configuring labels for records management* section.

With that said, there are some more settings to consider when it comes to disposition reviews. For example, the default email notification sent to reviewers can be customized from the Microsoft Purview Compliance Portal:

1. From the **Records management** page, select **Records management settings**:

Figure 12.33 – The location of the Records management settings button

2. Select the **Disposition notifications** tab, where we can see the default message and add content to the default message to clarify it for the reviewers:

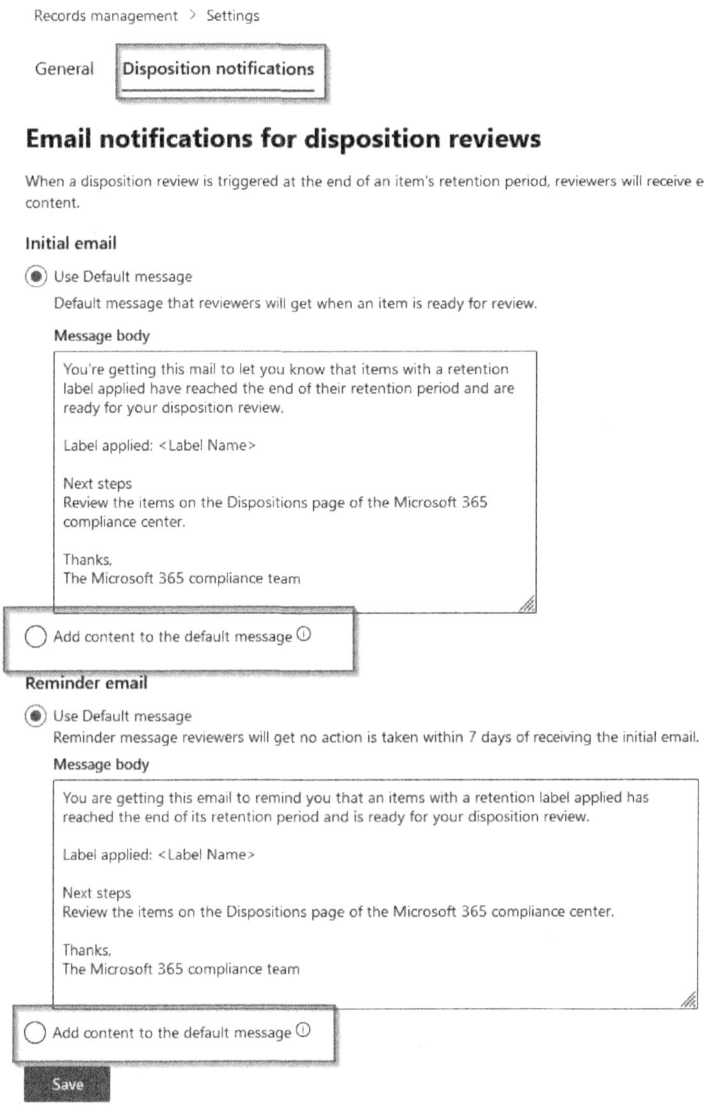

Records management > Settings

General | **Disposition notifications** |

Email notifications for disposition reviews

When a disposition review is triggered at the end of an item's retention period, reviewers will receive email notifications content.

Initial email

(●) Use Default message

Default message that reviewers will get when an item is ready for review.

Message body

> You're getting this mail to let you know that items with a retention label applied have reached the end of their retention period and are ready for your disposition review.
>
> Label applied: <Label Name>
>
> Next steps
> Review the items on the Dispositions page of the Microsoft 365 compliance center.
>
> Thanks,
> The Microsoft 365 compliance team

( ) Add content to the default message ⓘ

Reminder email

(●) Use Default message

Reminder message reviewers will get no action is taken within 7 days of receiving the initial email.

Message body

> You are getting this email to remind you that an items with a retention label applied has reached the end of its retention period and is ready for your disposition review.
>
> Label applied: <Label Name>
>
> Next steps
> Review the items on the Dispositions page of the Microsoft 365 compliance center.
>
> Thanks,
> The Microsoft 365 compliance team

( ) Add content to the default message ⓘ

Save

Figure 12.34 – The email notification settings for disposition reviews

With the basics of disposition reviews covered, let's look at how to use the feature in practice.

Viewing and disposing of content

When a reviewer is notified that they have content to review, they can click the link in the email provided or navigate manually to the Microsoft Purview Compliance Portal and the **Disposition** page. There, reviewers can see how many items for each label are waiting for disposition with **Pending disposition** displayed under **Type**:

Figure 12.35 – The Disposition page in the compliance center showing the Pending disposition type

From the **Pending dispositions** page, the reviewers can see all pending dispositions for a specific label and select an action to take on the items listed:

Figure 12.36 – The Pending dispositions page showing the files pending a disposition review

And that is it for managing dispositions of records. If you are searching for even more information on the topic, stay updated with docs.microsoft.com and keep on learning!

Summary

Wow! What an end to the book. This chapter has been all about Microsoft Purview Records Management, and as you might see, there is much to it with new features added frequently. We hope that this book helps you conquer the SC-400 exam, and by following the chapters within, they should help you to achieve the 700 points required to clear it and become an information protection administrator.

Practice Exam

This section will have example exam questions that are similar to the test so that you can become acquainted with the format and how to read and answer a question within the allowed time frame.

Test questions

1. You have implemented three sensitivity labels named SC-LB-01, SC-LB-02, and SC-LB-03 and executed the following customizations:

   - Implemented an auto-labeling policy for SC-LB-02

   - Published SC-LB-01

   You want to configure a file policy called SC-FP-01 with Microsoft Defender for Cloud Apps. Which sensitivity label are you able to apply to SC-FP-01?

   A. SC-LB-01 and SC-LB-02 only

   B. SC-LB-01 only

   C. SC-LB-02 only

   D. SC-LB-01, SC-LB-02, and SC-LB-03

2. You are configuring a solution for data classification. The development department need documents containing code to be labeled as confidential. You are provided with a sample of the code by the development manager. Your solution must decrease the amount of administration overhead. What do you need to do?

   A. Use the source code classifier

   B. Create a custom classifier

   C. Create a sensitive information type that uses a regular expression

   D. Create a sensitive information type that uses **Exact Data Match** (**EDM**)

3. You are an administrator for a Microsoft 365 tenant. You need to make sure that custom trainable classifiers can be created in your tenant. Following least privilege access, which admin role do you need to be granted to complete this configuration?

    A. Compliance administrator

    B. Security administrator

    C. Global administrator

    D. Security operator

4. You are going to implement a custom trainable classifier to identify organizational product codes in Microsoft 365 content. You identify 150 documents that can be utilized as seed content. In which location should you store the content?

    A. Azure File Share

    B. Microsoft OneDrive for Business folder

    C. SharePoint Online folder

    D. Exchange Online shared mailbox

5. Your organization has several product groups that need to show a specific product logo in encrypted emails rather than the Office 365 logo. Which task should you perform to create the branding template?

    A. Create an RMS template

    B. Create a transport rule

    C. Run the `New-OMEConfiguration` cmdlet

    D. Run the `Set-IRMConfiguration` cmdlet

6. Which custom sensitivity information type feature allows you to manage reused keyword lists for matching large amounts of business information and supports up to 1 MB of keywords in any language?

    A. Document fingerprinting

    B. Keyword dictionaries

    C. **Exact Data Match (EDM)**

7. Which feature allows you to scan and protect data within your on-premises infrastructure, including file shares, local SharePoint servers and NAS storage devices?

    A. Universal labeling

    B. Unified labeling

C. Global labeling

D. Local labeling

8. You have recently implemented a custom sensitive information type that utilizes **Exact Data Match** (**EDM**). You want to intermittently update and upload the content utilized by EDM. What is the highest rate at which that content can be uploaded?

A. Two times per hour

B. Two times per day

C. Two times per week

D. Once every 6 hours

9. Your manager has sent you a list of phrases that need to be used for a sensitive information type. You are required to produce a file that will be used as a source for the keyword dictionary. Which format do you need to save this list in?

A. CSV

B. JSON

C. XML

D. DOCX

10. You have been asked to test **Office 365 Message Encryption** (**OME**) capabilities by your manager. You need to verify the following:

* Encryption and decryption verification status

* Obtained default template names

    Identify which PowerShell cmdlet you need to run:

    A. `Test-Mailflow`

    B. `Test-ClientAccessRule`

    C. `Test-OauthConnectivity`

    D. `Test-IRMConfiguration`

11. You are an administrator for a Microsoft 365 tenant that utilizes **Office 365 Encryption (OME)**. You need to make sure that all emails that contain an attachment and that are sent to `OfficeAdmin@iamitgeek.com` are auto-encrypted using OME. Which task do you need to implement to achieve this?

    A. Configure an auto-apply retention label policy

    B. Create a new sharing policy

    C. Create a safe attachments policy

    D. Create a mail flow rule

12. You have been asked to configure sensitivity labels for Microsoft Teams. You need to make sure that you are able to read and apply sensitivity labels to new Teams sites. Which task do you need to complete first?

    A. Create a new sensitivity label scoped to groups and sites

    B. Run the `Execute-AzureAdLableSync` cmdlet in PowerShell

    C. Run the `Set-SPOSite` cmdlet in PowerShell

    D. Implement the `EnableMIPLabels` Azure AD setting

13. You manage a Microsoft 365 tenant. It has been reported that emails are not utilizing **Office 365 Encryption (OME)**. You need to make sure that OME is being applied to emails. Which task do you need to implement first?

    A. Configure an Azure Key Vault

    B. Activate **Azure Rights Management (ARMS)**

    C. Activate Azure Information Protection

    D. Enable Defender for Office 365

14. You are an administrator for a Microsoft 365 tenant. One of your teammates has configured the following:

    • An auto-labeling policy

    • A sensitivity label

    You need to verify that the sensitivity label is applied to all content that is found by the auto-labeling policy. Which task should you complete first?

    A. Configure a trainable classifier

    B. Run the policy in simulation mode

    C. Turn on insider risk management

    D. Run the `Enable-TransportRule` cmdlet in PowerShell

15. A sensitive information type based on a trainable classifier has been implemented by your colleague. You are dissatisfied with the output of the rule of the trainable classifier and want to retrain the classifier. What do you need to utilize in the Compliance Center to complete this task?

    A. Content search

    B. Labels from Information Protection

    C. Content explorer from Data Classification

    D. Labels from Information Governance

16. Your company's Microsoft 365 tenant utilizes 150 **data loss prevention (DLP)** policies. Blocked emails due to DLP violations are regularly reviewed by Exchange administrators. You are required to recommend which DLP report the Exchange administrator needs to utilize to recognize how many emails were blocked based on each separate DLP policy. Which report do you need to recommend?

    A. DLP incidents

    B. False positive and override

    C. DLP policy matches

    D. Third-party DLP policy matches

17. You have been asked by your manager to grant a team member access to read DLP alerts in the Compliance Center. Your answer needs to use the principle of least privilege. Which role do you need to assign to your team member?

    A. Security reader

    B. Compliance administrator

    C. Security operator

    D. Compliance data administrator

18. You have a requirement to be informed when a user shares sensitive content from OneDrive to people outside your organization. Which task should you complete?

    A. Create a DLP policy from the Compliance Center

    B. Create an Azure Information Protection policy from Azure Policy

    C. Start a data investigation from the Compliance Center

    D. Create an insider risk policy from the Compliance policy

19. You have recently configured multiple DLP policies. Once the policies were created, the support team received a larger than normal volume of DLP alerts. You have been asked to find the rules that are creating the alerts. Which report should you utilize?

   A. DLP incidents

   B. DLP policy matches

   C. Third-party DLP policy matches

   D. False positive and override

20. Which feature ensures that original copies of files, prior to any updates or deletions, are preserved in Microsoft 365 Preservation Libraries?

   A. Preservation Lock

   B. Library Hold

   C. Library Lock

   D. Preservation Hold

21. In SharePoint Online and OneDrive, how many versions are retained by default?

   A. 250

   B. 100

   C. 500

   D. 1,000

22. Which feature of **Messaging Records Management** (MRM) allows you to apply sets of retention tags to standard user mailboxes?

   A. Personal tags

   B. Default policy tags

   C. Retention policies

   D. Retention policy tags

23. Which PowerShell cmdlet allows you to show the existing default retention policy?

   A. `Get-RetentionPolicy`

   B. `Set-RetentionPolicy`

   C. `Update-RetentionPolicy`

   D. `View-RetentionPolicy`

24. In Exchange Online, which type of mailbox hold prevents mailbox data that matches a specific search criterion from being purged or modified?

    A. Shared mailboxes

    B. eDiscovery Hold

    C. Litigation Hold

    D. Meeting room mailbox

25. Which fundamental component of a sensitive information type is typically identified by a regular expression but can be keywords?

    A. Confidence level

    B. Character proximity

    C. Primary pattern

26. You plan to implement sensitivity labels for Microsoft Teams. You need to ensure that you can view and apply sensitivity labels to new Microsoft Teams sites. What should you do first?

    A. Run the `Set-SPOSite` cmdlet

    B. Create a new sensitivity label scoped to groups and sites

    C. Run the `Execute-AzureAdLabelSync` cmdlet

    D. Configure the `EnableMIPLabels` **Azure Active Directory** (**Azure AD**) setting

27. You need to automatically apply a sensitivity label to documents that contain information about your company's network, including computer names, IP addresses, and configuration information. Which two objects should you use?

    A. An information protection auto-labeling policy

    B. A custom trainable classifier

    C. A sensitive information type that uses a regular expression

    D. A **data loss prevention** (**DLP**) policy

    E. A sensitive information type that uses keywords

    F. A sensitivity label that has auto-labeling

28. You have a Microsoft 365 tenant. You discover that email does NOT use Microsoft **Office 365 Message Encryption** (OME). You need to ensure that OME can be applied to email. What should you do first?

    A. Enable Microsoft Defender for Office 365

    B. Activate Azure Information Protection

    C. Activate **Azure Rights Management (Azure RMS)**

    D. Create an Azure Key Vault

29. You have a Microsoft 365 tenant that uses Microsoft **Office 365 Message Encryption (OME)**. You need to ensure that any emails containing attachments and sent to user1@contoso.com are encrypted automatically by using OME. What should you do?

    A. From the Exchange Admin Center, create a new sharing policy.

    B. From the Microsoft 365 Security Center, create a safe attachments policy.

    C. From the Exchange Admin Center, create a mail flow rule.

    D. From the Microsoft Purview Compliance Portal, configure an auto-apply retention label policy.

30. You have a Microsoft 365 tenant. You create the following:

    - A sensitivity label

    - An auto-labeling policy

    You need to ensure that the sensitivity label would be applied to all the data discovered by the auto-labeling policy. What should you do first?

    A. Enable insider risk management

    B. Create a trainable classifier

    C. Run the `Enable-TransportRule` cmdlet

    D. Run the policy in simulation mode

31. You implement Microsoft 365 **Endpoint data loss prevention (Endpoint DLP)**. You have computers that run Windows 10 and have Microsoft 365 Apps installed. The computers are joined to **Azure Active Directory (Azure AD)**. You need to ensure that Endpoint DLP policies can protect content on the computers.

    Solution: You onboard the computers to Microsoft Defender for Endpoint. Does this meet the objective?

    A. Yes

    B. No

32. You have a Microsoft 365 tenant that uses 100 **data loss prevention (DLP)** policies. A Microsoft Exchange administrator frequently investigates emails that were blocked due to DLP policy violations. You need to recommend which DLP report the Exchange administrator can use to identify how many messages were blocked based on each DLP policy. Which report should you recommend?

    A. Third-party DLP policy matches

    B. DLP policy matches

    C. DLP incidents

    D. False positive and override

33. Your company has a Microsoft 365 tenant that uses a domain named `contoso.com`. You are implementing **data loss prevention (DLP)**. The company's default browser is Microsoft Edge. During a recent audit, you discover that some users use Firefox and Google Chrome browsers to upload files labeled as confidential to a third-party Microsoft SharePoint Online site that has a URL of `https://m365x076709.sharepoint.com`. Users are blocked from uploading the confidential files to the site from Microsoft Edge. You need to ensure that users cannot upload files labeled as confidential from Firefox and Google Chrome to any cloud services. Which two actions should you perform?

    A. From the Microsoft 365 **Endpoint data loss prevention (Endpoint DLP)** settings, add `m365x076709.sharepoint.com` as a blocked service domain.

    B. Create a DLP policy that applies to the device's location.

    C. From the Microsoft 365 Endpoint DLP settings, add Firefox and Google Chrome to the unallowed browsers list.

    D. From the Microsoft Purview Compliance Portal, onboard the devices.

    E. From the Microsoft 365 Endpoint DLP settings, add `contoso.com` as an allowed service domain.

34. You recently discovered that the developers at your company emailed Azure Storage keys in plain text to third parties. You need to ensure that when Azure Storage keys are emailed, the emails are encrypted. Solution: You configure a mail flow rule that matches a sensitive information type. Does this meet the objective?

    A. Yes

    B. No

35. You are creating an advanced **data loss prevention (DLP)** rule in a DLP policy named Policy 1 that will have all locations selected. Which two conditions can you use in the rule?

    A. Content contains.

    B. Content is shared from Microsoft 365.

    C. Document size equals or is greater than.

    D. Attachment's file extension is.

    E. Document property is.

36. You need to provide a user with the ability to view **data loss prevention (DLP)** alerts in the Microsoft Purview Compliance Portal. The solution must use the principle of least privilege. Which role should you assign to the user?

    A. Compliance data administrator

    B. Security operator

    C. Compliance administrator

    D. Security reader

37. You need to be alerted when users share sensitive documents from Microsoft OneDrive to any users outside your company. What should you do?

    A. From the Microsoft Purview Compliance Portal, create a **data loss prevention (DLP)** policy.

    B. From the Microsoft Purview Compliance Portal, start a data investigation.

    C. From the Microsoft Purview Compliance Portal, create an insider risk policy.

    D. From the Azure portal, create an Azure Information Protection policy.

38. You need to protect documents that contain credit card numbers from being opened by users outside your company. The solution must ensure that users at your company can open the documents. What should you use?

    A. A sensitivity label policy

    B. A sensitivity label

    C. A retention policy

    D. A **data loss prevention (DLP)** policy

39. You have a Microsoft 365 tenant that has devices onboarded to Microsoft Defender for Endpoint as shown in the following list:

- Device 1 – Windows 8.1

- Device 2 – Windows 10

- Device 3 – iOS

- Device 4 – macOS

- Device 5 – CentOS Linux

    You plan to start using Microsoft 365 **Endpoint data loss prevention. (Endpoint DLP)**. Which devices support Endpoint DLP?

    A. Device 5 only

    B. Device 2 only

    C. Device 1, Device 2, Device 3, Device 4, and Device 5

    D. Device 3 and Device 4 only

    E. Device 1 and Device 2 only

40. You have a Microsoft 365 tenant and 500 computers that run Windows 10. The computers are onboarded to the Microsoft Purview Compliance Portal. You discover that a third-party application named `Tailspin_scanner.exe` accessed protected sensitive information on multiple computers. `Tailspin_scanner.exe` is installed locally on the computers. You need to block `Tailspin_scanner.exe` from accessing sensitive documents without preventing the application from accessing other documents. Solution: From the Cloud App Security portal, you create an app discovery policy. Does this meet the objective?

    A. Yes

    B. No

41. You have a Microsoft 365 tenant and 500 computers that run Windows 10. The computers are onboarded to the Microsoft Purview Compliance Portal. You discover that a third-party application named `Tailspin_scanner.exe` accessed protected sensitive information on multiple computers. `Tailspin_scanner.exe` is installed locally on the computers. You need to block `Tailspin_scanner.exe` from accessing sensitive documents without preventing the application from accessing other documents. Solution: From the Microsoft 365 **Endpoint data loss prevention (Endpoint DLP)** settings, you add a folder path to the file path exclusions. Does this meet the objective?

    A. Yes

    B. No

42. You have a Microsoft 365 tenant and 500 computers that run Windows 10. The computers are onboarded to the Microsoft Purview Compliance Portal. You discover that a third-party application named `Tailspin_scanner.exe` accessed protected sensitive information on multiple computers. `Tailspin_scanner.exe` is installed locally on the computers. You need to block `Tailspin_scanner.exe` from accessing sensitive documents without preventing the application from accessing other documents. Solution: From the Microsoft 365 **Endpoint data loss prevention (Endpoint DLP)** settings, you add the application to the unallowed apps list. Does this meet the objective?

    A. Yes

    B. No

43. You are planning a **data loss prevention (DLP)** solution that will apply to computers that run Windows 10. You need to ensure that when users attempt to copy a file that contains sensitive information to a USB storage device, the following requirements are met:

    - If the users are members of a group named Group1, the users must be allowed to copy the file, and an event must be recorded in the audit log.

    - All other users must be blocked from copying the file.

    What should you create?

    A. Two DLP policies that each contain one DLP rule

    B. One DLP policy that contains one DLP rule

    C. One DLP policy that contains two DLP rules

44. You have a Microsoft SharePoint Online site that contains employee contracts in a document library named Contracts. The contracts must be treated as records in accordance with your company's records management policy. You need to implement a solution to automatically mark all the contracts as records when they are uploaded to Contracts. Which two actions should you perform?

    A. Create a sensitivity label

    B. Create a retention label

    C. Configure a default label on the Contracts document library

    D. Create a retention policy

    E. Create a file plan

    F. Create a retention lock

45. You need to create a retention policy to delete content after 7 years from the following locations:

    - Exchange Online email

    - SharePoint Online sites

    - OneDrive accounts

    - Office 365 groups

    - Teams channel messages

    - Teams chats

    What is the minimum number of retention policies that you should create?

    A. 1

    B. 2

    C. 3

    D. 4

46. You have a Microsoft 365 tenant that uses records management. You use a retention label to mark legal files stored in a Microsoft SharePoint Online document library as regulatory records. What can you do to the legal files?

    A. Remove the retention label of the files

    B. Edit the properties of the files

    C. Move the files to a different folder within the document library

    D. Delete the content from the files

47. You have a Microsoft 365 tenant. All Microsoft OneDrive for Business content is retained for 5 years. A user named `User1` left your company a year ago, after which the account of `User1` was deleted from **Azure Active Directory (Azure AD)**. You need to recover an important file that was stored in the OneDrive of `User1`. What should you use?

    A. The `Restore-SPODeletedSite` PowerShell cmdlet

    B. The OneDrive recycle bin

    C. The `Restore-ADObject` PowerShell cmdlet

    D. Deleted users in the Microsoft 365 Admin Center

48. At the end of a project, you upload project documents to a Microsoft SharePoint Online library that contains many files. The following is a sample of the project document filenames:

    - `aei_AA989.docx`

    - `bci_WS098.docx`

    - `cei_DF112.docx`

    - `ebc_QQ454.docx`

    - `ecc_BB565.docx`

    All documents that use this naming format must be labeled as Project Documents. You need to create an auto-apply retention label policy. What should you use to identify the files?

    A. A sensitive information type

    B. A retention label

    C. A trainable classifier

49. You need to create a retention policy to retain all the files from Microsoft Teams channel conversations and private chats. Which two locations should you select in the retention policy?

    A. OneDrive accounts

    B. Office 365 groups

    C. Team channel messages

    D. SharePoint sites

    E. Team chats

    F. Exchange email

50. You have a Microsoft 365 tenant that uses records management. You use a retention label to mark legal files stored in a Microsoft SharePoint Online document library as regulatory records. What can you do to the legal files?

A. Rename the files

B. Edit the properties of the files

C. Change the retention label of the files

D. Copy the content of the files

Answer key

1. A

2. A

3. A

4. C

5. C

6. B

7. B

8. B

9. A

10. D

11. D

12. A

13. B

14. B

15. C

16. C

17. A

18. A

19. B

20. D

21. C

22. C

23. A

24. B

25. C

26. B

27. A and B

28. C

29. C

30. D

31. A

32. B

33. C and D

34. A

35. A and B

36. D

37. A

38. D

39. B

40. B

41. B

42. A

43. A

44. B and C

45. A

46. C

47. B

48. C

49. A and D

50. D

Packt.com

Subscribe to our online digital library for full access to over 7,000 books and videos, as well as industry leading tools to help you plan your personal development and advance your career. For more information, please visit our website.

Why subscribe?

- Spend less time learning and more time coding with practical eBooks and Videos from over 4,000 industry professionals

- Improve your learning with Skill Plans built especially for you

- Get a free eBook or video every month

- Fully searchable for easy access to vital information

- Copy and paste, print, and bookmark content

Did you know that Packt offers eBook versions of every book published, with PDF and ePub files available? You can upgrade to the eBook version at packt.com and as a print book customer, you are entitled to a discount on the eBook copy. Get in touch with us at customercare@packtpub.com for more details.

At www.packt.com, you can also read a collection of free technical articles, sign up for a range of free newsletters, and receive exclusive discounts and offers on Packt books and eBooks.

Other Books You May Enjoy

If you enjoyed this book, you may be interested in these other books by Packt:

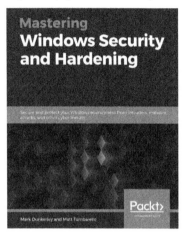

Mastering Windows Security and Hardening

Mark Dunkerley, Matt Tumbarello

ISBN: 978-1-83921-641-1

- Understand baselining and learn the best practices for building a baseline

- Get to grips with identity management and access management on Windows-based systems

- Delve into the device administration and remote management of Windows-based systems

- Explore security tips to harden your Windows server and keep clients secure

- Audit, assess, and test to ensure controls are successfully applied and enforced

- Monitor and report activities to stay on top of vulnerabilities

Mastering Microsoft Endpoint Manager

Christiaan Brinkhoff, Per Larsen

ISBN: 978-1-80107-899-3

- Understand how Windows 365 Cloud PC makes the deployment of Windows in the cloud easy

- Configure advanced policy management within MEM

- Discover modern profile management and migration options for physical and cloud PCs

- Harden security with baseline settings and other security best practices

- Find troubleshooting tips and tricks for MEM, Windows 365 Cloud PC, and more

- Discover deployment best practices for physical and cloud-managed endpoints

- Keep up with the Microsoft community and discover a list of MVPs to follow

Packt is searching for authors like you

If you're interested in becoming an author for Packt, please visit `authors.packtpub.com` and apply today. We have worked with thousands of developers and tech professionals, just like you, to help them share their insight with the global tech community. You can make a general application, apply for a specific hot topic that we are recruiting an author for, or submit your own idea.

Share Your Thoughts

Now you've finished *Microsoft Information Protection Administrator SC-400 Certification Guide*, we'd love to hear your thoughts! Scan the QR code below to go straight to the Amazon review page for this book and share your feedback or leave a review on the site that you purchased it from.

`https://packt.link/r/1801811490`

Your review is important to us and the tech community and will help us make sure we're delivering excellent quality content.

Index

Printed in Great Britain
by Amazon

37466379R00183